Experiencing Architecture in the Nineteenth Century

Experiencing Architecture in the Nineteenth Century

Buildings and Society in the Modern Age

EDITED BY
EDWARD GILLIN AND
H. HORATIO JOYCE

BLOOMSBURY VISUAL ARTS
LONDON • NEW YORK • OXFORD • NEW DELHI • SYDNEY

BLOOMSBURY VISUAL ARTS
Bloomsbury Publishing Plc
50 Bedford Square, London, WC1B 3DP, UK
1385 Broadway, New York, NY 10018, USA

BLOOMSBURY, BLOOMSBURY VISUAL ARTS and the Diana
logo are trademarks of Bloomsbury Publishing Plc

First published in Great Britain 2019
Paperback edition first published 2020

Cover design: Eleanor Rose
Cover image © RMN-Grand Palais (Musée d'Orsay)/René-Gabriel Ojéda

A catalogue record for this book is available from the British Library.

A catalog for this book is available from the Library of Congress.

ISBN: HB: 978-1-3500-4594-1
PB: 978-1-3501-5970-9
ePDF: 978-1-3500-4596-5
eBook: 978-1-3500-4595-8

Typeset by Deanta Global Publishing Services, Chennai, India

To find out more about our authors and books
visit www.bloomsbury.com and sign up for our newsletters.

CONTENTS

ACKNOWLEDGEMENTS

This volume is largely the product of the conference 'Architecture and Experience in the Nineteenth Century', held at St John's College, Oxford, in the spring of 2016. From the quality of papers delivered we could have filled this book three times over and, as editors, our hardest job has been to select just twelve chapters. We would like to thank all who participated in the original conference and contributed so positively to the early development of this work.

Financial support for that event was provided by a number of generous bodies, including the British Association of Victorian Studies (BAVS), the Faculty of History at the University of Oxford, the John Fell Oxford University Press (OUP) Research Fund, the Society of Architectural Historians of Great Britain (SAHGB), and St John's College, Oxford – our sincere thanks to them all.

We would like to acknowledge our debts to friends, colleagues, and families for their constant support and inspiration along the way. In particular, we are grateful to Peter Budden for his input and assistance, and to Silke Muylaert for her help in developing the Introduction. In the case of Chapter 10, a specific debt is also owed to Jane Garnett for early encouragement on Trollope and Parliament.

We have very much appreciated all the support from Bloomsbury, who have made the production of this work a great pleasure. To our editor, James Thompson, who saw the potential of the project, we can only express gratitude, while we greatly value the hard work that Sophie Tann, Leeladevi Ulaganathan, and Giles Herman have put into this book. Thank you also to the two anonymous reviewers of this volume who helped sharpen its analysis and structure. We very much hope that we have done their feedback justice.

Finally, we would like to express our thanks to our contributors, who have all been models of efficiency and rigour. We are both hugely proud to include every one of these chapters and will always be thankful for the contributors' generosity in allowing us to publish their work. Although perhaps unorthodox, the editors would like to dedicate this book to one of the contributing authors, their mutual supervisor and friend, William Whyte.

LIST OF FIGURES AND TABLES

NOTES ON CONTRIBUTORS

Emma Anderson is an interior designer, working largely in historic or listed buildings, for both commercial and residential clients. She holds an MSc in historic conservation from Oxford Brookes University. She is currently studying for a DPhil at the University of Oxford, entitled *The Hotel de Luxe: The Social and Architectural Significance of the Grand Hotel in London in the later Victorian and Edwardian Period.*

G. A. Bremner is senior lecturer in architectural history at the University of Edinburgh. His research focuses on the history and theory of Victorian architecture, with a special interest in the architecture and urbanism of the British Empire. His principal publications include *Imperial Gothic: Religious Architecture and High Anglican Culture in the British Empire, c.1840–1870* (Yale University Press, 2013), and ed. *Architecture and Urbanism in the British Empire* (Oxford University Press, 2016).

Caitlin DeClercq holds a PhD in architecture from the University of California, Berkeley, and an MS in education from the University of Rochester. Her doctoral research investigated the social, historical, and built environment contexts of bodily education in nineteenth-century and twentieth-century American institutions of higher education, an endeavour that integrated her interests in health, education, and architecture. Currently, she is a postdoctoral researcher for the Interdisciplinary Center for Healthy Workplaces at UC Berkeley. She is a published author with articles in the *Journal of Academic Librarianship* (2014) and *Planning for Higher Education* (2016) as well as a contributed chapter in *Ethnography for Designers* (Routledge, 2016).

Edward Gillin is a research fellow at the University of Cambridge and postdoctoral associate member of Trinity College. A cultural historian of nineteenth-century Britain, his research interests include Victorian architecture, science, technology, and politics. Along with articles on the Cunard steamship company, geology in architecture, and Isambard Kingdom Brunel's *Great Eastern* steamship, he is the author of *The Victorian Palace of*

Science: scientific knowledge and the building of the Houses of Parliament (Cambridge University Press, 2017). He was awarded the 2015 Hawksmoor Medal from the Society of Architectural Historians of Great Britain and the 2016 Abbot Payson Usher Prize from the Society of the History of Technology.

Graeme Gooday is professor of the history of science and technology in the School of Philosophy, Religion and History of Science at the University of Leeds, UK. He has written extensively on the history of laboratories – for example, Robert Fox and Graeme Gooday (eds) *Physics in Oxford, 1839–1939* – and more broadly on the history of technology in late-nineteenth-century Britain, including *The Morals of Measurement* (Cambridge University Press, 2014), *Domesticating Electricity* (Pickering & Chatto, 2008), *Patently Contestable* (with Stathis Arapostathis, MIT Press, 2013), and *Managing the Experience of Hearing Loss in Britain, 1830–1930* (with Karen Sayer, Palgrave Macmillan, 2017). His current research project concerns the historical development of acoustic ecologies and of related technologies to assist hearing.

H. Horatio Joyce was born in New York City, and educated at the Universities of Chicago, Boston, and Oxford. From 2015 to 2018, he was a PhD Scholar of the Society of Architectural Historians of Great Britain. He is currently writing a social and architectural history of gentlemen's clubs in Gilded Age New York.

Ayla Lepine is a visiting fellow in art history at the University of Essex. Her research focuses on architecture and theology in modern Britain. Following her PhD at the Courtauld Institute of Art, Lepine held postdoctoral fellowships at Yale's Institute of Sacred Music and the Courtauld's Research Forum. She is a trustee of art and Christianity and arts editor for the *Marginalia Review of Books*. She has published in journals including *Architectural History* and *Visual Representations* on the Gothic Revival and Kenneth Clark, modern monasticism, and pre-Raphaelite medievalisms. Her edited collections include a collaborative project on the Hereford Screen for the journal *British Art Studies*, *Gothic Legacies* (2012), *Revival: Memories, Identities, Utopias* (2015), and *Modern Architecture for Religious Communities, 1860–1970* (2018). She is currently completing *Medieval Metropolis*, a book exploring transatlantic modern Gothic architecture, forthcoming with Bloomsbury in 2019.

David Frazer Lewis is an architectural historian. He received his doctorate from the University of Oxford in 2014 and, in 2017, completed a postdoctoral research associateship at the Yale Center for British Art in New Haven, US. His current research focuses on British and American architecture of the nineteenth and twentieth centuries, particularly the way architects thought about psychology and religion. He is editor of the Pugin Society's peer-reviewed journal, *True Principles*.

Valerie Mendelson holds a doctorate from the Graduate Center of CUNY in art history and teaches at The New School and The Brearley School in New York City. Her research and publications focus on the history of collecting, especially in nineteenth-century France. Her articles have been published in the *Open Library of Humanities*, *Antipodes*, and the *International Journal of the Book*, among other places and she has presented widely on topics related to architectural space and museum history.

Henrik Schoenefeldt is senior lecturer in sustainable architecture at the University of Kent and an AHRC leadership fellow. He trained as an architect and specialized in the history of environmental design with an MPhil and PhD from the University of Cambridge. He is currently seconded to the Palace of Westminster Restoration and Renewal Programme to lead a research project, 'Between Heritage and Sustainability – Restoring the Palace of Westminster's nineteenth-century ventilation system.' His recent publications include a chapter in *Gothic Revival Worldwide*, published by Leuven University Press, and he has a forthcoming article in the *Journal of the Society of Antiquaries* entitled 'The Historic Ventilation System of the House of Commons, 1840–52: revisiting David Boswell Reid's environmental legacy.'

Geoffrey Tyack grew up in London, where he first developed an interested in the history of architecture by exploring the city's buildings, and he went on to read history at St John's College, Oxford, and to gain a PhD from the University of London. He has taught architectural history and the history of urban planning for many years, both in Britain and the United States. He is an emeritus fellow of Kellogg College in the University of Oxford, a fellow of the Society of Antiquaries and of the Royal Historical Society, and president of the Oxfordshire Architectural and Historical Society. His books include *Sir James Pennethorne and the Making of Victorian London* (1992), *Oxford: an Architectural Guide* (1998), and an edited volume on *John Nash: Architect of the Picturesque* (2013). He is editor of the *Georgian Group Journal* and coedited the revised volume on Berkshire in the Pevsner *Buildings of England* series (2010). He is currently writing a book on the history of the British urban landscape.

William Whyte is professor of social and architectural history and a fellow of St John's College, Oxford. His publications include *Redbrick: a social and architectural history of Britain's civic universities* (Oxford University Press, 2015) and *Unlocking the Church: the lost secrets of Victorian sacred space* (Oxford University Press, 2017). He is currently writing *The University: a material history*, for publication by Harvard University Press.

Introduction

Experiencing Architecture in the Nineteenth Century

H. Horatio Joyce and Edward Gillin

In the nineteenth century, more than ever before, architecture was built to be experienced. This is the chief claim of this book. Throughout the following twelve chapters we argue that how individuals experienced the buildings around them was central to society and culture. How architecture was seen, smelt, felt, heard in, interpreted, and how it evoked emotions and conjured up memories, was inseparable from the ways in which contemporaries perceived their rapidly industrializing societies to be modern and progressive. Buildings were constructed not only to be lived, worshipped, or worked in, but also to embody specific cultural values, including political and religious beliefs. They could also be used to project new understandings of nature or visions of society. Along with new building types, such as grand hotels, clubs, railway stations, and museums, architects employed new materials, historically-informed styles, and diverse skills in their work. This was a moment of profound social and economic change, through rapid industrialization, urbanization, and population growth. Mechanized forms of labour, new electrical communication apparatus, and increasingly fast transportation accompanied the growth of global networks through colonial expansion. And the built environment was very much part of this changing world. Architecture was absolutely crucial to how people lived, what they believed, how they envisaged nature, and how they ordered society. *Experiencing Architecture in the Nineteenth Century* provides a showpiece of how architectural history can enhance our understanding of the nineteenth century. In doing so, we address the waning interest in nineteenth-century architecture which has become increasingly marked in recent years.[1]

Architecture and users in the nineteenth century

Our focus on the experience of architecture is inseparably bound to the broader social-economic contexts of the nineteenth century. From the mid-eighteenth century, growing industrialization and increasingly self-consciously empirical approaches to knowledge production were implicitly associated with ideas of progress and modernity. The nineteenth century was an age of iron and coal, but also of growing urbanization, mechanization, and experiment, following from the Industrial Revolution and Enlightenment of the eighteenth century.[2] Architecture was very much part of this change. The study of past architecture and nature, in many ways an effort to produce an empirical science of architecture, encouraged new stylistic forms, such as the neoclassical of the 1820s and 1830s and the Gothic of the mid-century. This use of history to shape architecture had parallels with the very latest natural philosophy of the day. Cambridge mathematicians William Whewell and Robert Willis, for instance, combined their study of nature with that of the development of architecture, constructing an empirical framework in their production of a narrative of progress in building.[3] At the same time, industry brought new materials, not only cast iron and industrially produced glass, but also an extended choice of stone and natural materials facilitated by new methods of transport, such as railways and canals. Building types also diversified, with hotels, hospitals, libraries, and museums just some of the responses to new ideas over society and how architecture should serve the demands of a modern industrial people. Architects had to deliver increasingly diverse buildings and master new specialist bodies of knowledge to bring these projects to fruition; indeed, our period witnessed the formation of what might be understood as the 'professional' architect.[4] In materials, forms, types, and understandings of history and nature, nineteenth-century architecture was noticeably different from that of previous centuries. As Barry Bergdoll puts it, architecture became 'self-consciously experimental as never before'.[5]

Certainly in Britain, architecture did take on an acknowledged increasing significance. John Ruskin (1819–1900) and Augustus Pugin (1812–52), perhaps the most influential nineteenth-century British commentators on architecture, both conceived of buildings as embodying and reflecting religious values. As typified in his 1841 *Contrasts*, Pugin argued that medieval buildings allowed their inhabitants to experience truth. The Gothic architecture of the Middle Ages, with its crucifix layouts, lofty naves, and celestial spires, provided instruction; divine Catholic architecture exhibited 'the triumphs of Christian truth' and played an active role in eliciting the 'wonder and admiration' of those who experienced it.[6] Pugin extended this idea beyond chapels and churches to architecture broadly, including poor houses, town halls, inns, and even entire towns. Likewise, Ruskin also emphasized that architecture was something that did things to its inhabitants.

Architecture reflected nature, with medieval Gothic embodying the rugged climate and landscape of Northern Europe. More importantly, it was an 'index' of religious and social values. The imperfections of Britain's Gothic structures, Ruskin alleged, revealed the freedoms of medieval Christian workmen and the very antithesis of nineteenth-century industrial precision and machinery.[7] Ruskin and Pugin were, nonetheless, only part of a more widespread interpretation of the past to understand architecture.

During the late-twentieth century, Michel Foucault asserted that at the end of the eighteenth century, architecture became something different to what it had been before. As he puts it,

> Previously the art of building corresponded to the need to make power, divinity and might manifest. The palace and the church were the great architectural forms, along with the stronghold. ... Then, late in the eighteenth century new problems emerge: it becomes a question of using the disposition of space for economico-political ends.[8]

The nineteenth century, then, is an important period for architectural historians, following on immediately from what Foucault identified as the crucial moment for architecture. In *Discipline and Punish* (1975), Foucault used the eighteenth-century philosopher Jeremy Bentham's panopticon design for a prison to explore how architecture acted in this new way, embodying power relations between dominant and subordinate subjects. In his analysis, disciplining power is architecturally inscribed through sites such as prisons, schools, factories, and asylums.[9] Foucault's call to examine space, and specifically architecture, has most frequently been taken up by sociologists, but architectural historians can, and indeed have, found much in his assertion that 'a whole history remains to be written of *spaces* – which would at the same time be the history of *powers*'.[10] Such a history would acknowledge the sort of agency nineteenth-century writers like Pugin and Ruskin ascribed to buildings, from the most ambitious institutions to the most intimate domiciles.

While Foucault provides some direction for architectural studies, his emphasis on the determining power of structural forms on inhabiting subjects is reductionist. Architecture does not simply exert power over the humans who occupy it; the subjects themselves shape not only the initial construction of a building, but its subsequent meaning and purposes. Just because a building is designed with specific intentions in mind does not mean that it will be used in that way; inhabitants have opportunities to ignore or subvert these original intentions. This is where experience can be useful: architecture is influential, but humans have agency over the spaces they inhabit, which means that any architectural analysis cannot be reduced to questions of power in a Foucauldian sense. Experience allows us to account for the relationship between inhabitants and buildings with more nuance and balance. Heghnar Watenpaugh has made this point well in his study of the urban experience of early-modern Aleppo, observing that while architecture can be used to project and forge identity, it has no determining power, but is instead encountered. As he surmises, while you can build a system to govern pedestrians, users can take shortcuts or make new routes: inhabitants always retain a degree of choice over how they use space.[11] Our volume combines the idea that architecture has agency, without reducing the human agents inhabiting these spaces to a passive role.

Building on ideas developed in constructivist approaches to the history of technology, Thomas Gieryn has considered this relationship between architecture and human agency by likening buildings to machines; they appear as both the consequence and structural cause of social practices. Just as machines are built to do things and cause certain results, so are buildings humanly designed for specific functions. And just as the extent to which machines perform the work intended varies subject to their users, so too does architecture's performance depend on its inhabitants and observers. As Gieryn puts it, if buildings and machines always operate as designed, then they would act 'as guarantees of a social structure beyond the reach of human agents', but this rarely happens. Architecture's structural impact, therefore, is contingent on the agency of its users.[12] Gieryn's analogy of the machine and questions of human agency has ramifications for a study concerned with experience. In a sense, we are dealing with how well buildings performed the intentions of their designers, as well as how users themselves encountered them, shaping both their meaning and purpose.

This volume, then, shares many of Henri Lefebvre's observations on the nature of space and how to examine it. In his *La Production de l'espace* (1974), Lefebvre challenges interpretations of space which build on the traditional Cartesian conception of space as an absolute geometric object. Kant complicated this understanding by conceiving of space as an *a priori* category, along with time, and therefore placing space within the realm of consciousness. In such philosophy, space is a structure: a passive container waiting to be filled with contents. To a volume concerned with the experience of architecture, such an account of space as a passive container with a single fixed meaning does not sit well. As Lefebvre puts it, space, and therefore architecture, cannot be reduced to 'the status of a *message*, and the inhabiting of it to the status of a *reading*'. Lefebvre argued instead for a spatial analysis which united the mental, social, and physical fields. Space was, for Lefebvre, both a physical and a mental category, and he argued that it was produced through human agency.[13] The idea of experiencing architecture takes us beyond readings of geometrical absolutes, but what Lefebvre shows is that this inhabiting of space is itself productive. When we deal with experience, we do not just examine how architecture could be encountered by inhabitants, but that the act of experiencing a building or built environment contributed and shaped the architecture itself.

In particular, we take inspiration from William Whyte's *Unlocking the Church* (2017), many of the arguments of which were delivered through his

Hensley Henson Lectures at Oxford which ran during Michaelmas Term 2014. It was, to some degree, these lectures which shaped the earliest concept of our present volume and its preceding conference, 'Architecture and Experience in the Nineteenth Century', held at St John's College, Oxford, in March 2016. Whyte explored Victorian churches in terms of what they meant, what they did, and how they were experienced. He examined the 'interplay of sight and sound, emotion and reason, considered thought and sudden impulse' within these sacred spaces. Whyte's complaint with traditional architectural histories is that they have often been preoccupied with architects rather than buildings, and when they have examined buildings, 'they have tended to remain so obsessed with their formal qualities that they fail to think about their function or their effect: they have studied *style* instead of *experience*'. However, as Whyte shows, churches were intended to perform functions; to achieve a certain effect on their congregations. They were devices, or technologies, central to nineteenth-century worship. How they were seen, smelt, felt, and sounded, as well as the emotional responses they induced, matter to our understanding of Victorian faith.[14] In putting the physical church at the centre of Victorian religion, Whyte provided a model of how architecture can, and indeed should, be put at the centre of our historical study of nineteenth-century society and culture. It seems clear, then, that now is the right moment to extend this idea of experiencing architecture beyond the church.

Similarly, Dana Arnold and Andrew Ballantyne's *Architecture as Experience* (2004) has offered valuable insights into how architectural sites provide contrasting experiences to different social groups. Their edited collection of essays demonstrates the volatility of meaning particular places can have, not only over time, but for various cultures. For example, Laura Hollengreen's study analysed how the meaning and social position of the Gothic cathedral of Notre-Dame at Chartres evolved from its construction in the thirteenth century, through the Middle Ages, and up to its de-sacralization in the revolutionary 1790s.[15] Our volume certainly does not disagree with these interpretations, but we want to engage more critically with this notion of 'experience'. Most obviously, it would seem that architectural experiences are not only different between cultures, but between individuals within these cultures. At the same time, we would place greater emphasis on the agency of an inhabitant or observer of architecture through their experiences.[16]

This notion that buildings do, in fact, do things, and cannot be treated as mere containers of human actions, has been productively taken up in histories of science which have concerned themselves with architecture. Works including Crosbie Smith and Jon Agar's *Making Space for Science* (1998) and David Livingstone and Charles Withers's *Geographies of Nineteenth-Century Science* (2011) place emphasis on the spatial settings of knowledge production and involve a strong architectural element.[17] In these works the place of scientific practice is not a passive background, but provokes intellectual innovation and shapes the formation and distribution of new science. In her brilliant *Nature's Museums* (1999) Carla Yanni demonstrates not only how Victorian museums were places in which to make new knowledge, but that these structures contributed to legitimize it. Architecture could be used to exhibit interpretations of nature, but also shaped the credibility of these interpretations with diverse audiences. As Yanni asserted, these museums did not present a single master narrative of science, but had coexisting meanings.[18] If laboratories, museums, and other places of experiment had a shaping role on the production of science, while varying visions of nature informed differing architectural meanings, then this is equally apparent for the broader experiences of society through churches, universities, clubs, art galleries, hospitals, schools, and homes.

The challenge for our volume then is how to explore this notion of 'experience'. As Whyte observes, it is a hard thing to recapture past experience; not only is it subjective, but it can differ for the same individual over time. As nineteenth-century architecture was often and in varied ways experimental, the problem might be compared to Heinz Sibum's classic reworking of historical experiments to build understanding of the practices and techniques employed in past scientific investigations. Sibum found, by replicating the nineteenth-century paddle-wheel experiments of James Joule to produce a measurable mechanical value for heat, just how important Joule's transfer of precision skills from his experience in the brewing industry were to this work. Just as we cannot identically recreate past scientific experiments, we cannot exactly re-enact how nineteenth-century audiences experienced their buildings, but we can connect the aesthetics and material form of structures with the documents surrounding their design, construction, and interpretation, to recapture a sense of how they were encountered. Indeed, it was this uniting of buildings with the novels, pamphlets, and memoirs which surrounded them which was of such value to Whyte's study of Victorian churches.[19] Throughout the following chapters we utilize this wealth of written material.

Our plan of work

In our opening section, 'Defining Experience', William Whyte identifies a nineteenth-century tradition of writing about architecture, focused on experience, before reviewing more recent historical, phenomenological, and sociological approaches to the architecture of the period, arguing that while these have sometimes been productive, they have also been immensely limiting. Whyte's chapter addresses the complex relationship between the concepts of 'architecture' and 'experience', suggesting that the nineteenth century saw a distinctive conjunction of them. And he suggests some ways in which future studies might use the insights of this volume to produce a more convincingly historical account of nineteenth-century buildings and those who experienced them.

Part Two, 'Producing Experience', provides a series of studies on how architecture was used to provide specific encounters for their users. From 1887, 186 Gwydir Street was the living space of the decorative painter David Parr, who was well connected with the Gothic Revival architect George Frederick Bodley and also with William Morris's design firm. In her chapter, Ayla Lepine shows how Parr used ecclesiastical art and design to create a unique site which offers a very personal contrast to better known artists' homes, such as Leighton House. 186 Gwydir Street was not only a place to live, but a place in which to experience religion. Parr's home, a singular example of a decorative Arts and Crafts working-class house, provides a very specific vision of modernity in which Christian faith was central.

In contrast to Lepine's analysis of what was a very private building for personal use, in Chapter 3, David Lewis explores the foundation and building of Stanford University and its campus in California. He demonstrates how the architecture of this institution was carefully cultivated to provide a certain pedagogical experience, in which the student encounter of art from all over the world was perceived to be crucial to the formation of character. Leland and Jane Stanford, whose fortune was made through railways, envisaged their university as a place that brought their cosmopolitan travels to the American West. The second half of the nineteenth century saw a host of new private universities in the States, founded and endowed by industrial magnets; Stanford provides an example of the central role of architecture for these new institutions. But while Stanford's architecture very much embodied the cultural values of a private couple and projected them to the University's students, architectural experiences could also be the result of state activity, as shown in Chapter 4. Another building type, new to the nineteenth century, was the provincial art school; these were a major focus of government initiatives and funding. Geoffrey Tyack shows how Westminster funds were employed to construct contrasting forms of this single building type. This chapter examines the planning, design and construction of some of the most notable schools of art built in Britain over the period from 1850 to 1914, laying special emphasis on their lighting, ventilation, and internal layout, but also looking at their relationship to the development of artistic and design culture as experienced and perceived by both students and teachers. A diverse variety of users attended these schools, Tyack points out, from artisans and middle-class women to amateurs and schoolboys.

While state-funded art schools were subject to increasingly diverse users, so too were art museums. Valerie Mendelson explores the different ways art came to be experienced in Paris in the late-nineteenth century, as public museums grew and professionalized, and smaller private art galleries proliferated as alternative venues for viewing paintings and sculpture. Both were places to encounter art, but this chapter emphasizes that the layout and structure of the buildings containing such works was central to how they were seen, analysed, and interpreted. Throughout the century the Louvre was continually reorganized, added to, and reimagined as the palace of the people. At the same time, private collectors were eager to house their collections. Their aim was to bring their artworks into relationships that mimicked conversation and intimacy, in contrast to the galleries and hallways of the museum. While the experience of the museum had become increasingly focused on visuality, the private collection allowed for a more holistic, sensual and fully corporeal experience that included, most importantly, touch. Similarly, while the long and narrow galleries of the Louvre created tiring and increasingly directed walks, informed by guidebooks, the private collection promoted impromptu 'sinuous paths' and extended absorptive observing and conversation. This chapter then demonstrates how architecture could be employed to shape the experience of the objects it housed.

In Part Three of this volume, 'Designing Experience', we analyse the practices, experiences, and knowledge behind architectural design. While Section Two looked at the diverse new range of building types and forms of architectural encounter prevalent in the nineteenth century, Section Three unpacks the immensely complex processes involved in efforts to produce specific responses to architecture and the roles of the actors behind these projects. Horatio Joyce begins by exploring the creation of an alumni culture of giving in the United States through the clubhouse building activities of Harvard graduates in New York City. This chapter examines how the collaborative work between alumni and their architect, the Harvard-educated Charles F. McKim, helped them to formulate a metaphor for a community of graduates in the city that ensured a robust philanthropic tradition which still survives today. Joyce's account, then, is not of how a building was itself encountered, but of the informative experience of the architectural design process behind it.

While Joyce explores the relationship between architect and client, Chapter 7 looks at the relationship between architect and knowledge. Through his study of the Sheffield-born architect Thomas Roger Smith, Graeme Gooday's inquiry into nineteenth-century acoustics provides an analysis of the different sorts of knowledge which could be employed to regulate experience. While the Harvard physicist Wallace Sabine produced an equation specifying the reverberation time for a room, based on its volume, area, and surface absorbency, Smith relied on his own practical architectural experiences to write about acoustics. This chapter, then, is not just about the experience of architecture itself, but about how experience contributed to the formation of new architectural knowledge. Smith's experience-grounded approach to acoustics was in stark contrast to Sabine's mathematically informed theoretical solution.

While architects, clients, and designers could fashion their buildings to achieve particular effects, the encounter of architecture remained subjective. This is the theme of Henrik Schoenefeldt's study of the Edinburgh chemist

David Boswell Reid's work to ventilate Britain's new Palace of Westminster, home to the Houses of Parliament, during the 1830s and 1840s. Reid's experiments to produce environmental control within the temporary Parliament, erected to house Britain's legislature after the destruction of the original building in a fire of 1834, were intended to produce knowledge that could secure the comfort of politicians in their permanent new debating chambers. However, while Reid claimed to be able to control the temperature and air quality of this structure, the experiences of its users varied. While some politicians found Reid's atmospheric system comfortable, others complained of excessive heat, draught, or of being too cold. Schoenefeldt reminds us that even with something as apparently mundane as temperature, the experience of architecture is completely subjective and differs from user to user. Reid's industrious efforts could not secure favourable responses from all of Parliament's inhabitants. Through their respective chapters, Joyce, Gooday, and Schoenefeldt all explore the expansion in the range of skills which were becoming increasingly important for architects, engineers, and designers of buildings during the nineteenth century.

In Part Four, 'Audiences and Experience', we look at the relationship between architecture and those who used it. Emma Anderson takes up the new building type of the grand hotel, exploring in particular the tension between public and private, and how to maintain a sense of exclusivity. Designers, she shows, necessarily had to become adept at curating experiences which seemed intimate, private, and luxurious, and yet were accessible to anyone who could afford to pay. Specifically, Anderson deals with the question of publicity which had to convey this sense of rarity while of course attracting custom. In late-nineteenth-century London, experience was very much something which could be commercialized and sold to both domestic and international audiences. Architecture could be fashioned to secure the patronage of the increasingly wealthy, cosmopolitan elites, who travelled to London.

These tensions between public and private spaces were equally apparent at Britain's new Houses of Parliament, and while Henrik Schoenefeldt's chapter deals with how politicians encountered this building, it was a place which the majority of British society never actually entered. Edward Gillin's chapter argues that to understand how Parliament was experienced by the broader population, we should look to the literature which surrounds it. The reading middle classes did not witness Parliament directly, but through the writings of authors, in particular Anthony Trollope, they could have a taste of life inside the House of Commons. This chapter offers direction on how we might think about the literary experience of architecture in the nineteenth century. Trollope provided his readers with detailed accounts of not only political debates within the building, but also its aesthetics and physical form. In the context of increasing enfranchisement following the 1867 Reform Act, as well as growing levels of literacy, few places were of so much interest to British society as Parliament, and it was through the printed word and fictional narrative of Trollope that it was most frequently experienced.

Often the relationship between audience and architecture could shape broader political debates, including over questions of gender. In the United States, the nineteenth century saw the emergence of women's colleges, beginning with Vassar College, New York, in 1861. Caitlin DeClercq uses the experiences of Vassar's gymnasium to explore the tensions over female education and the changing place of women more broadly in society. While Vassar's student body used this space for physical education, and female physicians and educators implemented regimes of bodily instruction and assessment within the structure, the public beyond the college encountered the building through the publicity surrounding the new institution. These groups experienced Vassar's spaces of physical instruction as ambivalent sites that both constrained and freed female bodies. Through Anderson, Gillin, and DeClercq's chapters, it is evident that there were new audiences for architecture in the nineteenth century. In many respects these audiences reflect the broader social changes of industrial populations, including an expansion in wealth, political representation, and role of women. How architecture was experienced was perceived to be crucial to informing and ordering these new social groups.

Drawing together the themes of this volume, Alex Bremner concludes our investigation by offering thoughts on where we should go from here. Bremner argues for the importance of the relationship between movement and architecture during the second half of the nineteenth century. Much of the architecture produced during this period was a new kind of experience in and of itself. Bremner considers the economy and processes of production involved in actually putting a building together. One of the most basic parameters of the changed nature of architecture during this period was the vastly increased input of energy surrounding the procurement and transportation of materials. This made Victorian architecture both objectively and conceptually a profoundly different type of architecture from anything that had come before. Mechanized movement in construction was central to this. The first part of this concluding chapter suggests that we must first ask what Victorian architecture *is* before we can fully appreciate the kinds of encounter people had with it. The second part considers further the consequences of the increased extension of movement. Here issues of displacement and disorientation come to the fore, as speed and distance of movement are considered as producing their own side effects with respect to how one can experience architecture vis-à-vis space and identity. This relates to the wider British world, including places as far afield as Australia and New Zealand. The increased frequency and extension of movement witnessed in the nineteenth century, Bremner shows, made the experience of architecture not only peculiar, but also an experience of global modernity. This chapter therefore draws out broad themes that arise from studying how architecture was experienced in the nineteenth century and argues for the importance and potential of the analysis developed in this volume.

Where, then, does all of this leave us? The theme of experience provides many valuable insights, as our contributors demonstrate, but perhaps there is yet another insight that we can glean – the particular contemporary resonance it holds. Architects in recent years have become increasingly interested in designing buildings that respond to their users on more than one level: to move beyond the dominance of vision and to embrace all senses. Architects are paying greater attention to taste, smell, sound, and especially touch in their work. This has brought them to engage with new areas of scientific research, including neurology, and to bring their clients, especially those institutional, deeper into the design process, such as through focus groups and questionnaires. As a leading contemporary architectural theorist in this growing discourse, Juhani Pallasmaa, argues, we do not just experience architecture through vision, but through an integration of mental and physical senses. In other words, buildings are encountered through touch, smell, sight, sound, and even taste, as well as through emotional responses.[20] It is this combination of thoughts and physical senses which constitutes experience. This is certainly evident in the nineteenth-century examples examined in this volume.[21]

PART ONE

Defining experience

CHAPTER ONE

Architecture and experience: Regimes of materiality in the nineteenth century

William Whyte

When writing about architecture and experience we seem to be discussing two concepts, but in fact find ourselves engaging with at least three. In the first place we have architecture, ostensibly solid and substantial, yet also protean and intensely problematic. 'Few questions are more frequently asked, and few have hitherto been more difficult to answer satisfactorily, than the enquiry, "*What is architecture?*,"' observed James Fergusson in his *Illustrated Handbook of Architecture* in 1859: and if that was true then, little has changed now.[1] Experience turns out to be an equally intractable concept. 'There is', claimed the philosopher Shadworth Hodgson in 1882, 'no larger word than *Experience*. … It is in this alone that both the material and the verification of all our enquiries and all our theorising, are found.'[2] As he went on to write four volumes, and numerous other essays, on the nature, function, and definition of experience, he knew whereof he spoke, and his caution should be a warning to anyone who uses the word 'experience' unthinkingly.[3] And then we come to the relationship between the perplexing categories of 'architecture *and* experience', a linkage which presumes agency, a sense that architecture is somehow constituted by experience and experience somehow shaped by architecture; an interrelationship, in other words, which implies that both are somehow affected by the other, and that exploring each will tell us something about both.

The fact that this volume is focused on a discrete period only makes these entangled themes all the more apparently intractable. We assume that architecture in the nineteenth century was distinct and different: the product, as a popular introduction to the subject puts it, of 'unprecedented social, intellectual and technological change'.[4] It has also been suggested that people experienced the world differently then.[5] But even these claims rest on the untested assumption that we already understand what architecture and experience actually were.[6] Moreover, there remains the question of whether there was something particular – and particularly nineteenth century – about the relationship between architecture (whatever that was) and experience (whatever that amounted to). Is there, we are forced to ask, a way of precisely delineating what architecture was, how experience was understood, and how both these complex concepts interacted?

Well, I am a historian. And for historians, the answer is always back to the texts. So let's begin with a text. Let's begin, in fact, with a text published just after the end of the nineteenth century. A text that is intimately concerned with recreating the experience of a lost, nineteenth-century past. A text, in other words, that is seeking to do very much what the chapters of this volume are all about. Let's begin with Proust, with *Du Côté de chez Swann*, the first volume in his epic *À la recherche du temps perdu*, first published in 1913. This is a book – or, rather, a series of books – saturated in architectural experience and in the experience of architecture. From the very start, buildings are as much characters in the story as the people who inhabit them. As David Anton Spurr observes, in one of the most interesting reflections on the subject, architecture 'runs parallel to and indeed intersects with what ... is in effect the search for the ground of his own being'.[7] So central was this architectural imagination, indeed, that Proust famously compared the whole work of *À la recherche du temps perdu* to a cathedral, and even contemplated giving the various parts of the books subheadings derived from cathedral architecture, so that one might be called the porch, the other the nave, yet another the windows.[8]

Looking for buildings in Proust is thus an endless and endlessly rewarding process. They are everywhere. But, to begin with, I want to concentrate on one particular place: the church at Combray. 'It is a building which takes up pages of description: from the old porch at the entrance – 'black, pocked like a skimming ladle, ... uneven and deeply hollowed at the edges' – to the tapestries; from the golden cross to the high steeple.' And Proust's description is not merely antiquarian or simply decorative. It is also, in a sense, metaphysical, with the architecture facilitating experience – an experience of profound, central importance to the author. The church was, he writes, 'something entirely different from the rest of the town: an edifice occupying a space with, so to speak, four dimensions – the fourth being Time – extending over the centuries'. It was a building, he later observes, 'distinguished ... from all other buildings by a sort of thoughtfulness that was infused into it'. It was a building with a steeple 'whose slopes of stone ...

approached each other as they rose like hands meeting in prayer' and which 'gave all the occupations, all the hours, all the viewpoints of the town their shape, their crown, their consecration'.[9]

Quite a church, then; quite a building. Indeed, it is not an exaggeration to say that Proust's reflections on the church at Combray contain within them many of the key themes which anyone working on nineteenth-century architectural history has of necessity to confront. There is the sense of architecture as a repository of time; the sense of buildings as a sort of vehicle for communication; the sense that the built environment was not passive, but active – that is, not static but rather infused with transformative energy. These, I suspect, were indeed distinctively nineteenth-century experiences of architecture.

For the moment, however, I want to make a far more facile point. I simply wish to attend to the very fact of Proust's reflections. It's important to do this: important to see that Proust was doing this, and important, too, to see that he was part of a continuous tradition of reflection on these themes that ran throughout the nineteenth century. Proust, as we know, was strongly influenced by the writer and social critic John Ruskin. He translated Ruskin and learnt much from him.[10] Although he would also go on to criticize him, Proust found, in the words of one critic, that Ruskin 'endowed him with precisely the insights into art and life for which he was looking'.[11] For Ruskin, of course, the experience of architecture was transformative: he himself experienced buildings as a sort of epiphany, with the cathedral at Amiens, for example, described as a place where it seemed impossible 'for imagination and mathematics together, to do anything nobler or stronger'.[12] This was, needless to say, a description which was to shape Proust's own account of the church at Balbec later in the *Lost Time* sequence.[13]

Nor, of course, was Ruskin the first to explore the impact of architecture in the nineteenth century. He drew on an older tradition, not least that of the English associational psychologists and romantic writers like Walter Scott, Samuel Taylor Coleridge, and Thomas Carlyle.[14] Moreover, although he seems to have been unaware of Kant, Goethe, and other German-language authorities, he was nevertheless part of a broader, pan-European intellectual movement which explored these themes and which stretched back to the late eighteenth century.[15] It was a tradition summed up in Arthur Schopenhauer's claim that

> architecture affects us not only mathematically but dynamically and that what speaks to us through it is not mere form and symmetry, but rather those fundamental forces of nature, those primary Ideas, those lowest grades of the will's objectivity.[16]

This was, obviously, intended as a critique of Kant, whose account of architectural experience stressed disinterested, objective appreciation rather than active, emotional engagement; and, as such, it marked a sharp break with Enlightenment thinking. But Schopenhauer's ringing phrases represent more than just a spat among the philosophers: they spoke to, and for, a major tradition in late-eighteenth and early-nineteenth-century thought, the belief that the experience of architecture was important and was worth studying in and of itself.

The later nineteenth century, especially in Germany, would also, of course, see a renewed interest in experience (both objective and subjective) and, most interestingly from our perspective, in the experience of architecture.[17] Drawing on – and also, following Schopenhauer by critiquing – Kant, the founders of what would become known as *Einfühlung* (or Empathy) Theory produced a series of staggeringly successful and hugely influential studies exploring just that.[18] From the 1870s onwards, indeed, the nature of architectural experience became a central question for historians, philosophers, and pioneers in the new subject of psychology. Indeed, the first psychological laboratory, established by Wilhelm Wundt in 1879, concentrated almost exclusively in its first years on precisely these subjects.[19]

It was the search for experience, and the empathy theory this promoted, which would create modern art history.[20] It was, in particular, this approach which shaped the work of figures like Heinrich Wölfflin, the founder of German architectural history and, in many respects, the originator of all that we are doing in this volume. 'As an art historian I am a disciple of Heinrich Wölfflin,' wrote Sigfried Giedion.[21] The same was as true of Erwin Panofsky and Nikolaus Pevsner as it was of Giedieon and Ernst Gombrich and dozens of others: the founding fathers of our discipline.[22]

Empathy theory also provides the underpinning for the revival of phenomenology at the end of the nineteenth century. It is especially important for understanding Edmund Husserl, who would become such a pivotal figure for the subject, whether by virtue of his own writings, or his role as Martin Heidegger's teacher, or his influence on and provocation of so many of the leading figures of twentieth-century phenomenological theory, from philosophers like Maurice Merleau-Ponty to architectural historians like Christian Norberg-Schulz. All of them took architecture deadly seriously; all of them took experience equally seriously. All of them were engaged in the same process as Edmund Husserl and those who helped to shape his approach. They all followed his injunction: 'auf die "Sachen selbst" zurückgehen', 'back to things themselves'.[23]

Proust, then, was just one voice among many urging the importance of objects, things, and in writing about the experience of architecture. That seems to me an important point: a reminder that this project is not merely the product of contemporary concerns, but grows organically out of questions that nineteenth-century writers were themselves asking. Indeed, there are two respects in which this nineteenth-century debate about buildings and the experience of buildings seems to me to be helpful: firstly, because it can help clarify our own questions about the nature and function of architecture, dealing with some very serious problems with what has become known as the material turn; and, secondly, because this nineteenth-century debate reveals a somewhat different understanding of architecture from our own: a difference which threatens to make our analysis of the nineteenth century profoundly anachronistic.

Husserl's call – the call to return to things, 'auf die "Sachen selbst" zurückgehen' – is, of course, one that we ourselves have heard repeated again and again in the last decade or so. We are operating after the linguistic turn: a turn that offered much, but also threatened to dissolve everything – everything including buildings, bodies, and the embodied experience of things – into discourse. Against this has been set the 'material turn': a turn towards things, or back to things – a material turn which has grown out of dissatisfaction with predominantly linguistic and discursive modes of analysis. The historian Ruth Harris spoke for many other historians – and for anthropologists and archaeologists – when, in 1999, she wrote of her 'growing unease with the totalistic way the "linguistic turn" reduced all human experience to language'.[24] The solution for her was a turn towards the body and then the history of emotions.[25] For others, it was a new emphasis on space and a 'spatial turn'.[26] Yet in all these cases material reality was called in to supplement or supplant linguistic abstraction.[27]

This new focus on things was articulated in several different ways. Indeed, there is a sense in which there has been not so much one material turn as many material turns. To some extent, this was the natural outcome of various different disciplines converging on the same subject. Hence, for example, the very real contrasts in approach exhibited in Dan Hicks' and Mary Beaudry's marvellous *Oxford Handbook of Material Culture Studies*, published in 2010, show just how distinct anthropologists, archaeologists, and science and technology specialists actually are in the ways that they work. The 'key texts', as Hicks and Beaudry observe, 'are read through disciplinary traditions, and their reception diverges as particular disciplinary methods are put into practice.'[28] Still more important than this disciplinary distinction, however, is the fact that the material turn draws on a range of sources; there is no one key text or established canon of literature. Instead, there is a multiplicity of different possibilities and, as interest in the material grows greater, so the range of possible influences expands in turn.

A move away from purely linguistic analysis has enabled scholars to rediscover authors like Georges Bataille, for example, whose conception of spectacular architecture – of buildings which 'speak to the multitude, or silence them' – has been brilliantly explored by Denis Hollier.[29] It has also encouraged an engagement with other literatures influenced by psychoanalytic theory, not least the work of Gilles Deleuze and Félix Guattari, whose architectural insights have been explored very fruitfully, not least in a helpful little book by the historian Andrew Ballantyne.[30] In his suggestive work on the agency of things – *What Do Pictures Want?* – the art historian W. J. T. Mitchell derives insights from authors as various as Benjamin, Baudrillard, Nelson Goodman, and Raymond Williams.[31] The writings of sociologists like Anthony Giddens and geographers like Nigel Thrift have also been deployed effectively to illuminate the material world, whilst Judith Butler's notion of 'performativity' has proved especially attractive to feminist scholars of material culture.[32] This does not, it hardly needs saying, exhaust the range of potential influences.[33]

This multiplicity of ideas can be found within the work of each of the two authors most frequently cited in the literature on material culture: Pierre Bourdieu and Michel Foucault. This is because the thought of both these influential writers evolved and changed throughout their careers, leaving an ambiguous legacy for those who follow them. Bourdieu's intellectual trajectory took him, famously, from structural anthropology to a post-structuralist sort of sociology. Both phases of Bourdieu's development have been influential, with some drawing inspiration from his early North African fieldwork, and especially his seminal article analysing indigenous architecture: 'The Kabyle House or the World Reversed'. This was a structuralist account, using a building (rather in the mode of Claude Levi-Strauss) as a text to reveal the social codes of a Berber people.[34] Other scholars have focused rather more on Bourdieu's later work, and especially his notion of 'habitus' – a term, it is worth remembering, that he first used in his translation of Erwin Panofsky's *Gothic Architecture and Scholasticism* (1967).[35] This conceptual framework suggested a rather more dynamic relationship between people and things, one mediated through the body.[36]

The uses made of Foucault's work likewise reveal the multiple perspectives his analyses offer. Initially seen as a key influence on the linguistic turn, it is only comparatively recently that his work on space has become more widely appreciated.[37] In the process, scholars have moved their focus from the specific, institutional contexts Foucault described in classic texts like *The Birth of the Clinic* and have begun to apply his notion of a materially grounded 'governmentality' to whole societies.[38] 'In short,' as Chris Philo puts it, 'there is now a "new" Foucault for academics to contemplate and a host of exciting new Foucauldian geographies to discern.'[39]

The problem for us here and now is not, however, that there are a huge variety of authorities we can draw on for insight into what buildings can do. That, surely, is a good thing. Rather, as I have argued elsewhere, the critical difficulty is that almost all of these authors – even when they deny doing any such thing – approach the material world as though it were textual.[40] This is even true of scholars who explicitly write on space. Thus Michel de Certeau argued that 'a spatial story is in its minimal degree a spoken language, that is, a linguistic system'.[41] So, too, in his *Postmodern Geographies*, Edward Soja complained that 'we still know too little about the descriptive grammar and syntax of human geographies, the phonemes and epistemes of spatial interpretation'.[42] Another key author, Henri Lefebvre, maintained that any attempt to use semiotic codes as a means of deciphering social space 'must surely reduce that space to itself to the status of a *message*, and the inhabiting of it to the status of a *reading*. This is to evade both history and practice.'

Nonetheless, just a few sentences later even he was claiming that just such a code had existed in the nineteenth century: a code 'which allowed space not only to be "read" but also to be constructed'.[43] The same is surely true of Bourdieu – even late Bourdieu – and, in fact, also of Foucault. It is even true of Amos Rapaport, whose *Meaning of the Built Environment* seems like a break with this literary analysis, but is in fact simply a revised version of the structuralism it presumes to critique.[44] In the end, literary scholars and social scientists alike find it very hard to escape a linguistic analogy or to abandon assumptions derived from the analysis of texts.

What this means is that the material turn endlessly threatens to degenerate into little more than a revision of the linguistic turn. That it has been driven, in large part, by scholars who are trained only to use textual sources simply makes this confusion all the more likely. The result has been that, firstly, there has been a continued emphasis on architecture's representational function above all else, even among those ostensibly working on what buildings do. There has been an assumption that buildings can be read for their meaning – and that contemporaries did just that. In the second place, and allied to this assumption, historians in particular have tended to conflate what was said about buildings with the buildings themselves: turning built structure into little more than metaphor. The effect of both approaches has been to dematerialize architecture. This tells us very little about what buildings themselves can do.

It is for this reason that in recent years many historians and sociologists have become attracted to another way of approaching the issue: the actor-network theory pioneered by Bruno Latour. Latour, of course, has radically rejected any approach that relegates the material world to the status of a text. Indeed, he goes further: imputing agency to the material world, refusing to distinguish between human and non-human actors. It is this approach which underpins pioneering studies like Timothy Mitchell's *Rule of Experts*, which opens with a chapter rather wonderfully entitled 'Can the Mosquito Speak?'[45] More pertinently still, it is clear that Latour has influenced many of the most recent and most interesting accounts of modern social history. Simon Gunn, for example, has described the Victorian city as a theatre in which the streets and buildings are actors as well as forming the backdrop to human drama.[46] Patrick Joyce, too, has moderated his early Foucauldian enthusiasm to embrace actor-network theory in a series of studies. A social historian, he has used Latour to interrogate the very concept of 'the social' itself, broadening the term to include material agency as well as human perception. 'The crucial intellectual move regarding agency and the social', Joyce argues, in a conscious echo of Latour's own claims, 'is one that moves away from notions of a coherent social totality, towards the erasure of familiar conceptual distinctions between the natural and the social, the human and the non-human, and the material and the cultural.'[47] Here is not a study of buildings as the representation of ideas, but rather a more profound critique of the assumption that buildings or things are different from humans at all.

Actor-network theory has certainly provoked some remarkable insights. By forcing us to rethink distinctions between the people and things which seem self-evident, yet turn out to be anything but, it has enabled scholars to say new and interesting things about buildings. It also buys into a wider re-enchantment of the material world.[48] Nonetheless, there are at least two reasons for thinking that, in fact, Latour's analysis does not go far enough and has only limited application for the study of architecture in the past.

Firstly, there is the familiar question of method. In a vivid image in *Reassembling the Social*, Latour sets out his approach: 'Once built', he writes, 'the wall of bricks does not utter a word.' The same is true of all objects, Latour goes on to argue. 'That is why specific tricks have to be invented to *make them talk*, that is, to offer descriptions of themselves, to produce *scripts* of what they are making others – humans and non-humans – do.'[49] How this might work in practice is made plain in Thomas Gieryn's deservedly much-cited article, 'What Buildings Do', which uses interviews and empirical ethnographical work to explore the consequences of a series of architectural decisions on the users of a biotechnology building.[50] It can also be seen in Latour's former student and current collaborator, Alberta Yaneva's fascinating work on *The Making of a Building*, in which she explores the 'turmoil' created by the design and production of architecture in a series of ethnographic essays.[51] Yet for historians, amassing such material is inevitably rather more difficult. Those who work on far older subjects, relying on what even they admit to be 'damaged', 'incomplete', and 'inadequate' – albeit 'tantalizing' – sources, are presented with a still more intractable problem.[52]

In the second place, and rather more importantly, it is questionable whether Latour and his followers go far enough in their redefinitions of architecture. His claim that 'once built, a wall of bricks does not utter a word' is not just a tellingly textual reference, which suggests that Latour has not quite abandoned the linguistic analogies he otherwise seems to eschew; it also suggests that he may still conceive of the built environment as a series of fixed bodies. Thomas Gieryn makes the point still more plainly in his account of 'What Buildings Do', suggesting that after construction buildings become a 'black box' which 'secures a material artefact *and* those social relations now built into its design'. On completion, a building, in his words, achieves 'closure'; it is 'sealed shut'.[53] This, as Tim Ingold has observed, is a strikingly impoverished account of architecture. Buildings, he argues – surely rightly – are never complete, they are continually being made and remade.[54] In the words of Stewart Brand, 'A building is not something you finish. A building is something you start.'[55] They are not static entities, simple artefacts. Indeed, the moment they stop being made is the moment they become redundant – in other words, the moment they die. In making a building an actor, Latour thus unwittingly turns it in to an object – an object, in his own words, that does not utter a word.

Latour, to be sure, has more recently sought to deal with this objection. In an important short article, co-written with Yaneva, he acknowledges that 'the problem with buildings is that they look desperately static'. Yaneva and Latour consequently argue that techniques need to be developed which will enable researchers to go beyond this – to study buildings and 'to grasp them as movement, as flight, as a series of transformations'.[56] But the techniques they propose do not in fact go far enough. For one thing, they further expose the peculiar paradox at the heart of actor-network theory as applied to architecture. While repeatedly attacking other approaches which 'reduce materiality to its objectivity', Yaneva and Latour nonetheless cannot escape their conception of buildings as 'concrete entities'.[57] Indeed, their approach effects an oddly static reification of 'the building project' as a thing: a black box which is brought into being by architects in their role as 'interpreters, of friends of this interpretable object'.[58] More importantly still, for our purposes, even this modified approach struggles to deal with the effects of change through time. It remains focused on 'building and design processes' – not what happens next.[59] As Tim Edensor has noted, actor-network theory struggles to make sense of actors outside of any given network.[60] In this case, that means that it is of little value to historians seeking to recapture the changing experiences of those who inhabit, visit, view, and as such, continually reshape buildings. Even in its modified form, Latour's approach is unduly reductive for our purposes.

But if actor-network theory offers us little by way of help in understanding the historical experience of architecture, then what alternative might we employ? In recent years, there has been a growth of interest in phenomenology. The insights of Heidegger, Maurice Merleau-Ponty, Gaston Bachelard, and, more recently, Edward Casey do indeed seem to offer an attractive way forward, not least for writers like Matthew Johnson in his article of 2013, 'What do medieval buildings mean?' Here, Johnson proposes 'a move away from "meaning" to "lived experience"' as the proper subject for architectural historians, and he advocates the use of phenomenological insights to achieve just that.[61]

It should certainly be admitted that phenomenology addresses some of the problems we have already identified with other ways of investigating architecture. In particular, the work of phenomenologists helps to break down the idea of buildings as fixed, stable, or sealed shut. For Merleau-Ponty, for example, a building is not a single entity but rather a collage of different experiences.[62] Indeed, for Heidegger, building is always the manifestation of deeper, existential realities and buildings not so much built structures as a means of defining location.[63] This is a long way away from any sense of a silent brick wall or a structure that really dissolves into text. Phenomenology's mode of enquiry is also distinct. It begins with the body and assumes that no analysis can exist outside subjective bodily experience.[64] '*Bodies build places*,' argues Edward Casey, and it can readily be seen that if this is the case then bodies are also necessary to understand them.[65] Perhaps, it might be thought, this circumvents the problems with evidence, the difficulties presented by absent or opaque sources that so stymy any attempt to apply actor-network theory to the buildings of the past.

It is a tempting thought, but also, I suspect, an illusory one. As William Taylor and Michael Levine have recently argued, the appeal to phenomenology is 'procrustean' in its effort 'to make a single theory account for all cases'. It rests, at one level, on a radically subjective set of experiences, and on the other, a totalizing assumption about 'universal and timeless sensibilities'.[66] It assumes, in other words, that what I experience now is the only thing I can experience and therefore the only way of experiencing it. 'History', as Merleau-Ponty puts it, 'is an object which is ourselves.'[67] The problems with this as a historical methodology are clear. Indeed, it must be said that the phenomenologists themselves tend to be rather less ambitious in their claims than those who would seek to use their work. Gaston Bachelard, for example, simply poses the question of how space acts on us. He scarcely seeks to answer it, much less propose universal mechanisms for addressing it. Each occasion, Bachelard suggests, is different; each occasion would require a different explanation – a different 'theorem of topo-analysis' – every time.[68]

As Jorge Otero-Pailos has observed in a brilliant book on the phenomenological turn in architectural history, it was precisely this ambiguity that attracted writers like Christian Norberg-Schulz and Kenneth Frampton in the last few decades of the twentieth century. As Otero-Pailos describes it, phenomenology had a twin appeal for these hugely influential postmodern theorists. In the first place, it seemed to rescue architecture from history – to 'free', as Joseph Rykwert puts it, 'architectural discussion and theory from historicist bondage', and enable the development of a truly authentic modern architecture.[69] In the second place, and still more importantly for us, this architectural phenomenology rescued architectural history from historians, enabling architects to claim precedence when it came to the analysis of buildings. If history, in Merleau-Ponty's terms, really was 'ourselves', it was reasoned, then who better than architects to determine how buildings were actually experienced? Historians, trapped by texts and ill-trained to analyse experience, were, it was concluded, incapable of an unmediated encounter with architecture.

The result of this approach is made fully apparent in Norberg-Schulze's most influential work, *Genius Loci: Towards a Phenomenology of Architecture*, published in 1979. A genuinely bizarre book, the product of a time which, although very close in calendar years, now seems very distant, *Genius Loci* reads far more oddly than many of the nineteenth-century texts explored in this volume, although it does share with many Victorian writers a strikingly, unselfconsciously colonial sensibility, with the architecture of Khartoum, for instance, described without any reference to the views or experiences of its inhabitants. Rather, Norberg-Schultz's own impressions – from the '*pitiless*' desert to the pronounced preference of 'the Arabs' for horizontal forms, to the uniformity of the buildings in a place where 'experiments and personal idiosyncrasies are meaningless' – provide the only interpretation. Even in his accounts of western towns, it is Norberg-Schultz's own impressions which matter. This is less history than a sort of travel journal. It tells us much about the author – and almost nothing about the places he visits or the history he seeks to evoke.[70]

Phenomenology has its value for historians. The work of David Leatherbarrow, for instance, seems to me highly suggestive in forcing us to pay attention to aspects of architecture which have been neglected by historians. Like Norberg-Schultz, indeed, he rejects a narrow focus on the building as a work of art, asking, 'Is it really the case that each building is seen as something "in itself," something that stands apart from its surroundings, noticeable because distinct?'[71] He challenges, too, a purely visual analysis, one that focusses unduly, obsessively, on the façade, and instead he argues

> that there are two ways of gaining knowledge in architectural experience: visual contemplation and bodily comprehension, the first disengaged and static, the second engaged and dynamic. Also, there seem to be two orders of time in architectural experience: the time of the façade, a changeless duration of the same *through* time, and there is the time of the site, interiors, and materials, a time of change, continuous alteration and difference.[72]

These insights seem to me interesting and valuable. But they are valuable chiefly because they pose new questions rather than because they offer new answers. Again – even though they echo some of the distinctions made in the nineteenth century between visual and bodily experience, and between different experiences of time – in the end even Leatherbarrow's analysis tells us more about him than it does about the past.

Phenomenology cannot offer us a securely grounded historical account of what buildings did because it cannot explain how contemporaries understood what buildings actually were. If, for instance, Edward Casey is right to argue that conceptions of place have changed profoundly throughout history, then why should we imagine that our modern subjective understanding of a place is the same as that of the people we study?[73] The same, one might say, is true of the concept of space, which as Andrew Sayer has persuasively argued, was one that writers until the twentieth century managed, on the whole, to do without.[74] As this suggests, the basic experience of architecture is likely to differ from time to time; from one analytical framework to another; from one building culture to another. Phenomenology teaches us to take experience and perception seriously. But phenomenological methods are inadequate for an understanding of the buildings of the past.

Ultimately, indeed, the problem with actor-network theory, and with phenomenology, and with other approaches to this subject is that none of them offer us a secure or convincing definition of what a building actually is: much less how this definition might have changed through time. In that way, both substitute anachronism for analysis. For we cannot take for granted that we understand buildings in the same way as those we study did. Buildings, as Howard Davies has insisted, are the product of particular building cultures, what he defines as 'the coordinated system of knowledge, rules, and procedures that is shared by people who participate in the building activity'.[75] What is true about the production of buildings is also true of their use and their effect on their users. Increasingly, it is becoming clear that there have been many different ways to conceptualize the built environment and that each model results in differing beliefs about what architecture actually amounted to: many different regimes of materiality.[76]

And if this was true in general, then it has specific consequences for the study of architecture. Notions derived from our assumptions may simply fail to grasp what contemporaries believed and experienced. The Gothic tradition, Robert Bork has recently argued, treated architecture as a 'dynamic design process', rather than an attempt to create a static or uniform edifice. The 'internal logic of the process', he contends, 'mattered more than the shape of the final product'.[77] This is a long way away from what Marvin Trachtenberg identifies as the modern – indeed, the modernist – conception of an ideal building as 'change resistant, immutably perfect': the coherent fulfilment of a stable, preordained plan.[78] If we are to understand what buildings can do, we need to understand what it was they were believed to be. As the architectural historian Anthony Geraghty puts it, 'At present, we struggle to understand what people were doing with buildings because we do not understand what they thought buildings were.'[79]

The solution to this problem will come from the sorts of research that this volume seeks to foster. It will also draw on the kinds of work done by historians of other periods, writers like the medievalist Mary Carruthers, who has used images and texts to illuminate attitudes that were long-thought lost. This does not mean a vulgar empiricism or narrow antiquarianism; nor does it mean ignoring insights derived from other disciplines. Carruthers's works *The Craft of Thought* and *The Experience of Beauty in the Middle Ages* make their theoretical positions absolutely explicit.[80] But their real strength comes from their attentiveness to what writers and thinkers in the Middle Ages actually wrote about architecture and actually believed architecture to be. She explores, then, not just the agency of architecture, nor just the phenomenology of architecture, but also, crucially, the ontology of architecture.

The success of this approach can be seen in the way in which it has been taken up by writers like Paul Binski, whose work on the architecture of medieval England reveals a real debt to Carruthers and offers a profoundly exciting new analysis of his subject.[81] He shows us that medieval people expected to experience architecture in a set of very particular ways: as a text designed to communicate ideas; as a dynamic space, designed to evoke particular emotions; as a thing which was not merely seen, but also felt. Architecture in this, medieval, understanding is not a static work of art, nor simply a space: but an experience designed to achieve certain effects.

That this view differed considerably from that which followed can be seen if we compare this medieval architectural imagination with, say, an Enlightenment view. For Kant, of course, this emotionally charged view of buildings was simply primitive, even barbarous. Later writers, like the anthropologists and art historians of the nineteenth and early twentieth centuries would concur, describing such a world view as animism, and seeing it as a long-dead, or happily exotic, tradition.[82] Such an assumption helps to explain what is otherwise a puzzle about much eighteenth-century writing on architecture. Compared to the rich vocabulary of the middle ages and the sensuous enjoyment of architecture it betokens, eighteenth-century architectural writing is curiously impoverished.[83] Description was often highly conventionalized and unspecific. Georgians lacked a vocabulary to account for buildings, even obviously important buildings, in anything but the most generic terms. Thus the Temple Church in London – one of the sights of the city – was simply, and repeatedly, described as 'a neat structure with pillars'.[84] Historians have often found this simply tiresome, but it is worth considering whether it doesn't, in fact, speak of a very different understanding of architecture itself: one in which buildings are static, not active; in which aesthetics, however conventional and conventionalized, matter more than feelings or sensations. A world in which experience doesn't matter because architecture itself has been conceptualized differently.[85]

What then, of the nineteenth century? Well, all of this brings us back to Proust; to Proust and to Ruskin; to the romantics and empathy theorists and the others who debated these ideas in the nineteenth century. For as I suggested at the start of this chapter, the remarkable thing about the nineteenth century is just how interested so many contemporaries were in the themes we are now exploring. It is relating these words to the buildings of the period that will enable us to comprehend just what architecture meant to contemporaries: what it did, and what it was believed to be able to do.

This efflorescence of writing was remarkable, and speaks of a renewed interest in the very nature of architecture and architectural experience – a big change from the unproblematic assumptions and reticent criticism of the preceding century. It was the product of what Jonathan Crary describes as the nineteenth-century 'crisis in perception': a new awareness, prompted by scientific investigation, that the eye was not an infallible organ.[86] It was also part of a broader movement questioning the very nature of experience itself. That experience was the basis for philosophy and science was a truism for many in an age in which inductive thought was privileged. This was especially true in Britain, where, as Shadworth Hodgson puts it, the 'English school' could be characterized as 'experientialism, the resolve to obtain experience pure and simple, and see it whole and without addition'.[87] Yet, as his qualification suggests, there was always doubt even among the 'experientialists' about experience and how best to understand it – hence, for instance, the arguments between the absolute empiricist John Stuart Mill and that great advocate of inductive reasoning William Whewell. For Mill, all knowledge was directly derived from experience; for Whewell, experience was processed by the mind.[88] Thus, again, questions of veracity constantly recurred.

This crisis in perception and this anxiety about experience fed into a still broader discussion about architecture. This is the debate recaptured by this book. I cannot, of course, encapsulate all of it in this chapter; nor does this volume cover all the very many areas of interest it might. But *Experiencing Architecture in the Nineteenth Century* will provide, I hope, encouragement to others to venture yet further into this field. There is work to be done on the ways in which architecture was reconceptualized in the nineteenth century – and how issues of experience helped to do that. I'm interested, too, in the difference between architecture and space. For it seems to me that the modern association of the two is one that was not, on the whole, shared by nineteenth-century writers, who stressed the facade and ornamentation much more than the volume or the spatial experience of buildings. Space, I increasingly think, is an issue created by and for the modern movement. It is also – with a marvellous circularity – the outcome of debates about phenomenology which began in the nineteenth century; though it seems to have taken some time to move from philosophical and psychological research into architectural practice.

Above all, I'm interested in exploring the relationship between the general regime of materiality and the specific experience of it – whether we can conceive of a 'nineteenth-century experience of architecture', or whether we should begin to think of architecture as something more protean, changeable, and problematic; as something which mutates in the minds of those who encounter it; as something that leads to very different experiences by very different people. Proust here is again important – he links subjectivity with experience, and architecture with subjectivity, thus suggesting that all are interlinked and each interdependent. As we go in search of this lost time, his example will always – I think – remain pertinent. Certainly it should serve an inspiration as well as a provocation, forcing us to consider, at both an individual and at a collective level, how architecture was experienced – and how it shaped experience – in the nineteenth century.

PART TWO

Producing experience

CHAPTER TWO

Touching heaven, crafting utopia: David Parr House in Cambridge

Ayla Lepine

In 1887, the painter David Parr (1855–1927) purchased 186 Gwydir Street, a small brick terraced house in Cambridge with a front and back garden. Frederick Leach and Sons employed Parr as a painter; they were based in Cambridge and produced complex interior schemes for churches throughout Britain, working especially closely with the Victorian Gothic Revival architect George Frederick Bodley and with William Morris's design firm.[1] Parr filled the interior of his own home using adaptations of the same designs he painted for major ecclesiastical commissions. His home is unique in the history of art and architecture. Parr's designs include Gothic Revival inscriptions from numerous sources such as hymns, well-known sayings often seen on early-modern-decorative art, and Shakespeare. This house is a space in which labour, art, medievalism, and modernity intermingle (Figure 2.1).[2] It also offers a legible and fresh story of late-Victorian and early-twentieth-century British modern life, and this building can be 'read' as a series of signals regarding historicism, knowledge, and imagination.[3] As Elizabeth Wilson writes, modernity 'refers to things both intangible and undeniably material: the atmosphere and culture of a whole epoch, its smells, its sounds, its rhythms. ... The term "modernity" makes possible the exploration of our subjective experience of it.'[4] By focusing on bodily experience and the senses in building a new

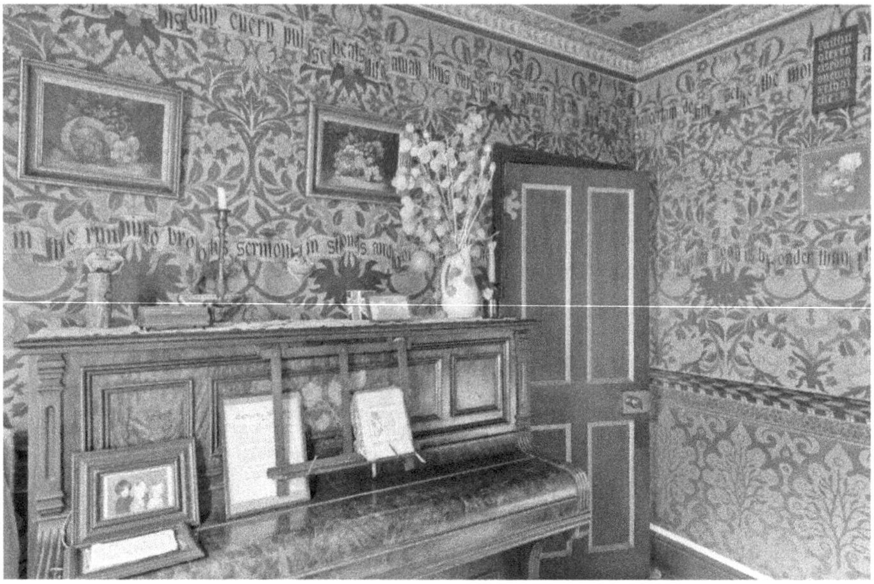

FIGURE 2.1 *David Parr House, Drawing Room wall paintings, c. 1892–1916 (photo: David Parr House).*

interpretation of David Parr House, the interiors of which only recently came to light among scholars and historians, the embodiment of modernity comes into play too.

This chapter explores the ways in which David Parr used his professional skills to create an architectural self-portrait and craft a domestic utopia. I seek to account for the motivations and multi-sensorial effects of this little-known, working-class artistic interior. Parr's home will be interpreted by focusing on experience and embodiment, the anachronic blending of past and present identities through historicism, and the unusual use of ecclesiastical architectural precedent to produce a new kind of domesticity which concentrated on eternity and sacramental theology within the framework of the everyday home. Parr's use of image and text brought the power of Christian thought into his familial spaces in a direct and visually accessible way. Parr's patterns and inscriptions make connections between the sacred and the everyday, referencing holy sites including local churches and their liturgies within the walls of his own dwelling. The longevity of the project is notable too: Parr fused the heavenly and the earthly through his artistic practice in his Victorian home over a four-decade period. Parr applied avant-garde revivalist ecclesiastical interiors to his own space and thus transformed the meanings of these bold patterns, making the familiar strange, and domesticating the monumental.

The Parrs in Gwydir Street

Gwydir Street is near the main railway station in Cambridge, approximately half a mile from the centre of the city. The street's houses indicate the presence of lower and higher levels of skill and a mixture of class backgrounds. No. 186, built in 1876, is part of a development known as Gothic Terrace, distinguished in the row by their ogee arches and dogtooth detail combined with otherwise conventional brickwork and a typical Victorian interior plan.[5] After David Parr purchased it in 1887, he renovated the house in minor ways and subsequent adjustments were made by his descendants (the alteration of a back bedroom to a bathroom as family needs changed, for example), but the schemes and furnishings from Parr's lifetime remain largely intact. The house is virtually unknown by scholars of Victorian and Edwardian British art and architecture, having come into the public eye gradually since 2014.

David Parr trained first as a joiner and was working for the decorative painting firm of F. R. Leach and Sons by the 1870s. He was also Anglican and probably worshipped locally. A small inscription near the west window of All Saints, Jesus Lane, a Gothic Revival church which George Frederick Bodley (1827–1907) designed in 1863 with interior paintings executed by Frederick Leach and Sons, includes Parr's name and the date 1871. Parr was a teenager when he joined this firm. Bodley's first designs for All Saints were devised in 1861, and the spire was completed by 1871. Painting the interior was a long-term project with numerous phases, and the first patterns – designed by Charles Eamer Kempe and Bodley, together with glass by Morris, Marshall, Faulkner and Company – began to appear in 1864.[6] The sense of labour involved in these projects and in Parr's own home can be discerned in a cluster of records and ideas. Crucially, Parr would not have been able to afford the middle-class pricing of Morris's own products. His access to this aesthetic world was made possible through Morris's own socialist ideals (which his business was often unable to achieve): instead of buying these patterned papers and textiles, Parr painted his own, much in the style of Morris' own Red House and the church interiors that Parr helped to create.[7] Leach and Sons' motto was the Benedictine motto 'labore est orare', which means 'to work is to pray'. Between 1871 and 1881 Leach more than doubled their workforce, to meet growing demand for their detailed and high-quality interiors.[8] Producing these patterns across churches, houses, and dining halls and even a palace was about more than paintbrushes, but it was a vocation, a devotion, and an art at the heart of the expression of something of the sacred.

David Parr's own insightful notebook contains descriptions of when and how work was done around his house, including one entry regarding the number of hours it took to paint patterns within one of the rooms. By costing his time as part of his own private record-keeping, Parr's personal project became incorporated into the experiential body of his working life, not only in terms of parallels in the patterns, but also in terms of wages and economics. Although he only recorded his work in this way this once, it suggests an oscillating self-awareness of the overall project in which decorating his home across the decades of his working life was a way of claiming agency as a professional and as an artist. Parr was not only keeping track of his work but also recognizing tangibly that his craft had worth and value. At the same time, his domestic decoration closely reflected the idiom of the designers with whom he worked. Parr was original, but also emulated the prominent figures of his day, such as Morris and Bodley. As the design historian Glenn Adamson writes in relation to feminism and craft, 'Agency, including whatever agency can be claimed through craft, is always compromised, always performed, never totally authentic. That, in fact, is the secret of its power.'[9] Adamson's point here is that the concept of 'craft' and its outcomes in art and architecture implies collaboration, the vernacular, and alliance with the 'decorative' as opposed to the 'fine' arts. Indeed the father of the Arts and Crafts Movement, Morris himself, wrote persuasively about the power and legitimacy of the decorative arts referring to them with a lack of irony as the 'lesser' arts in an influential essay in 1882.[10] Parr's sense of being his own client contributed to the concept of his house on Gwydir Street as a manifestation of his values and expertise. David Parr's house is, and always was, a self-portrait of a highly skilled arts and crafts worker together with his growing family, as Parr's work sought to provide for his household not only financially but also artistically.

Morris, Leach and Parr

Leach and Sons, a firm similar to but smaller than London-based Clayton and Bell or Lavers, Barraud and Westlake, carried out a large number of commissions for Morris and Bodley through the 1870s and 1880s. Primarily known for artisanal painting, they were also able to execute designs in glass, and almost certainly had commission overlaps with the Cambridge-based firm of Rattee and Kett, nationally known for their ecclesiastical and domestic woodwork. In Cambridge, Leach and Sons executed the interior schemes for the hall at Queens' College, Jesus College Chapel, the ceilings of St Michael's and St Botolph's churches, the interior of All Saints Church on Jesus Lane, and the chancel and sanctuary of St Barnabas on Mill Road, close by what would become Parr's residence on Gwydir Street. Paul Thompson has described the working relationship as one of growth and prosperity through the key decade of the Gothic Revival and the Aesthetic Movement as Morris and Bodley's respective firms grew in status and number of commissions. Leach and Sons carried out 'two to three jobs a year for the firm between 1867 and 1870. In 1871 there were nine jobs, the next year fourteen, and by 1878 forty-eight.'[11] Leach and Sons, with David Parr as a key artist in the firm, also carried out Morris's designs for the staircase at St James's Palace in the early 1880s.[12] These designs became an important inspiration for Parr's own home in the decades that followed. However, by the turn of the twentieth century and into the Edwardian period, designs from the heyday of the Aesthetic 1870s and 1880s began to fall out of fashion in favour of lighter and brighter spaces, less florid and intense in their ornamental surfaces. And then with the outbreak of the First World War, there were fewer commissions and far fewer artists and labourers to carry them out. Throughout, Parr continued to paint; from about 1914 his house increasingly becoming an echo, legacy, and afterlife of the productivity and style of the last decades of the nineteenth century. Indeed, Leach and Sons were wound up in 1916, and Parr's employment after that date is unknown.[13]

There are moments in the house's interior in which the painted walls operate as simultaneous self-portraits of David Parr, and portraits of Parr's family, his ideals, and of Morris himself, as well as of the Leach and Sons firm. Furthermore, Parr's interiors and his status as a working artist – indeed, a craftsman – within the Leach and Sons firm complicates Morris's own views on craftsmanship, industry, and politics. Morris identified a strong relationship between craftsmanship, nostalgia, and utopia, as his many lectures, practices, and publications such as *News from Nowhere*, completed in 1890, amply demonstrate. He desired political revolution and he also desired an artful escape route from the industrial pressures of modern Victorian culture. An alternative view of Morris's ideals and their challenging presumptions is offered by Glenn Adamson, who focused on Morris's deep concern about the death of craft and the death of dignity in artistic labour (inspired significantly by John Ruskin), in order to show that Morris's rhetoric was not consistent with the world around him and the milieu with which he frequently engaged.[14] Beyond Morris and Co.'s own workshops for textiles, glass, and the like, he also outsourced much of his work to firms such as the wallpaper printers Jeffrey and Co, and the painters Leach and Sons. The romantic ideal of the craftsman, paradoxically both the lone genius and the collaborative socialist art-worker, comes into stark contrast with the working life of a highly skilled art-worker like David Parr.[15] This is not because Morris idealized craft while Parr (and indeed Leach) did not. It is because Parr's labour was integrated with the work of thousands of Victorian art-workers invested in, and supported by, the very industrial processes that so frustrated and concerned Morris. It is worth remembering that Morris experimented briefly with an early version of linoleum, that most man-made and industrial of materials, and that Morris got into trouble with the Master and Fellows of Jesus College in Cambridge when they queried whether he truly was the designer of the chapel ceiling paintings because they saw Leach and Sons' workmen and not Morris himself on the job.[16] By living his life in the presence of motifs like these, Parr was integrating more than domesticity and public labour within a dialectic of design. As David Morgan explains, creating a likeness is an act of mimetic sympathy: 'a structure of relations, a way of seeing that is a way of feeling'.[17] Indeed, Parr also aligned his identity with those of his colleagues and mentors through the production of multi-sensorial spaces in which to sleep, pray, eat, and entertain. Parr complicates our understanding of Morris by translating and re-innovating his ideas into a truly working-class artist's domestic spaces. Parr's house is the only known example of this.

Art of beauty, labour of love

From the outside, there is no indication that David Parr's family home contained the level of domestic artfulness that it does. In this sense, it is not so different from the grander bespoke statements of London artists' houses, such as Leighton House or William Burges's Tower House. Both are plain brick on the outside – granted in monumental and distinctive forms – and they reveal the treasures within both slowly and conscientiously by appealing to the discerning eye, from wall paintings and architectural sculpture to ceramics and bespoke furnishings. David Parr's house was an artistic house among the best of the early and bold examples of Aesthetic Movement and Arts and Crafts Houses, though Parr was working within his means much in the same way that the wealthy Burges worked within his. Parr's interiors invite comparison with Caroline Dakers's research into the so-called Holland Park Circle, fully within the scope of Parr's own hand's capacity to design, create, and offer a narrative of beauty, history, and cultural sophistication.[18] Parr's home shows that art and architectural discourses on beauty and taste need not be limited to middle-class, aristocratic, and affluent examples. Indeed, Parr's project puts Ruskin and Morris's ideals into practice. Burges, of course, had skilled workmen with whom he collaborated or who carried out his designs in different materials from mosaic to semi-precious stones.[19] Parr, working on a different scale and with different pressures and priorities, did it himself.

Parr's approach to the relationship between nature and culture, as well as ornament and form, is manifestly Ruskinian. In the chapter 'Beauty' in John Ruskin's *Seven Lamps of Architecture*, published in 1849, he writes,

> What is the place for ornament? Consider first that the characters of natural objects which the architect can represent are few and abstract. The greater parts of those delights by which nature recommends herself to man at all times, cannot be conveyed by him in his imitative work. He cannot make his grass green and cool and good to rest upon, which in nature is its chief use to man; nor can he make his flowers tender and full

of colour and scent, which in nature are their chief powers of giving joy. Those qualities which alone he can secure are certain severe characters of form, such as men only see in nature on deliberate examination, and by the full and set appliance of sight and thought.[20]

Ruskin concludes that the experience of nature directly is the only route towards the design of successful ornament that seeks not to replicate nature but to distil it, calling to mind the joys and sensorial pleasures of nature's beauty: 'A man must lie down on the bank of grass on his breast and set himself to watch and penetrate the intertwining of it, before he finds that which is to be gathered.'[21] Particularly in the front room of Parr's house on Gwydir Street, the lessons of nature distilled in ornament and the pleasures of nature recalled by descriptive text are bound together in an immersive experience of beauty, creation, and morality. Shakespeare's evocative words of water and wildlife flutter in scrolls across the intertwining leafy plants Parr devised across the span of this interior; the blending of these approaches to nature through culture attest to Parr's sophistication and knowledge.

Following architectural historian John Maddison's invaluable chronology based on Parr's own records, the sequence of Parr's projects began with the entrance hall in 1887–8. The upper walls here were finished in 1891. The drawing room ceiling was painted in 1892–3, and the dining room acquired a dado of Gothic ornaments in the same painting campaign. The drawing room and dining room were painted in 1894–5. The next major phase was the entrance hall, staircase, and landing in 1909–10. The most impressive and complex scheme, the walls of the drawing room were completed in 1912–13, and the diaper dado was finished in 1916. In the same year, the inscription in the smallest front bedroom was also completed. In 1918–19, the green and red diaper patterns were completed. The final recorded design was Parr's blue flower design in the kitchen in 1920.[22]

Entering the house, patterns based on northern Renaissance damasks and late-medieval wall paintings festoon the upper and lower regions of the walls. Though some have been covered with emulsion paint in recent years, in Parr's time the entrance hall would have been an inviting spectacle, with deep russet tones of the dado zone giving way to freer-form foliage designs which recall Morris's 'Willow' pattern. The curving stalks and blossoming motifs of the pattern beneath the dado reference Pugin's work as well as Watts and Company's designs for textiles and wallpaper including Pugin's 1840s patterns for the Houses of Parliament and Watts's patterns including 'Pine' and 'The Pear'; the strong central stalk element is reminiscent of the river patterns running through Morris's designs such as 'Wandle' or 'Cray'. Close design relations are for public rather than private spaces, namely the walls of Queens' hall, All Saints Church, and wallpaper designs for the New Palace of Westminster. Turning 180 degrees, the stained-glass lunette above the front door reveals a roundel of a bird in a wood, singing in full voice, in a relatively naturalistic depiction. The natural world is more stylized in the surrounding quarries, letting in maximum light and contrasting with the carefully detailed rendering of the bird. Windows like these were not uncommon in Cambridge, and may have been produced by Leach and Sons. Whether this warbling reminder of nature's vibrancy in the midst of an expanding and increasingly urbanized Cambridge was Parr's decision to install or whether it was an earlier feature is unknown.

The drawing room contains several distinct zones and several inscriptions running around the room on scrolls painted to indicate a robust three-dimensionality against the flattened stylized floral patterns. It is the most sumptuous room in the house, and the varying scales of the patterns and intensity of the variation create a symphony of stimulation similar to entering All Saints on Jesus Lane or Queens' College Old Hall, both of which were painted by Leach and Sons just prior to Parr's acquisition of 186 Gwydir Street. The all-over patterns are typical of Bodley's churches throughout this period, from St Salvador's in Dundee to St John's Tue Brook in Liverpool. As Maddison observes, the back wall of the drawing room, which is one of the most spectacular passages of painted pattern in the house, bears close comparison with Morris and Co.'s designs for the window embrasures of Old Swan House in Chelsea, a project which Parr may have worked on as part of Leach and Sons.[23] The drawing room also features small wood and lead gilded elements that may have been salvaged from project sites, including a rose-en-soleil, floriated portcullis, and tiny plaster flowers adorning the painted patterns to create a three-dimensional effect. This latter strategy, generally not used in Bodley's church interiors, recalls the plaster relief across the walls of Morris, Webb, and Burne-Jones's groundbreaking Green Dining Room, designed for the South Kensington Museum in 1867 and their first civic commission. In this room, Morris and Bodley's schemes for churches and domestic and collegiate interiors are stretched, compressed, concentrated, and interlaced with texts in Gothic script that were particular to Parr's life, tastes, and Anglican beliefs.

There are four inscriptions in Parr's drawing room. As they run around the walls from left to right, they tell a story. Parr's designs for this space create a narrative of honest labour, delight in creation, and the value of time as a fleeting gift. To the left of the window reads, 'If you do anything, do it well.' Beginning to the right of the window is a popular verse that Maddison has attributed to Sunderland lustreware and to the seventeenth-century Anglican priest and poet George Herbert.[24] The 'Sunderland' text is: 'Swiftly see each moment flies see and learn be timely wise, every moment shortens day every pulse beats life away thus our every heaving breath wafts us on to certain death. Seize the moments as they fly, know to live and learn to die.'[25] The inscription by Herbert is, 'He who knows nothing doubts nothing.'[26]

The next wall, to the left of the door, features an inscription from *As You Like It*. Parr captioned this one (and only this one), perhaps doing so to demonstrate his knowledge of Shakespeare or to clarify its source as the others would have been instantly recognizable. The inscription reads, jubilantly, 'Tongues in trees, books in the running brooks, Sermons in stones and good in everything.' These 'sermons in stones' and 'books in the running brooks', combined with carefully stylized repeating ornament, strike a harmony between the natural world and its decorative interpretation. As discussed above, there is a Ruskinian effect in the conjunction of these texts and images, allowing for the particularity of the natural world to mingle with the imaginative fount of English literature and historicist interior design. The final inscription is on the lower portion of the wall opposite the window. It is a line from a popular Victorian hymn, 'There's a wideness in God's mercy': 'Now the Love of God is broader than the measure of man's mind and the heart of the eternal is most wonderfully kind.'[27] This is a profoundly tender and optimistic hymn, in which the writer warns that when we consider God, humanity tends to 'make his love too narrow by false limits of our own', offering an alternative of radical hospitality and capacious spiritual liberation.[28] Parr himself concludes the sequence of texts, from adage and classic domestic wares' moralizing aphorisms to Shakespeare, George Herbert, and hymn-writer Frederick Faber. The concluding word he chose was not 'amen', but 'alleluia'. The note is one of praise and of perpetual continuation (rather than the completion that 'amen' would imply), inviting the viewer-beholder-reader to contemplate afresh, to turn again, to explore the room and its cultural references anew in this bespoke mixture of histories and values. The flow of texts and their references bear comparison with numerous inscriptions integrated within Leach and Sons' projects. These include biblical inscriptions from Matthew's Gospel and Revelation at All Saints, Jesus Lane and the hymn 'Vexilla Regis' held by angels and floating through trees along the borders of the nave ceiling painting at Jesus College, which was completed by Leach and Sons and designed by Morris and Webb in 1867. The collection of texts in the Parr Drawing Room spans nearly 300 years and unites a canon of English poetry, prose, and devotional writing across a couple of metres against a flowingly complex array of floral and vegetal decorative painting.

At the end of the entrance hall, the pattern Parr painted on the kitchen chimney breast features small blue flowers surrounded by willow-type leaves, their springing boughs woven into lightly microarchitectural forms similar to patterns by Owen Jones or Christopher Dresser, rather than curling and curving as Morris's do in his willow pattern.[29] The dining room is dominated by a pattern of scrolling foliate designs in green and red on a white background with details of deep brown and yellow. The bedroom above the dining room features walls with a virtually identical pattern. Maddison points out that the Morris-like pattern, carried out in 1893, is closely related to a pattern published by Lewis F. Day three years after Morris's death, in 1899.[30]

Paintings in the back bedroom are nearly identical to those in the dining room. Here the undulating broad leaves of green and red are offset by darker hatched patterns, which create an effect of all-over decoration with a bold rhythm (Figure 2.2). Close study of these surfaces suggests that this room may have been used as a space for teaching, though it is unclear whom may have been at work here as David Parr's son, David, Jr. was in his 30s and already an accomplished worker with Leach. While some areas of paint are crisp and in an assured freehand, some are far less precise around the edges, and the darker hatched areas are much rougher. As a less significant room in the house, the back bedroom's painted scheme, carried out in 1919 according to Parr's records, is no less impactful than the dining room but less accomplished in some areas. If this was indeed a space in which teaching took place, this is a particularly significant room in the linkage of experience and architecture, passing traditions on from one person to another through touch and pedagogy.

Smaller than the other bedrooms in the house, the front bedroom was wallpapered with a basic commercial pattern of small pink flowers. It is also the only room in the house to have a painted inscription at the top of the wall rather than an ornamental frieze (Figure 2.3). In scale and in stylistic detail it is a close relation to many of the biblical texts encircling painted schemes for, among others, All Saints and the Old Hall at Queens' College. This use of text was a hallmark of Bodley and Garner's interior designs from the 1860s until the turn of the twentieth century. That this tiny bedroom hosts this monumental design, the lettering overpowering the room's scale, contributes to a sense of paradoxical hospitality and uncanny oppression.

FIGURE 2.2 *David Parr House, Dining Room, c. 1918-19 (photo: David Lewis).*

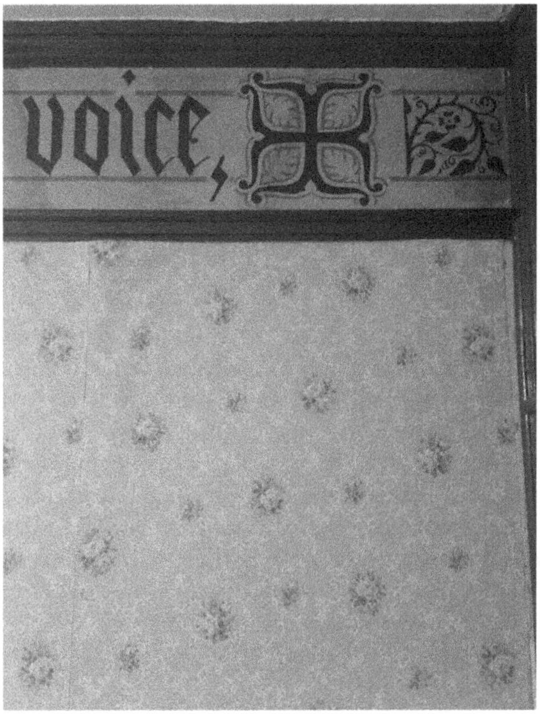

FIGURE 2.3 *David Parr House, Front Bedroom, 1915 (photo: David Lewis).*

It reads, 'May I always be ready when my Saviour calleth me. May I in sight of heaven rejoice, when I hear my Saviour's voice.' Completed in 1915, the lettering scheme is on a scale typical for lofty church interiors, not for small-scale intimate bedrooms. The conjunction gives the text an intensively moralizing effect, reminding the reader that a life of Christian devotion is lived in the midst of a longing for heaven and an ease with the anticipation of death and resurrection. It is not a dissimilar theology of domestic design than the influential American Gothic Revival architect and artist Ralph Adams Cram's bed for his child, surrounded by angels and topped with a crucifix, reminding the sleeper of the close relationship between protection in rest and anticipation of eternal rest in heaven.[31]

Domesticity and identity

Though the initial intensity of Arts and Crafts idealism born in the 1860s had waned somewhat through the turn of the twentieth century, the Arts and Crafts world in which Parr lived and worked continued through the

Edwardian period. As Cheryl Buckley notes, 'Consolidated before the First World War, aspects of Arts and Crafts design evoked stability, longevity and tradition.'[32] Buckley also notes that changing roles of women in relation to histories of design, both domestic and in the wider social sphere, impacted on aesthetics, economics, and understandings of family life. Little is known about the extent to which Parr's family participated in the production of 186 Gwydir Street's unique home environment, but it would be incorrect to suggest that his wife and children were mere passive spectators as his painting endeavours took shape around them. It is possible that the inscriptions in the front room, for example, reflected the family's ideals as a whole, or particularly those of the family's circle, rather than Parr's beliefs alone. Parr's work epitomizes much of the rhetoric at the turn of the century regarding domestic utopia and Arts and Crafts ideals on both a small and large scale. The architectural writer Ethel Unwin, describing the beliefs shared with her husband, the utopian urban planner and designer Raymond Unwin, wrote that they 'wanted the home to be a setting for a life of artistic worth'.[33] With designs for Letchworth Garden City and idealized cityscapes, the Unwins were a major voice in debates regarding healthy homes and better modern urban planning.[34] The infinite worth of humanity could be displayed in the finite gestures of beautiful and conscientious design, which worked out the pleasures of life itself – both nature and culture – in visible interior domestic details.

In some senses, the Parr house is the inverse of Bodley and his network's vision in the 1870s of creating ecclesiastical spaces that reflected qualities of ideal Aesthetic domesticity. In Parr's case, the decorative programme throughout No. 186 Gwydir Street is a series of domestic spaces underpinned by ecclesiastical texts and imagery mingling with the more conventionally domestic. Designs with direct and more distant references to textiles and painted patterns that could be used for ecclesiastical and domestic purposes combine in these spaces, blurring the boundaries between these worlds with a canny attentiveness to both design and meaning. Some of Morris and Co.'s design schemes and trials, such as the nave walls at Jesus College Chapel in Cambridge, are connected to domestic textile and wallpaper patterns. Watts and Company, which the architects George Frederick Bodley, Thomas Garner, and George Gilbert Scott, Jr. established in 1874, deliberately blended together the ecclesiastical and the domestic in their designs and in their showrooms. A pattern could be made into a silk cope for a priest or an upholstered chair for an earl, or wallpaper for a middle-class drawing room.[35] The intentional and artistically innovative Victorian merge of the motifs and atmospheres of both home and church through late Gothic design. Bodley noted the parallels between Aesthetic homes, the first stirrings of the Arts and Crafts Movement among Webb and Morris, and late-medieval ecclesiastical palettes and materials. Indeed, he explained the domestic quality of his church interior designs in the 1878 notes he produced describing All Saints, Jesus Lane:

> The later and more developed Gothic styles adopted the system of darker and richer painting on the walls, while the glass was made delicate and silvery in tone, much white being used ... the interior of an old church being treated with the same intention, so to speak, as we treat the rooms in our houses.[36]

Sacred and domestic themes intertwine with the quotidian to create a unique portrait at 186 Gwydir Street. In art historian James Elkins's study of methods of looking at everyday objects and phenomena (from postage stamps to sunrises), he concentrates briefly on fingerprints.[37] Noting the complexity of recording and understanding fingerprint details and patterns, and exploring the difference between the 'core', 'delta', and 'whorl' of a given fingerprint, Elkins's study is a helpful metaphor to explore David Parr House not merely as an example of an artist's late-Victorian home but as a place in which art, life, the touch of the artist's hand, and the specificity of unique individual identity interlace. In the front hall on the left side as one enters, there are looped intertwined initials of Parr himself; as he signed his work he also welcomed in his guests in an unusual way, alerting them to his presence in the painted walls by encouraging them to seek and find Parr's own logo-signature in the merged decorative loops of a distinctive D and P. The patterns of Parr's home are closely related to Morris, Pugin, and other designs in this aesthetic ethos of the Gothic Revival and the Arts and Crafts Movement. The house itself is a personal and highly complex portrait of Parr as an artist, and it is not simply an homage to these high-profile Victorian designers. The patterns adorning the Parr family home express a unique identity, closely related to, but utterly distinct from, Morris and his circle. The patterns are Parr's 'whorl', a unique design fingerprint underscoring the interior as a self-portrait. Initially, fingerprints from two different people look very similar. With closer attention, their relatedness remains apparent but it becomes easier to spot the differences in the details. Parr's own 'fingerprint' – his own home – is closely related to, but not an intentional copy of, Morris or Pugin. Parr's interiors – the wall patterns, the colours, the use of three-dimensional relief, and the inscriptions – are wholly his own and are closely connected to the design-world in which he trained and worked. The very nature of influence, style, and originality in ornament, pattern, text, and image is interrogated in these meticulously painted surfaces. Taken together, each of these rooms forms an element in the fingerprints of Parr's own artistic hand.

Parr's room designs, especially the front room and the bedroom above it, use scale to create a sense of stimulating immersion and even unease. The painted patterns Parr worked with in schemes for churches, civic projects, and St James's Palace were meant to be used on a grand scale. By adapting them to his own relatively small terraced house but only partially diminishing the scale, a sense of grandeur and intimacy are paradoxically and simultaneously achieved. The initial observation of a plant, perhaps, is scaled up, stylized, intertwined, granted movement and dynamism in swirling repeated patterns, offered opportunities to range across surfaces of holy and grand spaces, and then in Parr's case these images are not miniaturized, but made grander still in their population of these small spaces, regarded by groups of two or three people, rather than a congregation or a party of hundreds. Parr's work collects the visual effects of these up-scale designs and concentrates them with an energy that vibrates in confined domestic Victorian worker space; the home references the castle, but itself stays at the scale of a workers' home. Moreover, the references to fragments of text, including Shakespeare, hymnody, and aphorisms, are mirrored in the references to fragments of pattern, drawn from Morris and possibly others with whom Parr was familiar. The house's walls constitute a cultural collection, reproduced and reinterpreted for the family's own labours and pleasures.

Across four decades, Parr and his family inhabited these small spaces as painted patterns slowly built up in vivid colours and layers of motifs and cultural references around them. From 1887 until his death in 1927, David Parr continued to paint, build, renovate, and dream within the walls of 186 Gwydir Street. For forty years, this working-class artist and his family participated in the production of a small home that became a microcosm for the most pertinent ideas and questions circulating in the final decades of the nineteenth century regarding domesticity, holiness, beauty, art, craft, and design. The house's small rooms, from the ambitious opulence of the variously scaled patterns and texts in the front room to the isolated and bold frieze reminding the viewer of mortality in the smallest bedroom, record a life of art and the art of life. Parr lived out St Benedict and Leach and Sons' shared motto, 'labore est orare'. In exploring the potential of pattern to express cultural meaning on a vast scale in both personal and professional settings simultaneously, Parr's experience as a painter, father, teacher, worker, and innovator is embedded within each pounce mark and brushstroke from the front door to the back bedroom within Gothic Terrace in Gwydir Street.

CHAPTER THREE

Architecture of the mind: Imparting Californian identity through architectural experience on the early Stanford University campus

David Frazer Lewis

In 1885, Leland and Jane Stanford decided to devote the majority of the fortune they had amassed from building the Transcontinental Railroad to the creation of a new university (Figure 3.1). The university would be named in memory of their only child, Leland Stanford, Junior, who had died of typhoid the previous year. 'The children of California shall be our children,' Leland Stanford famously declared. The story is familiar, but a point that bears further investigation is the relationship between the Stanfords' vision for the future of California and the way they intended the art and architecture of their campus to transmit that vision. In fact, the Stanfords placed considerable emphasis on student experience of the physical campus environment as a key component of the education provided by the new university. The Stanfords aimed to create a uniquely Californian experience by immersing students in a uniquely Californian visual culture.

The Stanfords are highly mythologized figures, whose golden hearts and golden pockets are eulogized in alumni literature; however, on the basis of surviving letters and scholarly histories of the university, it is safe to

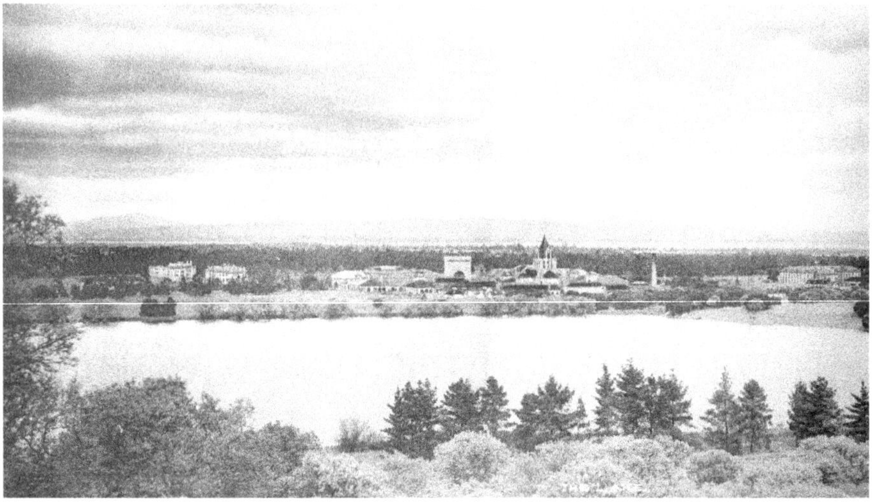

FIGURE 3.1 *A general view of the Stanford University campus, c. 1903. Author's collection.*

say that they intended the university to support a three-pronged vision for the future of California.[1] Firstly, the Stanfords chartered a university that was multicultural and would admit women. Rapid population growth was essential to the economic development of the state, and they wanted an environment in which all could thrive. Secondly, they wanted to emphasize that this was an environment different from the eastern United States, especially an east badly scarred by recent civil war and sectional difference. The American West's sublime landscapes and Spanish architecture instantly marked it as a different sort of place, and thus these images could be used to create an environment in which a new kind of American identity could be forged. Crucially, these sublime images could also be used to imply vast emptiness and vast resources in order to attract immigrants. In the mythology of the West that the Stanfords were helping to build, California was a land of vast untapped potential. Thirdly, the Stanfords envisioned a California that was a centre of culture and science. The development of technology and the arts would improve the economic potential of the state. The Stanfords sought to use the art and architecture of their campus as a vehicle for these messages. As the buildings began to take shape, they filled the campus with one of the largest collections of art in the United States. The idea was not only to provide a vast library of objects for teaching, but to develop students' character and intellect through the constant experience of art and architecture in the campus environment.

The new university was carefully and holistically planned. From the railroad station, a straight boulevard of palms led to a triumphal arch that marked the beginning of a series of quadrangles. Rejecting landscape designer Frederick Law Olmsted's initial proposal for gently curving roads that mirrored the contours of the landscape, Leland Stanford instead requested the 'rational' axial arrangement of City Beautiful planning. The landscape was then heavily sprinkled with 'improving' art. Terraces were lined with sculpture, walls filled with carving and stained glass; the subject of every artwork was selected or approved by Jane Stanford herself. The whole campus became a vast assemblage, where the experience of particular works of art, it was hoped, would feed into a larger message. The entire programme was mediated through two key buildings. At the centre of the campus, the church, for training the soul through art, and near the entrance, the museum for training the mind.

Environmental immersion had long been a strategy in American campus architecture. In 1814, polymath third president of the United States, Thomas Jefferson, had begun building the University of Virginia as an 'academical village' in which students and professors dwelt in classical pavilions ordered in an Arcadian natural landscape. These pavilions were each small Palladian structures, built to demonstrate the different orders of architecture: a physical manifestation of the sort of Enlightenment book learning that Jefferson hoped to impart to the young gentlemen of the new republic.[2]

The vision for Stanford was considerably different. The campus consisted of a series of interconnected quadrangles built of yellow sandstone and crowned with red-tile roofs, nestled in the foothills of the San Francisco Peninsula. The buildings were designed to be flexible: they were mostly one-story spaces, with column-free, reconfigurable interiors.[3] The grid of quadrangles could be infinitely extended as the university grew. The campus projected a strongly regional image of California with its boulevard of palms and Mission Style architecture. In fact, Leland Stanford claimed to have been the first to revive the Mission Style so that his university could be uniquely Californian.

The buildings themselves were stylistically and materially uniform, but the art and ornament that adorned them was a collage of different subjects, cultures, and media. This artistic program, of which little remains, formed a key part of the Stanfords' intentions for the campus. The early Stanford campus was littered with art: from statues of Ben Franklin, Faith, Augustus Caesar, and the Stanfords' favourite race horses, to Japanese bronze lanterns and stained-glass windows of Moses, Confucius, and Jesus, *The Light of the World*, to name a few of the hundreds of items that cluttered the interiors of campus buildings and lined pathways around the grounds. In many ways, this variety was in keeping with the more multicultural, individualistic United States that had emerged over the course of the century. In contrast with the monolithic, Enlightenment vision for the University of Virginia, Stanford University was an assemblage.[4] Whereas the University of Virginia's educational model was about a search for universal abstract laws, Stanford's was about the direct study of the vast variety of the material world. It was a commerce-driven philosophy that believed the best way to understand the natural and man-made substance of the world was by gathering as much of it together as possible for students to experience.

A pluralistic vision underpinned the Stanfords' utopian aims. The art displayed on campus was various in the hopes that it would capture the interest of different types of students at different times in their lives. From the start, the diverse range of students at Stanford included women and students of Asian and Hispanic heritage. From its location on the Pacific Rim, the campus was looking both east and west. Jane Stanford included Asian art in the decoration of the campus, just as she made provision for Buddhist religious practice, so that all members of the university community would feel included.[5] Around 1902, Jane Stanford placed four large Japanese bronzes in Memorial Court, as 'illustrative of higher Japanese life'.[6] This was not only a statement of her support for Japanese students, but an assertion of the link she considered to exist between art and the spiritual. She wanted the students to see themselves in the art, both as potential subjects and potential makers. Jane specifically asked for a higher number of women in the mosaics and stained glass that decorate the church, so that there would be figures to inspire both women and men.[7] She also made a point of patronizing women artists, for instance commissioning eight portraits from the American painter Georgina Campbell.[8] In her mind, art and student experience were directly linked.

As mentioned above, the choice of an architectural style inspired by the California missions was suggested by Leland Stanford. At his request, the Richardsonian Romanesque buildings designed by Rutan, Shepley, and Coolidge, were given red-tile roofs and covered arcades. The Stanfords had played an important role in restoring the California missions, providing much of the funding that paid to reroof and repair the ruinous mission buildings.[9] They regarded these buildings as essential monuments of California history, crucial for the sense of independent Californian identity they were helping to shape and for the future of tourism in the state. Leland later claimed to have been the first person to introduce the traits of the California missions to American architecture, thus setting a precedent for generations of California buildings.

However, in reality, Stanford had seen the Spanish Revival architecture in Florida and brought it back to California. The Stanfords had attended the grand opening of Henry Flagler's Spanish Revival fantasy, the Hotel Ponce de Leon in St Augustine, Florida, in January 1888.[10] At this time, they were deeply involved in planning the architecture of their university, and it is clear that Flagler's resplendent hotel made an impression. It was an exotic vision – the first Spanish Revival building in the United States and one of the most luxurious resorts in North America. Designed by New York architects Carrère and Hastings, who would go on to design the New York Public Library, it was the first and grandest hotel that Flagler would build on his new railroad line along the east coast of Florida. The hotel was designed to entice wealthy northerners to make the two-day railroad journey to the mostly undeveloped area. It was also the first high-style American building to have exposed concrete walls.[11] The Stanford University Museum would be perhaps the second. Henry Flagler was a fellow railroad magnate and the following year, he would add an associated memorial church to his St Augustine developments. Like the eventual Stanford Memorial Church, it was constructed in memory of a beloved child and claimed the inspiration of St Mark's, Venice. It was perhaps the closest architectural precedent to the final design of the Stanford campus, and it must not be a coincidence that the Stanfords saw it right as they were developing the architectural design of their university.

The Stanfords had long been collectors and patrons of public arts and sciences in California. They were actively involved in showing their art collection, especially when it served to promote California. For instance, they had sent prize-winning canvases of California landscapes by Thomas Hill to the 1876 Philadelphia Centennial Exposition.[12] However, California boosterism still had much to learn from Florida, which was actively creating a new image for itself, centred around its warm climate and its attendant opportunities for agriculture and tourism. In order to attract northern tourists, Florida needed an image that was distant from the sectional tensions of the recent Civil War; its traditional plantation architecture was too closely associated with the Confederacy. The solution lay in its Spanish past.[13] During his visit to St Augustine, Stanford must have realized that California could follow suit: it too needed an image that would attract Americans from all over the country (and beyond). The state needed to develop a mythology that it was inclusive while still being broadly American.

When seeking an ideal Californian identity for their students, the Stanfords went so far as to put themselves forward as role models. They had developed their family life as a setting for Leland Stanford Junior's education, and they now sought to bring that family experience to a broad swath of California's most promising young people – complete with Jane Stanford living on campus as 'campus mother' hosting teas on her lawn. By moving the interiors of their San Francisco house to the campus museum as a series of room installations, complete with furniture, art, and architectural features, Leland, Jr.'s educational experience could become the students' experience.[14] The setting that Leland and Jane had carefully crafted to shape their son into the ideal Californian could be made available to all worthy young Californians. The saying, 'The children of California shall become our children,' turned out to be fairly literal.

In this context, the frieze of *The Progress of American Civilization* on the towering arch that originally marked the entrance to the Inner Quad becomes important. It showed the Stanfords riding triumphantly through the mountain pass that was the Transcontinental Railroad's last hurtle before reaching the Pacific coast, accompanied by the genius of engineering.[15] This was not merely a bit of Stanford family self-aggrandizement, but an allegorical example of the ideal Western family. Here they were making sublime landscapes profitable through science and human endeavour; here they were linking America to a global world. On passing through the arch, campus visitors were greeted by a bronze statue of the Stanford family, with Jane and Leland flanking their son, their devotion creating a shining example of domestic virtue.

The art museum at the heart of the university

The Stanfords were devotees of Swiss–American biologist Louis Agassiz, and his theories of material examination and comparison would be a dominant idea in the planning and design of the campus. As such, they aimed to provide a wealth of material specimens for students to experience and study, ranging from art objects to historical artefacts to geological specimens. These collections, Jane Stanford wrote, would form the backbone of the university.[16]

Agassiz was one of the most important natural scientists of the Victorian era. He was credited with being the first to propose that the Earth had experienced an Ice Age, and he made important contributions to the taxonomy of fish. He taught natural history at Harvard through the use of comparative specimens. He founded the Harvard Museum of Comparative Zoology and also the United States' first marine lab, so that comparative zoology could be taught from living examples. Although Agassiz's offensive late writings on race are often discussed today, these writings were not central to his fame at the time. As demonstrated by their multicultural and inclusive vision for the university, the Stanfords did not subscribe to this aspect of his work.

They were, however, very interested in his ideas about pedagogy. Even greater than his influence as a scientist, was Agassiz's legacy as a teacher. Agassiz believed in an empirical approach to learning. Students would best learn any subject, he believed, whether that be arts or sciences, not primarily through reading, but by close study of the material world. As the president of the California Academy of Sciences would explain when eulogizing Agassiz in 1873, he 'gathered facts from observation, combined and correlated them, then deduced order and placed them lucidly before the learned and unlearned'.[17] This approach to teaching from objects was considerably indebted to a British tradition of 'object lessons'. The naturalist James Rennie in particular had popularized the concept of learning by looking earlier in the nineteenth century.[18] Aggasiz gave the concept a more rigorous scientific framework, and his philosophy of teaching with objects consequently became one of the most influential ideas in late-Victorian pedagogy. He regarded perception as an essential skill for all intellectual discovery, one that he felt would be the basis of a programme of cultural revitalization.[19] Agassiz's ideas would transform university teaching in the

United States, and his influence would echo into the twentieth century. As late as 1934, Ezra Pound's 'Parable of the Sunfish' situated Agassiz as the central figure in truly modern thought.[20]

Stanford's first president, David Starr Jordan, recorded that Mr and Mrs Stanford regarded Louis Aggasiz and his educational theories with 'almost veneration'.[21] According to Jordan, Aggasiz had sparked Leland Stanford's interest in founding a museum in California during an 1872 visit to Sacramento.[22] Not long afterwards, Leland Stanford was among the founders of San Francisco's Agassiz Institute for the Promotion of Interest in the Arts and Sciences.[23] David Starr Jordan was himself appointed by the Stanfords because he was an ichthyologist and follower of Agassiz. Reflecting its devotion to his methods, Stanford University would found the Hopkins Marine Station on the Agassiz model in 1892, only the third marine station in the country.

Perhaps because Agassiz offered a model of learning that was both pragmatic and attainable without access to elite universities, Aggasiz's ideas were particularly revered in late-Victorian California. Leland Stanford may have been present at the December 1883 meeting at which the president of the California Academy of Sciences called for institutions on the Agassiz model to be built in California. Agassiz, the president explained, 'contended for broader studies than those prescribed in the old, dogmatic curriculum; for something more than heavy, reiterated book-learning'.[24] He also popularized the lecture (with visual aids) as a democratic means of sharing knowledge:

> [The lecture] humanizes and expands the minds of men of power whose business habits and pursuits have kept them apart from study since their school-boy days; it quickens the memory of the student and reader; and from humbler walks of life, it will call out latent talent from many a gifted but timid youth whose instincts and aspirations would have been chilled by the old formal school.[25]

In the same speech, the president of the Academy called for the creation of Agassiz-inspired collections in California and for more universities and museums in the West.[26] The meeting's next speaker, Professor D.C. Gilman, declared that Agassiz had discovered a method of teaching that addressed 'the practical wants of Americans', and he was followed by a speech by Rev Dr Horatio Stebbins explaining that Agassiz placed religion at the centre of his scholarly pursuits because 'man's science is the discovery of God's law'.[27]

This appeal could have been custom-made for Leland Stanford, who particularly aimed to improve California business and manufactures and to provide educations for those many Californians who otherwise might not have been able to seek one in the East. Stanford himself, denied much formal education, had to pursue knowledge through books and public lectures. He regarded himself as a self-taught man of learning, choosing to have his portrait painted by Paris artist Ernest Meissonier surrounded by his books and papers as well as images from the scientific study of motion that he had commissioned from photographer Eadweard Muybridge. In 1882, Leland Stanford responded to the California Academy of Sciences' appeal by purchasing a significant collection of natural history specimens, with the hope that it would form the nucleus of a new 'British Museum' for San Francisco.[28] This vision for a great new San Francisco museum was one that members of the Stanford family would often refer to from that point onwards.

Their son, Leland, Jr., was especially interested in art and archaeology. His parents considered regular trips to Europe a key part of his education, and there they encouraged him to begin collecting. As he built his collection, his tutor, as directed by his mother, had him catalogue and organize it; his education was built around the analysis of material culture. His parents wanted Leland, Jr. to grow up immersed in art – absorbing an understanding of design and manufactures from his surroundings. The Stanfords' house on San Francisco's Nob Hill was filled with Chinese, Japanese, American, British, Continental, and ancient art. One of its most prominent features was an art gallery which included an electric orchestrion music machine and automaton birds, white marble neoclassical sculptures, grand Western landscapes, Victorian genre pictures, copies of Old Masters, and authentic Old Masters. The influence of Agassiz, coupled with Leland, Jr.'s growing interest in art led the Stanfords to begin thinking more broadly about the ways their collections could benefit the state through the museum they envisioned founding. They also hoped that Leland, Jr. would dedicate his life to this cause. When asked about his future by the director of the Metropolitan Museum of Art, Leland, Jr., aged twelve, exclaimed that he wished to be involved in 'the art-training of our American people'.[29] By 1882, the museum had become the interest to which to the family devoted the majority of their philanthropic efforts and around which they would build their plans for the future of their only child.

It was this dream of a great museum that would form the kernel of the idea for a university in memory of their son. The museum was not an appendage to the plans for the campus, but essential to its very genesis. It was to form the pedagogical centrepiece around which a curriculum and learning environment was built. In the Stanford's conception, the university was, in many ways, to be a museum with teaching attached. The museum was meant as an educational resource built around the European tradition of object lessons, and the addition of the university, that is providing expert instruction from the collections was, from that perspective, a natural expansion of the Stanford's initial vision. The university offered the full range of humanities and sciences, and the intention was that students would take a broad range of subjects, as many of which as possible would benefit from the university collections.

The Stanfords intended for students to be immersed in the university's collections at all times, experiencing them in their coursework but also in their everyday environment. Jane Stanford made it clear that she intended the university collections to be used in coursework; when she acquired the world's second-largest collection of Cyproit pottery, she decreed that it was intended for use in conjunction with lectures by the professor of Latin and Archaeology.[30] She later took the professor with her on a buying trip to Egypt, so that he could help select artefacts that would be most useful for his courses.[31] Jane herself held that the university was founded on its collections, and that those collections were the 'connecting link' between the institution and its namesake.[32] At the first celebration of Stanford University's Founders' Day in 1909, university president David Starr Jordan declared, 'Great libraries and great collections the university should have, but libraries and collections should be chosen for their fitness in the training of men.'[33]

From the beginning, the Stanford University Museum was a Herculean conception (Figure 3.2). When it opened in 1894, it was larger than either the Metropolitan Museum of Art or the Boston Museum of Fine Arts, and was the largest private museum in the world.[34] By 1905 it had grown even further into a large quadrangle containing 290,000 square feet of floor space (over five acres).[35] The building, designed by San Francisco architects George Washington Percy and Frederic Hamilton, was inspired by the Archaeological Museum in Athens, which Leland Stanford, Jr. had particularly admired. Following a European trend the Stanfords had encountered in Britain, Germany, and Greece, the building was neoclassical, the first neoclassical museum building in the United States.[36] Like so much of the art and architecture on campus, this innovation was rooted in the

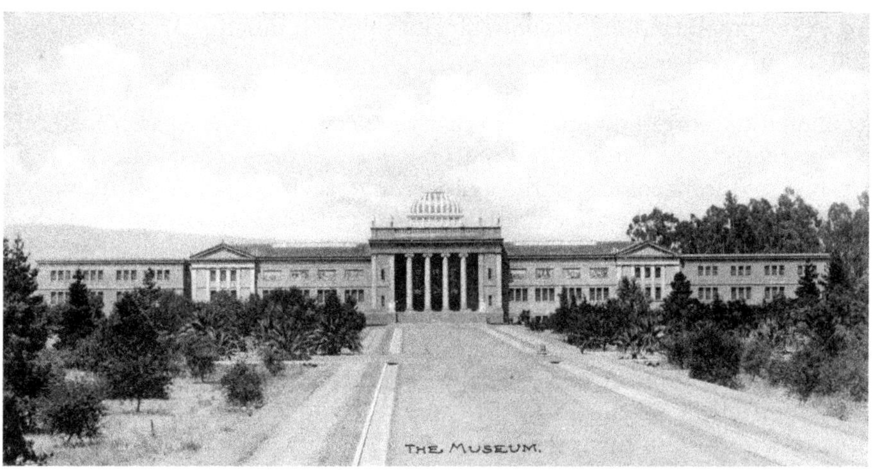

FIGURE 3.2 *The Stanford University Museum at an intermediate stage of its development, photographed c. 1900. It would be extended once more before the 1906 earthquake. Author's collection.*

extensive scrapbooks kept by Jane Stanford: she had sent the architects photographs of the museums in Athens, Greece, on which she wanted the design of the building to be based and had long had the British Museum in mind as a model for the projected art museum in San Francisco.[37] The museum was also, incidentally, the first public building in the United States made entirely of concrete (walls and floors) – another reflection of the experimental spirit of the institution.[38] At Leland Stanford's suggestion, the shafts of the ionic columns were made in a single pour in order to make them more earthquake resistant.[39]

The presence of the giant museum, the first major building encountered on the journey from the gates of the university towards the Main Quad, made a striking statement of the place of art in the new university's educational programme at a time when very few American universities had dedicated art museum buildings, and those that did were very small. Princeton's Museum of Historic Art, built in 1889, consisted only of a few rooms.[40] Yale's Street Hall, the home of America's oldest university art gallery was not much bigger. Harvard's similarly pint-sized Fogg Museum would not open until 1896, and in Britain, only Oxford and Cambridge had dedicated art museums, neither of which compared with the sheer size of the Stanford Museum. Although the Stanfords were at the crest of a wave of university art museum building and a number of additional museums would open on American campuses during the 1890s, the Stanford Museum was on a different order of magnitude.

Like most American museums of the period, particularly the Metropolitan Museum of Art, whose director was a friend, consultant, and art dealer to the Stanfords, the Stanford Museum borrowed the industrial arts model of London's South Kensington Museum, with specimens organized by type.[41] An 1886 pamphlet about the museum, for instance, described cases of Greek pottery in rows, organized 'from the highest plane of art to the rudest'.[42] This arrangement gave the collections a sense of scientific authority and facilitated the sort of comparisons that were central to the Agassiz method.

The idea of the campus centred on art collections reflects the birth of art history, archaeology, anthropology, and their cognates as academic disciplines during the nineteenth century, and the rise of the idea that material culture could tell the story of the world's history as well as text. In the Stanford Museum collection the 1886 pamphlet explained, 'Every student and traveler recognizes … landmarks of history and civilization.'[43] As Stanford curator Carol Osborne has noted, this was a time before colour slides, and Jane Stanford ordered copies of Old Masters from all over Europe to be used in the teaching of art history.[44] In the Stanford model, art also became a substitute for travel: culture and history, even of faraway lands, could be experienced by the student through these objects.

Over a period of less than ten years between 1885 and 1893, Jane Stanford added 15,000 items to the collection – a prodigious feat of shopping.[45] In her search for objects that could teach the students of California, she bought the Censola collection of Cyproit pottery, William McAdam's collection of Native American mound relics, the DeLong and van Reed collections of Japanese art, Greek antiquities from Athanasios Rhousopoulos, Korean objects gathered by the missionary Henry G. Appenzeller, William Flinders Petrie's Coptic textiles, John Daggett's collection of artefacts from the Pacific Northwest, numerous Egyptian artefacts, Neolithic tools, and all of these is not to mention commissions for vast amounts of new art ranging from Salviatti mosaics to copies of European masterworks to additions to the Stanford family's pioneering collection of contemporary photography. And this was just by 1893. The museum kept growing at the same voracious pace until Jane Stanford's death in 1905.[46] And it was not only a Stanford family enterprise; as the premier museum of the entire region, meant to function on much the same model as the Metropolitan Museum of Art, it also attracted donations from prominent San Franciscans.[47] The collection was more Pacific-facing than most other American collections; it included East Asian art, Native American art, Western landscapes, and the only survey collection of Australian art in the United States. The multicultural, in fact broadly global, focus of Stanford was a contrast with the University of Virginia's focus on Western forms of knowledge and art – marking a major change in American thinking over the course of the nineteenth century.

Memorial Church: Moulding the spirit through art

Stanford University was explicitly without religious affiliation. The Stanfords wanted everyone to feel welcome and to preclude any meddling with the substance of their vision by church authorities. However, Jane Stanford believed that ideals were not taught in classrooms, and hoped to leave a legacy of her beliefs in the physical fabric of the campus.[48] The Stanfords felt that the life of Christ would provide a good example for students of any religion. The centrepiece of the campus was therefore a non-denominational church: 'My heart is in the university, but my soul is in that church,' Jane Stanford declared. Alongside the museum, it was the focus of her greatest efforts. The hope was that the physical presence of the building and its contents would have a psychological effect on the student body.

The idea that environment had a psychological effect on its users even appeared in early Stanford guidebooks. Willis Hall's guidebook to Memorial Church, which was reprinted several times in the first decades of the twentieth century, quoted English architect G.E. Street: 'Over and over again, when at Venice, one must go to St Mark's, not to criticize, but to admire, and if ever any building in which the main object is the study of art, assuredly here it must also be to worship. I think I never saw an interior so thoroughly religious and religion-inspiring as this.'[49] By including this telling quotation in reference to their own church, the Stanford guidebooks point not only to the campus philosophy of being immersed in the study of art, but to an understanding that art shapes actions and character. University president David Starr Jordan also drew connections between student character and campus architecture, declaring that the character of students should rise out of their activities just 'as the great church towers above the red tiles of the lower buildings'.[50] Jordan's successor, John C. Branner too would make analogies between material objects and values. The idea of an allegorical setting has ancient roots in architectural design, but the addition of Aggasiz's ideas gave it a new scientific basis. The material world was an influence for spiritual development.

The subjects for the decorative programme for the campus buildings, which consisted of marble statuary, Salviatti mosaic, and stained-glass windows executed by the Lamb Brothers firm, were all selected or approved by Jane Stanford. Sources for decoration were often chosen from albums she had gathered over the course of her life and travels. Jane Stanford's scrapbooks thus became a collection of artistic specimens on the Agassiz model, and the campus became an enormous act of assemblage. She would have photographs or prints translated into glass, marble, or paint. Each item was carefully selected to impart certain ideas and values that she felt would help the students to live meaningful and productive lives. For example, Jane Stanford had copies of famous Madonnas in European collections made with the intention of hanging them in a special gallery of the museum so the students could experience them. She even had the frames copied. The experience of these images together, she hoped, would not only help students to understand art history, but by repeated exposure to images of Divine Motherhood, would inspire its emulation in the students.[51]

The range and number of Jane's sources was enormous. *The Eye of God* fresco on the ceiling of the crossing in Memorial Church was inspired by a similar fresco she had seen in a Greek church. For Memorial Church alone, paintings selected to be copied in stained glass included works by Ernst Deger, Anton Deitrich, Gustave Dore, Axel Ender, William Holman Hunt, Antonio Paoletti, Sybil Parker, Edward A Hoffmann, Frederick James Shields, and even the Spanish Baroque painter Bartolome Esteban Murillo (whose work Leland, Jr. had admired).[52] Involving a total of forty windows, it was perhaps the largest single order of stained glass yet placed in the United States.[53] Jane also selected the art to be displayed in each building. The university's first purpose-built Library, on the front Quad, featured stained glass portraying Moses, Christ (from Holman Hunt's *Light of the World*), Confucius, a statue of George Washington, an array of marble busts, and painted portraits of university trustees. It must have felt almost like a state capitol and was meant to be equally as inspiring of civic virtue.

Objects were selected for the meanings they were held to embody, and Jane Stanford sometimes made her choices without having seen the object in person. Bertha Berner recorded that she ordered a marble copy of *The Angel of Grief* for the campus arboretum, for instance, based only on having seen a photograph of the original.[54] The Angel served as a memorial to Jane's brother, but spoke to the broader campus theme that great things could be born out of virtuous lives. When commissioning mosaics for the church, she showed Maurizio Camerino, the head of the Salviati Company, photographs of art that was meaningful to her and took him to visit precedents in Venice and Paris.[55] Just as decoration was selected from her scrapbook, the inspirational inscriptions in Memorial Church came out of her commonplace books.

The process of 'scrapbooking' was not only applied to the decoration, but even to the architecture itself. As already mentioned, Leland Stanford asked that the buildings feature the red-tile roofs and covered arcades of the California missions. The basic design for the men's dormitory, Encina Hall, was borrowed from a hotel the Stanfords had visited in Switzerland. On seeing the hotel from the road, the Stanfords had stopped and asked the hotel manager for a tour and a copy of the floorplan, then returned to their carriage to write a description and post it to the campus architect.[56] The selection of architectural precedents was often linked to Jane's personal story: the places she had visited with her son or husband, the Missions which she and her husband had helped to preserve and restore. In case the students did not realize this, it was all explained to them in a special gallery of the Stanford Museum dedicated to the plan and architecture of the university.[57] Here they could be taught to appreciate and understand the intentions behind their environment.

The partial destruction of the campus and its legacy in American design

The Stanfords' vision would not long remain intact, however. Many of the buildings and much of the art would be destroyed in the 1906 earthquake. The buildings of the Main Quad, designed by Shepley, Rutan, and Coolidge, survived because of the broad footings under the walls; an innovation the firm said Leland Stanford had suggested as a way of resisting earthquakes.[58] The buildings commissioned by Jane Stanford from more affordable local architects after her husband's death, however, all collapsed. Jane's extensive cultural programme was destroyed in a blow. At the vast museum, the galleries pancaked, crushing the collection of Cyproit pottery, and statues tumbled from their pedestals shattering on the floor. Over two-thirds of the enormous building, including the art storage areas, was destroyed and never rebuilt. The art collection in the Stanfords' San Francisco house, where it had been left to await transit after Jane Stanford's death in 1905, was destroyed by the fire that raged through the city after the earthquake.[59] The Stanford Museum, intended to be the centrepiece of artistic and humanistic study in the American West, was abandoned shortly afterwards, its building given over to the storage of fish specimens. This allowed the university to focus on sciences, developing the great science programmes that would give birth to Silicon Valley, but its arts and humanities programmes would not regain their strength for decades.

During the earthquake, the statue of Aggasiz on the second-story façade of the Outer Quad tumbled from its pedestal, and its head punched through the concrete path below (Figure 3.3). Coming across it later, one of the professors quipped, 'Agassiz was always better in the abstract than in the concrete.' This was not merely a good joke. The fate of the statue was a perfect metaphor for the way the post-earthquake university shifted away from the Agassiz-inspired cluttering of the campus with 'specimens' of art. What the earthquake did not destroy, changing taste did. The church was rebuilt with a simpler façade. The twelve large marble statues around the altar were not replaced; their niches remain empty. The fresco of the *Eye of God*, with its giant teardrop poised to splash down on the congregation, was omitted in favour of a skylight that considerably brightened the interior. In 1914, the Olmsted Brothers landscaping firm wrote to recommend removing the statue of Faith from the oval in order to clear the vista to Memorial Church.[60] The dark and clutter of late-Victorian aesthetics was receding in favour of the simplicity, brightness, and order of the American Renaissance.

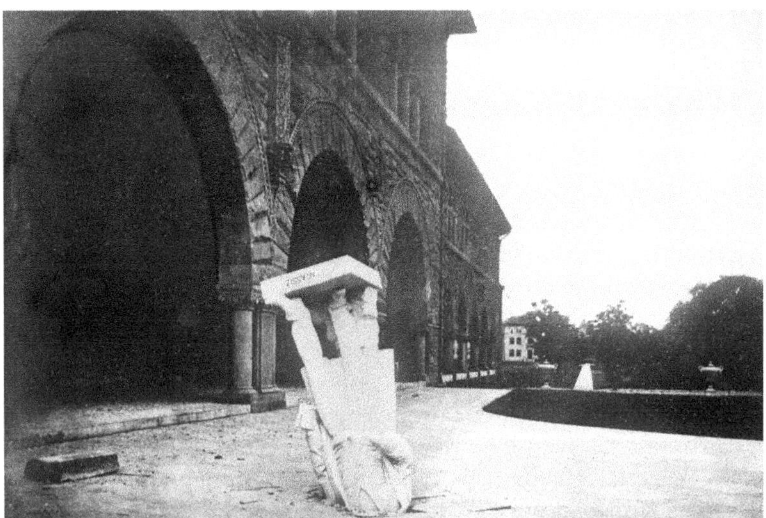

FIGURE 3.3 *The statue of Louis Agassiz that once stood on the façade of the Outer Quad, after tumbling from its pedestal during the 1906 Earthquake. Courtesy of Getty Images.*

'We are not trammeled by old traditions,' Jane Stanford had once declared to the assembled campus community, and perhaps she would have approved of the university shifting elements of its vision with changing times.[61] Stanford University's focus on art and, by extension aesthetics, though, was on the leading edge of a wave in American campus design.

Aesthetics, conceived as the spirit-building, character-developing power of material beauty, was at the heart of the conception of America's most ambitious and idealistic campuses in the decades immediately following the founding of Stanford. The planners of these universities believed they were not only transferring skills and knowledge, but moulding ideal citizens – the civic leaders of a flowering democracy. 'Artistic' settings were felt, as they were at Stanford, to play an important role in shaping character. This idea formed an enormously important strand in American thinking about art, and it was a strand that developed outside of the country's nascent art museums. Aesthetic immersion came to be seen as essential to imparting identity (whatever that identity might be) in American educational environments. After Stanford, American campuses had looser and looser ties to Enlightenment concepts of rational design, instead creating environments that focused on provoking emotional reactions through settings tempered, as all identity narratives are, by fantasy and myth.

In 1910, Rice University would commission Ralph Adams Cram to design its campus as a single, unified aesthetic vision. Like the Stanfords, Rice's founder, William Marsh Rice, wanted to create an institute of free higher education to benefit the city and state where he had made his fortune (in this case Houston, Texas), and intended the university to be co-educational from the beginning. He conceived the idea in the late 1880s, around the same time the Stanfords' plans were being made public. Like Stanford University, the campus of Rice features red-tile-roofed quadrangles set in an arboretum. Rice's campus, however, was much more exotic – drawing on Middle Eastern precedents as well as Spanish ones. The goal was not the literal evocation of a foreign model, but simply beauty: a Persian–Byzantine conception of a university with a hint of Maxfield Parrish. The intense specificity of Stanford's vision of comparative material culture had given way to something more abstract, concerned less with perception of a vast library of artistic material than with a search for beauty. It says something about the intentions of Rice, that the founders invited Benedetto Croce to speak on aesthetics at the inauguration of the university in 1912.[62] The Italian philosopher's major treatise on aesthetics, *Brevario di estetica*, was written for the occasion. A central idea of the book is his assertion that 'only art edifies us'.[63] He claimed that human knowledge could be reduced to logical and imaginative thought. Beauty, he wrote, was fundamentally a formation of inward mental images, and thus art too was about cultivation of the mind.

By 1933, the American concern with the aesthetic campus was considered so standard that the Master of Berkeley College, Yale, could write that the purpose of Yale's new residential college system, with its expensive and heavily decorated buildings, was to allow undergraduates 'to develop first of all their intellectual and esthetic interests'.[64] American campuses have always been able to claim to be places in which the scholarly and aesthetic are purposefully intertwined, but for the two to be weighted equally when considering the function of university buildings was only possible after Stanford had paved the way. Student experience of an art-filled environment was now considered to be an essential component of their education.

CHAPTER FOUR

The architecture of art education: Provincial art schools in Britain, 1850–1914

Geoffrey Tyack

'Art is on the town,' proclaimed James McNeill Whistler in his 'Ten o'clock lecture' at the Prince's Hall in London in 1884. He was referring to avant-garde art and the cult of celebrity that it engendered, of which he was a prime exponent. But the phrase could also be applied to the burgeoning of public art education in late-Victorian Britain. This was not primarily inspired by a desire to encourage the mass of the population to become artists, in the sense that we understand the term; private art schools had existed for this purpose since the early eighteenth century. The main aim was the utilitarian one of improving the quality of British design, which it was believed would have beneficial economic results as industry faced increasing foreign competition. By the end of the nineteenth century there were some two hundred publicly funded schools of art in Britain. With the exception of one world-famous example – Charles Rennie Mackintosh's Glasgow School of Art – their architecture has received little scholarly attention.[1] But they helped, both directly and indirectly, to form the taste and enrich the lives of the urban population, and they present an intriguing case study of the interaction of function, design, and technology out of which much of the best architecture of this highly fertile period emerged.

Private academies were established in some of the larger provincial towns, such as Birmingham, in the early nineteenth century, and art classes were also given in some of the Mechanics' Institutes that sprang up in the 1820s.[2] But British governments, unlike some of their Continental counterparts, did not begin to take a systematic interest in art education until 1835, when a Parliamentary Select Committee recommended granting aid to schools of design, the first of which was established in Somerset House in London two years later; others soon followed, initially in the larger cities, and by 1852 there were twenty-one in all.[3] Then in 1852, a year after the Great Exhibition, a new government department was created in order to promote 'practical art' in public art schools; it was renamed the Department of Science and Art in the following year. The schools, which included the existing schools of design, were to receive some of their funding from government grants, in return for which those receiving grant aid had to follow a Gradgrindish common curriculum, based, at least at first, on repetitive copying, and leading to examinations.[4] The system, lampooned by Charles Dickens in the second chapter of his novel *Hard Times* (1854), was anathema both to artists like Whistler, the product of Parisian *ateliers*, and to his nemesis John Ruskin, who, responding to a request to give a lecture at the Derby School of Art in 1873, wrote: 'If you only come to the Art School to get your living, you may or may not get your living; but you will never get, or learn, any Art.'[5] That was not an argument that carried much weight with politicians and civil servants who, by means of the Public Libraries Act (1855) made it possible for local authorities to help fund the construction of museums and 'schools for science and art' out of the rates (local property taxes), the remaining funds being left to the generosity of local donors and subscribers. By 1884 there were 34,000 students in 'systematic training' in 177 schools, and an act of Parliament of the same year gave local authorities the power to acquire land for new art schools and libraries.[6] It also offered grant aid for new buildings, provided the schools followed the government-approved central curriculum, and in 1902, under the Balfour Education Act, the local authorities took over the whole system.[7]

Publicly funded art schools were set up primarily to train artisans in the principles of good design. The Manchester School of Art, founded in 1838, to take one example, was intended to 'enhance the value of the manufactures of this district; to improve the taste of the rising generation; to infuse into the public mind a desire for symmetry of form, and elegance of design; and to educate for the public service a highly intelligent class of artists and civil engineers'.[8] But the schools would never have been financially viable without the fees of middle-class students, mostly women, who did not need formal qualifications and did not take examinations. Women constituted the majority of the daytime clientele in most schools, most of the male students attending evening classes after work ended. In the early years, classes also contained schoolchildren, who attended early morning classes; at Exeter in the 1870s, some 40 per cent of the 250 or so students were still schoolboys, most of them only attending two or three times a week.[9] Here, as elsewhere, their art education was eventually taken over by elementary schools, and their place in the art schools taken by trainee teachers and other members of the aspirational artisan and lower middle classes, most of whom attended part-time; payment was pro rata for a term's instruction, and there was no obligation to complete the whole curriculum. The initial aim of educating the working classes in design was only partially realized, due mainly to long-working hours and low incomes, inadequate even for the modest fees charged to grant-aided students. Of 368 students at the Manchester school in 1863, only 46 were described as artisans, 73 as teachers or prospective art teachers, and the remainder schoolboys and amateurs.[10] At Nottingham, the lacemaking capital of England, there were thirty-nine clerks or managers in 1868, along with twenty-nine lace designers, twenty-four builders and cabinetmakers, eighteen architects' clerks, and a handful of others; only twelve students described themselves as artists.[11] By 1884, according to J. C. L Spokes, the first principal of the central school of art and design at South Kensington, about three quarters of the pupils in British art schools were would-be artists and designers (including future art teachers); the rest were mostly women who attended 'for the purpose of turning their talents to profitable account, and not for mere amusement'.[12]

The first schools were unpretentiously housed in older buildings adapted for the purpose; the Nottingham school, for instance, used rooms in the town's Mechanics' Institute before moving in 1843 to a plain-brick eighteenth-century building, originally a private house, in Heathcote Street, to the north of the town centre.[13] The Brighton school, founded in 1859, was housed in a room next to the kitchen of the Royal Pavilion before moving in 1877 to the upper floor of a new building (since demolished) in Grand Parade.[14] Other schools shared their buildings with privately funded institutions; the classes in Manchester were held for many years in the basement of Charles Barry's Royal Institution (now the City Art Gallery) in Mosley Street. The Bristol school was handsomely housed in what was arguably the first purpose-built provincial art school: the privately funded Royal West of England Academy, a classical structure, containing a picture gallery, built to the designs of J. H. Hirst and Charles Underwood in 1854–7 close to the recently built Victoria Assembly Rooms, on the edge of the prosperous suburb of Clifton. At Leeds the school, first founded in 1846, moved in 1868 into a monumental classical building of 1860–5 in the city centre (now the City Museum) by Cuthbert Brodrick, architect of the equally impressive Town Hall, close by; the art school occupied one side of the building, separated by a circular lecture theatre from the art gallery and the library, reading room and offices of the Mechanics' Institute on the other side.[15] The much smaller Exeter school was squeezed into the upper floor of a multipurpose Gothic building of 1861–9 (now the Royal Albert Memorial Museum) designed by the local architect John Hayward, and devoted, as an inscription over the doorway states, 'to the purposes of art, science and literature'; it also housed a museum and public library.[16] And at Burslem, in the Potteries, the art school occupied part of Wedgwood Institute (1863–9), its impressively Gothic façade elaborately adorned with decoration designed by Robert Edgar and John Lockwood Kipling, father of the writer Rudyard Kipling; some of it is in terracotta, including panels on the upper floor – occupied by top-lit studios – depicting pottery manufacture. Ambitious buildings of this type, like the town halls and administrative buildings that they sometimes resemble, were among the products of a public culture of 'improvement' in mid- and late-Victorian Britain which could hardly avoid having an impact on those who taught and learnt in them.[17]

Until the last years of the century the curriculum taught in public art schools was not very different from that of the Royal Academy Schools in London, founded in 1768, or of Continental schools like those in Berlin and Düsseldorf.[18] As in the Italian Renaissance, drawing (*disegno*) was regarded as the basis of art: outline drawing came first, initially copied from set designs illustrated in a manual prepared by the artist William Dyce in 1842–3; then came drawing from casts (and flowers), followed by drawing from life; and finally painting and the making of three-dimensional models. From 1856 onwards the management of art education nationwide was based in London at South Kensington, where studios, finished in 1863, were built for training art teachers, linked to a library and a museum (the present Victoria and Albert); a mosaic portrait of the civil servant Henry Cole, the director of the Museum and guiding spirit behind the government-sponsored system of art education, still adorns the ceramic staircase leading up to what were originally the studios, discreetly hidden away in utilitarian brick buildings behind the façade of the present main courtyard.[19] The curriculum proceeded through twenty-three stages, starting with 'Linear Drawing by aid of instruments' via shading, drawing from casts and life, to modelling and technical studies.[20] The future Dame Laura Knight, who entered the Nottingham school on a scholarship at the age of thirteen in 1895 as 'the only serious girl student', resented the fact that women were obliged to draw the male nude from plaster casts and not from life, writing in her autobiography that 'the hatred of those plaster figures stays with me to this day'; her own enigmatic self-portrait of 1913, next to a nude female model, now hangs in the National Portrait Gallery in London.[21]

By the 1890s the curriculum had begun to broaden out from the rigid straitjacket imposed by Cole and his associates under the influence of the Arts and Crafts movement and, more specifically, the Technical Instruction Act of 1889, which allowed support from the rates to fund extra 'artisan classes'.[22] This led to a greater emphasis on working directly with materials, as in bookbinding, woodcarving, pottery, needlework, and other crafts. The effect was transformative, and by 1904 Hermann Muthesius, the Prussian cultural attaché, could write as follows: 'For many years now, hundreds of draughtsmen, modellers, architects, teachers of drawing and artistic craftsmen of all kinds have been pouring from [the art] schools and working and creating in the new tradition, which has thus maintained an entirely unified image in England and is no longer questioned in any quarter.'[23] This development could hardly fail to influence the planning of new art schools.

The government's requirements for the layout of art schools were set out in a form issued by the Science and Art Department in 1859, and periodically revised afterwards. As a bare minimum, the schools were expected to contain three high-ceilinged classrooms: an elementary drawing room, which could be divided by a curtain separating the male from the female students; a modelling room containing plaster casts; and a painting room for the more advanced students, along with the fee-paying middle-class women. An exhibition room for the students' own work was also thought desirable.[24] As in the board (elementary) schools which went up throughout the country under the 1870 Education Act, classrooms and studios were expected to be well-lit, well-ventilated, and grouped together in a coherent manner so as to allow easy access from one part of the building to another. Studios and classrooms were expected to have glare-free light, so, wherever possible, new buildings were aligned so as to face north, with as much top-lighting as possible for the upper-floor studios where the more advanced teaching took place: an essential consideration in smoky, polluted cities. Art schools can nearly always be identified, even when they have been turned over to other uses, by the glazing in their pitched roofs. The other important functional requirements were for adequate heating and ventilation. Until the 1890s the rooms in art schools were heated from open fireplaces, and lighting for the evening classes was provided by gas; the first school to be lit by electricity was that at Glasgow, begun in 1897. Gaslighting made an adequate system of ventilation essential, usually through ducts in the walls. One example which attracted the attention of the contemporary building press was the new school at Liverpool, begun in 1882, ventilated by 'Tobin tubes', previously used in the police courts at Leeds; here the foul air was 'extracted by vitiated air-flues, carried up with the smoke-flue from each fireplace, and also by additional flues in the outer main walls, connected to Boyle's air-pump ventilators on the ridges of the roofs, by air-tight trunks'.[25]

New purpose-built schools funded (at least in part) by public resources and dedicated solely to the teaching of art did not appear until the 1850s. The first seems to have been at Sheffield, where a new building containing classrooms, studios, and a sculpture gallery went up in Arundel Street, close to the city centre, in 1855–7, to the designs of the London-based partnership of J. R. Manning and F. Mew, its stripy façade and Byzantine/Romanesque round-arched windows clearly showing the influence of Ruskin's *The Stones of Venice*.[26] Schools in other towns and cities followed in the 1860s, the size and grandeur of the buildings depending on the generosity of local donors; only a tenth of the £7,400 cost of the new Nottingham school (now the Waverley Building of Nottingham Trent University), opened in 1865, came from public funds. Its handsome classical building of stone was designed by a local architect, Frederick Bakewell, on an open suburban site near the Arboretum, laid out in 1852. The palazzo-like façade, with its central turret and cupola, has large round-arched windows, and more light entered through the glazed roof, and a conservatory for studying plants – an important part of the curriculum, especially in an institution whose main purpose was training employees in the lace industry – was added in 1881.[27] The need for good lighting sometimes led to innovative architectural solutions. At Gloucester the art school occupied the first floor and the whole of the north wing of a new Gothic building of 1871–2 by the local firm of Fulljames, Waller and Son, with a curved, conservatory-like iron-framed roof lighting the advanced drawing and painting rooms on the upper floor; a science laboratory was placed in a separate pavilion to one side.[28] The Derby school (1876), by the same firm, had a similar curved roof for its painting and cast rooms, placed in a wing over the machine-drawing and ladies' elementary drawing rooms; here, as in most art schools down to the 1890s (and in elementary schools for much longer), the male and female students were segregated, with separate entrances for each.[29]

Art schools attracted growing numbers of students in the last two decades of the nineteenth century, as real wages rose and economic and cultural aspirations increased, putting pressure on what were still in many cases inadequate premises; some 1,320 students were enrolled in the Birmingham school, the largest in the country in 1880, but by 1900 the number had risen to 4,268, many of them educated initially in classes in branch schools held from 7 to 9 am in local elementary schools.[30] When the Manchester school finally escaped from the lower regions of the Royal Institution it was rehoused by the local authority in a handsome new building of 1880–1 in Grosvenor Square, within a residential neighbourhood largely made up of artisan terraced housing to the south of the city centre. The architect, G. T. Redmayne, was the brother-in-law of Alfred Waterhouse, whose formidably impressive Manchester Town Hall (1867–77) epitomizes the civic aspirations of the time, as do his new buildings for the University of Manchester, begun in 1879 on a site to the south of the art school. Redmayne first wanted to give the art school an elaborately detailed neo-Romanesque façade not unlike that of Waterhouse's Natural History Museum in London. But the funds failed to materialize, and it was built with a plainer, symmetrical Gothic façade of stone, with two storeys over a basement, a prominent central entrance surmounted by naturalistic detailing, and gabled wings: a loosely medievalist reinterpretation of an essentially classical design. The formal and hierarchical internal layout was not unlike that of many contemporary board schools. An axial corridor gave access to offices, a library and classrooms for elementary drawing lessons – the foundation of the curriculum – for male students in the west wing; a room for architectural and mechanical drawing was in the corresponding position to the east, and there were workshops for modelling and casting in the basement (Figure 4.1).

Female students taking the elementary classes went upstairs to a classroom of their own in the west wing; the corresponding room in the

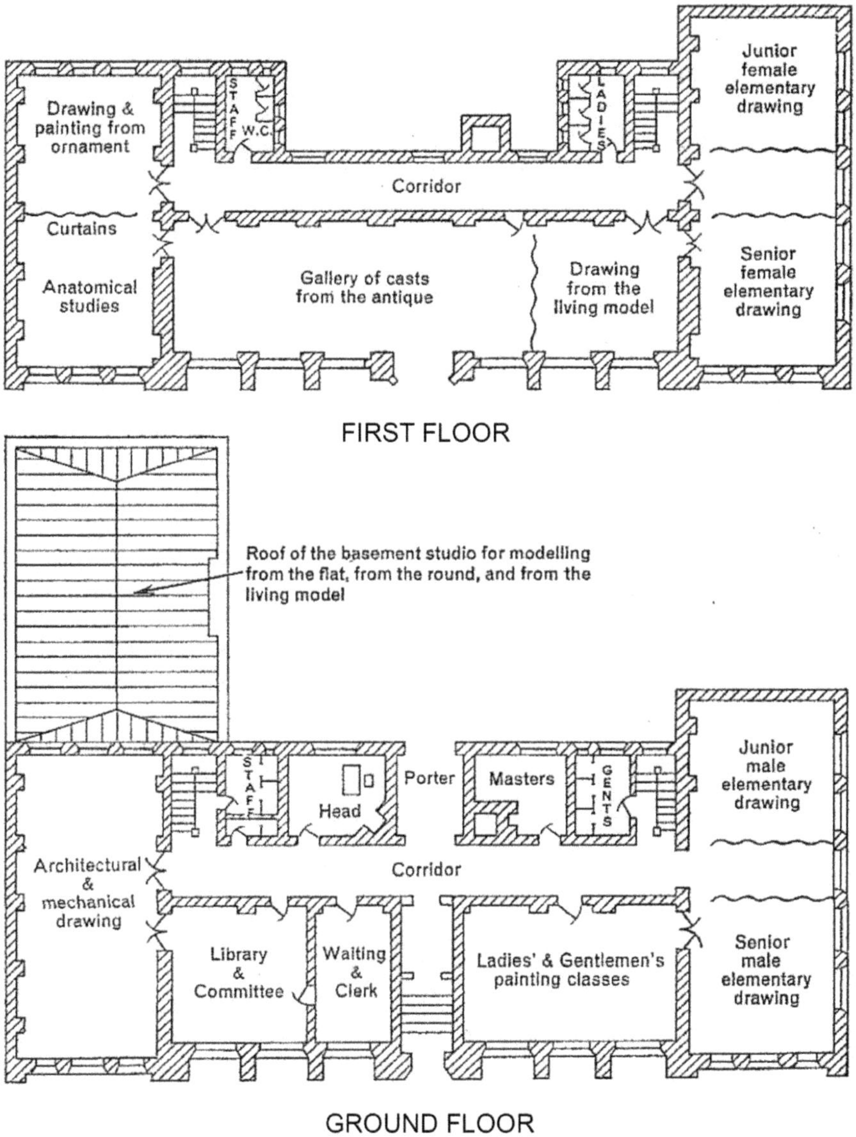

FIGURE 4.1 *Ground- and first-floor plans of the Manchester School of Art before the building of the 1893–6 extension (S. Macdonald,* The History and Philosophy of Art Education *(London: University of London Press, 1970), p. 184).*

east wing was given over to drawing from ornament and anatomical studies (the two separated by a curtain), and the large first-floor room in the centre contained a gallery for plaster casts, with a curtained-off section at the end devoted to life drawing, lit from above by windows in the roof.[31]

New craft-based classes were introduced in the 1890s, accompanied by lectures from, among others, Walter Crane ('visiting director' from 1893–6), C. R. Ashbee, W. R. Lethaby, and William Morris's daughter May. Then in 1896–8, an extension (the present Holden Gallery) went up behind the original building, to the designs of another Manchester-based architect, Joseph Gibbons Sankey, best known for designing one of the massive warehouses (the Tootal, Broadhurst and Lee Building of 1896–8 in Oxford Street) that transformed the southern part of the city centre in the late-Victorian period. Reached from the old building through a tiled corridor, its plain-brick exterior was enlivened by grouped lancet windows on the south elevation, adorned with angels in the spandrels by the terracotta artist W. J. Neatby. The ground floor was largely given over to exhibition space, freeing the existing building for studios, and there were workshops in the basement. The top-lit central galley was originally devoted to textiles, appropriately in a city that owed its prosperity to the cotton industry; an early photograph shows glass cases for museum exhibits and a Burne-Jones tapestry on one of the end walls.[32] The Italian and Gothic courts on either side were filled with plaster casts, and were reached through Romanesque arches, featuring more of Neatby's medieval-inspired work: a tangible illustration of the aesthetic philosophy that underlay the new spirit in art education in the late nineteenth century.

A similar migration to new premises took place at Birmingham. Here the rehousing of the art school formed part of a wider project of city centre urban improvements encouraged by the local authority, one of the most energetic in the country. The corporation took over the management of the art school in 1877, and moved it from New Street to a site donated by Cregoe Colmore, one of the main local landowners, at the corner of Edmund Street and Margaret Street, close to the newly created civic 'forum' with its new Museum and Art Gallery and Gothic monument to the politician Joseph Chamberlain, arch exponent of Birmingham's 'civic gospel' of municipal activism. Begun in 1884, the art school's strikingly 'Ruskinian' character reflects the sympathies of the architect, J. H. Chamberlain (no relation of the politician), the chairman of the management committee, and his professional partner and successor F. W. Martin, already displayed in their numerous local schools (e.g. Oozels St, now the Ikon Gallery, 1877) and their branch libraries.[33] It may also reflect the taste of the industrialists who contributed the bulk of the £21,254 cost; it certainly expressed the artistic aspirations of the city, which numbered among its inhabitants a notable concentration of talented craftspeople in embroidery, leatherwork, stained glass, wood engraving, and bookbinding, many of them, including Arthur Gaskin, Kate Bunce, and Joseph Southall, trained, or teaching in, the art school. For Janet Ashbee, wife of C. R. Ashbee, one of the foremost arts and crafts practitioners, Birmingham was 'a wonderful place: a curious mixture of bourgeoisie and romance, dullness and intellectual activity; materialism and spirituality'.[34] The Arts and Crafts theme – already anticipated in buildings like the Wedgwood Institute at Burslem – is proclaimed in the roundel in the left-hand gable, designed by Chamberlain, with a pattern of lilies in terracotta by the Leicester-based Samuel Barfield, an 'architectural sculptor' who was responsible for the sculptural enrichments of the Joseph Chamberlain memorial not far away. It is also apparent in the wrought-ironwork on the Edmund Street front and in the Doulton tile patterning both there and along the wing facing Cornwall Street, added in 1891 at a cost of £15,000 to accommodate extra classrooms and 'art laboratories' needed for the increasingly craft-based curriculum[35] (Figure 4.2).

Stairs lead up from Margaret Street to a medieval-inspired aisled hall which bisects the building and doubles up as a museum; it is flanked by Gothic arches on cylindrical columns, with light entering from windows in the steep-pitched open timber roof. Students taking elementary classes in the late nineteenth century turned right into a transverse corridor leading to a classroom; more advanced students could take a left turn into a 'light and shade' room – the second stage of instruction after outline drawing – and a lecture room. The central hall is flanked by staircases leading to first-floor studios set aside for design, painting, and drawing from casts; their glazed roofs, allowing the maximum top-lighting, are supported on pointed cast-iron arches, successfully marrying Gothic form with modern technology. A second-floor studio on the south side, facing Edmund Street, was used for life-drawing, and the modelling and machine-drawing studios were sunk into the semi-basement.[36] By the early 1900s, following the building of the

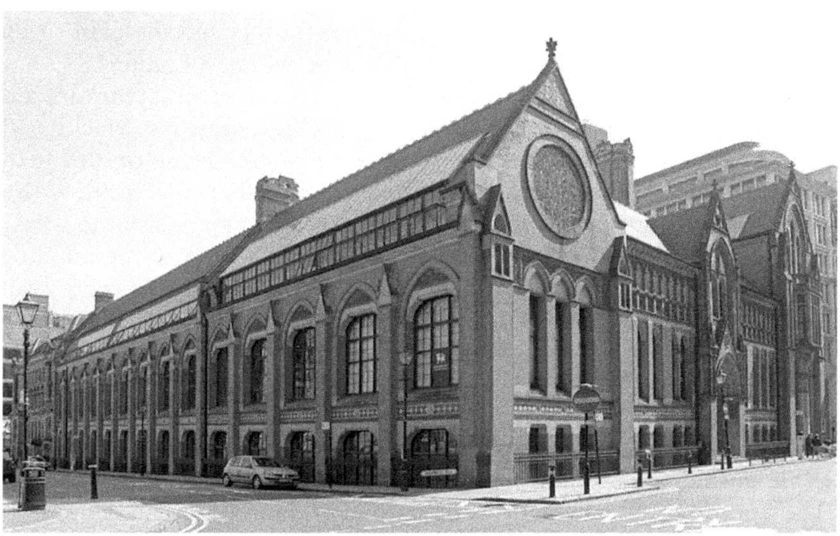

FIGURE 4.2 *The Birmingham School of Art from the north-west, showing the extension along Cornwall Street on the left and the glazed roof lighting to the upstairs studios (Wikipedia Commons).*

wing along Cornwall Street, four of the basement rooms were being used for metalwork, two for modelling and casting, one for woodcarving and another for bookbinding. There was an 'animal room' on the ground floor (a contemporary photograph shows men seated at benches modelling lions and horses) along with a room for lectures on building construction and another for brass-working and elementary modelling, and upstairs were studios for stained glass, 'design applied to flat surfaces and gesso', needlework, copying from antique casts, fashion plate drawing, and architecture, with a storehouse for plants on the roof.[37]

In 1896 Francis Newbery, the head of the Glasgow Art School, visited the schools at Manchester and Birmingham before compiling a detailed brief and settling on an architect for a new building to replace his school's existing cramped premises, shared with the city's art gallery, in Sauchiehall Street, leading from the city centre towards the affluent western suburbs.[38] The young Charles Rennie Mackintosh, a former pupil in the art school working in the office of Honeyman and Keppie, was chosen as architect because his scheme conformed most closely to Newbery's own ideas of a building which would not only be functionally efficient but would also reflect well on the cultural aspirations of the self-styled 'Second City of the Empire' (and, by the 1890s, the sixth largest city in Europe). Glasgow had already hosted a successful international exhibition in 1888 and had seen the rise of a much-admired group of local artists, the 'Glasgow Boys', some of whom, including George Henry and William Macgregor, were alumni of the School of Art.[39] The new building went up on a long, narrow site facing north onto a side street (Renfrew Street), running east to west on a steep hillside to the north of Sauchiehall Street, and the site to some extent dictated the plan of the main block, the first part of which was built between 1897 and 1899 at a cost of £14,000. Like the Manchester school, it has a central entrance and long transverse corridors giving access to the classrooms, but Mackintosh cunningly departed from a strictly symmetrical treatment of the main elevation, and he adopted a slightly different internal arrangement, with a single staircase beyond the small entrance hall leading straight up to a cast-filled museum, physically as well as symbolically the heart of the building, and lit by large windows in the timber roof. The ground slopes steeply away to the south, and here Mackintosh's scheme allowed for the building of wings, four-and-a-half storeys high in contrast to the two and a half of the main block. They allowed the building to accommodate the larger number of rooms, especially studios for small-group teaching and individual work, needed for the expanded curriculum which Newbery, like his counterparts in the English schools, had recently introduced.

The specification issued to competitors in June 1896 mentioned an Ornament Room for elementary and advanced students; a lecture theatre; a design room; a library; an architectural drawing room with an architectural lecture room adjoining it (a relative novelty in art schools of the time); two rooms for still life and flower painting; two antique (cast) rooms, one for elementary and the other for advanced students; two life rooms, one for male, the other for female students; three modelling rooms; 'technical studios' for stained glass and china painting, metalwork, woodcarving, and needlework; a room for the Headmaster with a studio adjoining it; three staff rooms, one serving as a studio, a janitor's office, a secretary's office and board room; a storage room; two lunch rooms, one for male, the other for female students; a heating chamber near the centre of the building; and cloakrooms. The studios were to be not less than 14 feet high, the corridors no less than 10 feet wide – a photograph of c. 1900 shows smock-clad female students working at tables and easels in the top-lit corridor on the first floor.[40] The east wing went up at the same time as the main part of the building, but the western part of the main block and the west wing were postponed until 1907–9, when a lightweight storey for extra studios, with greenhouse-like glazed exteriors, invisible from the street, was built on top of the main block; the total cost was in the region of £28,000. The west wing, externally evoking the Scottish tower-houses that Mackintosh admired, contained the famous library, another inspiring, light-filled space filled with dark Japanese-inspired woodwork, along with a lecture room underneath and a studio above.[41]

The Glasgow school has sometimes been seen as a proto-modernist building, and in a sense the main Renfrew Street façade, of smooth local stone, exemplifies Louis Sullivan's adage of 'form follows function'. Its huge plate-glass windows, insisted on by Newbery, anticipate Van de Velde's celebrated School of Arts and Crafts at Weimar (1905–8) and even, more distantly, the Bauhaus at Dessau. But the superficially functionalist effect (never Mackintosh's intention) is diluted by the quasi-Art Nouveau ironwork, both the railings along the street front and the platform for cleaning the first-floor windows: an essential consideration in the smoke-polluted atmosphere. Mackintosh believed that iron and glass would 'never worthily take the place of stone because of the defect of the want of mass' and of what he called 'stability'. So the iron girders supporting the floors rest on load-bearing walls. Inside, though, there were important technical innovations: electric lighting, and ventilation – or 'air conditioning', a word first used in c. 1904 – from the plenum system, invented by Glasgow engineer William Key. A heating chamber was placed next to a boiler in basement, with a fan circulating warm air which rose and was expelled through ducts (fatal in the devastating fire of 2014) behind grilles in the spine walls and through turrets in the roof; Glasgow, as Reyner Banham remarked, is 'a chill city for nude models'.[42] The natural light for the library was filtered through tall windows, supplemented by hanging electric lights to illuminate the wooden desks; wood was also used for the galleries, and elsewhere for roofing and furnishings throughout the building.[43]

Late-Victorian and Edwardian art schools were stylistically as varied as any other type of public building in that extraordinarily prolific and inventive period. Some were externally reticent, even self-effacing. The Leeds school, costing only £12,000, went up in 1902–3 behind Cuthbert Brodrick's Institute (on a site partly occupied by a school playground, replaced by a covered gymnasium) to the designs of the local firm of Bedford and Kitson. They were instructed to 'design a building of plain character, which, by its proportions and architectural outline and patterns, will not only harmonise with the existing Institute, but will also look appropriate for its intended use. The interior should also be of a plain and simple character, and all plaster and other mouldings liable to catch and retain dust are to be carefully avoided.'[44] The ingenious design made the most of the limitations imposed by the confined site, concentrating the accommodation into a compact L-shaped brick-built block with the classrooms and studios grouped around a central, top-lit staircase. Students entered through a classical doorway framed in a 'Gibbs surround', above which is a large mosaic by Gerald Moira featuring the name of the school against a gold background flanked by two brawny, Michelangelesque female figures representing Painting and Sculpture. As in most schools of the period, the workshops were placed in the basement, and the rooms arranged hierarchically on the floors above, with the elementary classrooms downstairs and the life, antique, and modelling rooms, lit by very large windows and roof-lights, on the top floor.

Most other art schools of the early twentieth century had a more assertive public presence, often expressed in the classical idiom. The Hull School of Art, built in 1902–5 on a cramped site just south of the main railway station to the designs of that most exuberant of 'Edwardian Baroque' architects, E. A. Rickards, has a similar plan to the Leeds school, with a central top-lit staircase, but its brick and stone façade is in a characteristically original version of the 'Wrenaissance' style of the late seventeenth century, intended no doubt to express the self-esteem of a thriving port which had recently been granted city status and had embarked on an ambitious programme of urban improvements.[45] The mosaic of 'the triumph of the arts over ignorance' in the pediment was designed by the illustrator Alfred Garth Jones and executed by the Bromsgrove Guild of applied arts, and the stone carvings over the semicircular porch are by H. C. Fehr, whose bronze statue of the late Queen presides over the civic centre in Queen Victoria Square: these embellishments may help explain the increase in the cost from £12,000 to £20,000.[46] The school at Liverpool moved in 1882 from the Neoclassical Mechanics' Institute of 1835–7 to a French Renaissance-style building designed by Thomas Cook on an adjoining site at the corner of Hope Street, but the exterior of its steel-framed extension, designed in 1910 by the local partnership (*sic*) of Willinck and Thicknesse is in the neo-Georgian style favoured by the newly founded Liverpool School of Architecture.[47] A stricter, Beaux Arts-inspired, version of classical architecture was adopted at the much larger Edinburgh College of Art, designed in 1906 by J. M. Dick Peddie, head of one of the leading Scottish practices, on the site of the former municipal cattle market, and completed in 1912 at a total cost of some £60,000: twice that of the better-known Glasgow school. The long rectangular building is entered through a monumental Doric frontispiece, with French-style pavilion roofs and a central top-lit ceremonial staircase flanked on either side by arcaded courtyards. Here too the quality of light played an important part in the way in which the building was experienced; the high-ceilinged, north-facing painting and drawing studios were described by the artist Elizabeth Blackadder, who taught there from 1962, as 'probably the best to be found anywhere. ... They have a quality of light even and subtle that makes them superb for their purpose.'[48]

The provincial art schools of late nineteenth- and early twentieth-century Britain played an important, if largely forgotten, part in the civic culture of the time, enlivening what were sometimes mundane urban environments and dignifying the lives of their students, who came with divergent aims and from differing social backgrounds. Their experience varied, not surprisingly, according to their level of proficiency and increasingly, as the curriculum broadened, their choice of classes. Architects, builders, designers, stained glass artists, brass workers, die sinkers, modellers, lithographers, and trainee teachers were among the students at the Birmingham school in 1890, and the curriculum in other towns and cities reflected their own trades and industries.[49] The daytime clientele in many schools remained predominantly female well into the twentieth century, and this is reflected in early photographs, which rarely show the more male-dominated evening classes. Those who took part in the elementary classes of the early twentieth century still sat, like their mid-Victorian predecessors, in rows of desks and performed repetitive tasks under the supervision of their teachers. But in the more advanced classes, whether for modelling and casting, or for life drawing and painting, the students, both men and women, sometimes intermingled, worked individually at their easels or stood at benches. Female students at the Manchester school are shown in photographs of c. 1900 drawing from a live, draped, model; others, both male and female, all of them well-dressed, stand at blackboards drawing daffodils.[50] A photograph of an embroidery class at Sheffield in 1905 shows the students, all women, sitting at desks in a well-lit interior hung with fabrics; at Derby a group of men and women are drawing from casts under the arched iron girders of the 'Antique Room', the light from the vast windows dispersed through draped curtains (Figure 4.3).[51] The mood, in so far as it can be judged from photographs, is decorous and intent: a far cry from the free-and-easy atmosphere that swept many art schools during the cultural revolution of the 1950s and 1960s.

Art schools proclaimed the value of the visual arts and crafts to the outside world, offering students the opportunity to experience an 'architectural promenade' – to use Le Corbusier's phrase – from shadowy entrances to light-filled upstairs studios: a metaphor perhaps for their artistic progress. Education at a provincial art school could pave the way to artistic fame, as it did for Laura Knight at Nottingham, for Henry Moore and Barbara Hepworth at Leeds, and for L. S. Lowry at Manchester, who learnt life drawing from Adolphe Valette, a largely forgotten artist whose moody,

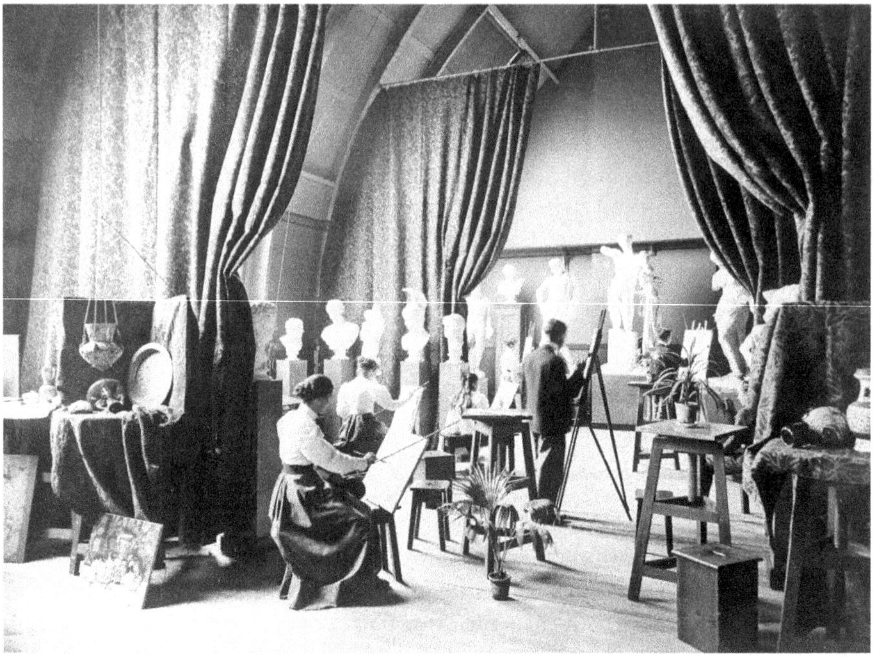

FIGURE 4.3 *Male and female students in the Cast Room at the Derby School of Art c. 1900. (Picture the Past, Derbyshire Record Office, DRBY200067, www.picturethepast.org.uk)*

Whistlerian canvases capture the misty atmosphere of the Cotton Metropolis in the early years of the twentieth century. More often it led to careers in industrial design, in commercial art, or in schoolteaching. In Arthur Conan Doyle's story 'The Naval Treaty' (1893), Sherlock Holmes, travelling out of London on a train from Waterloo Station, draws Dr Watson's attention to the recently erected elementary schools put up by the London School Board: 'those big isolated clumps of building rising above the slates, like brick islands in a lead-coloured sea … . Light-houses, my boy! Beacons of the future! Capsules with hundreds of bright little seeds in each.'[52] The same can be said of the art schools of Victorian and Edwardian Britain.

CHAPTER FIVE

Rooms and galleries: Spaces of art in the nineteenth century

Valerie Mendelson

By the end of the nineteenth century, the Louvre had become an exhausting place. Henry James, looking back in 1913 at his childhood impressions, described how in the Galerie d'Apollon, with its 'long perspective, the tremendous, glorious hall', the space itself overwhelmed the artworks within.[1] The more casual private art collection, often installed in the new neighbourhoods rising up around the Parc Monceau, invited a longer stay, one mixed with conversation, perhaps a meal, and with friendship. These two competing architectural forms, one intimate and one overwhelming, provided contrasting experiences for audiences eager to enjoy Paris's artworks.

Paris, as the international centre for avant-garde art, as well as a magnet for collectors and art lovers, serves as an important case study for the experience of art in the nineteenth century. By the mid-century, Superintendent of Buildings Baron Haussmann was renovating Paris by tearing up old slums, installing new sewers and lighting systems, and creating wide boulevards flanked by uniform apartment buildings that worked to erase the medieval city and bring Paris into the industrial era. Newly wealthy industrial magnates, among others, were building lavish mansions to house their art collections, and even the magnificent Louvre museum was being renovated and reinstalled.[2] Other new spaces of art exhibition such as the huge universal exhibition halls, burgeoning private galleries, and the ever-busier Drouot auction house offered new viewing experiences. This chapter, concentrating on Paris, examines the perceived tensions between museum and private collection, as observed in novels, memoires, and sales catalogue essays. Throughout the century, the Louvre, former palace of kings, was continually reorganized, extended, and reimagined as a palace of the people. At the same time, private collectors were eager to house their collections in their own hotel particulier. Their aim was to present art in a manner which inspired conversation and intimacy, in contrast to the galleries and hallways of the museum.

While the experience of the museum had become increasingly focused on looking as a mode of experience, the private collection allowed for a more sensual, and fully corporeal experience that included, most importantly, touch. Similarly, while the long and narrow galleries of the Louvre demanded tiring and increasingly directed walks, informed by a growing proliferation of guidebooks, the private collection promoted impromptu 'sinuous paths' and extended absorptive observation and conversation. Often visiting a private collection would involve a private, individualized tour with the owner.

While scholars have addressed the history and ideology of the museum, the art market, and the literary discourse around collecting, an experiential comparison of the museum and the private collection has yet to be drawn.[3] Some recent scholarship has focused on the way that spaces where art was displayed in the past were designed to engage all the senses. Timothy O'Sullivan has shown how in ancient Greece and Rome, strolling with a friend while viewing frescoes was believed to promote understanding of the art and encourage philosophical conversations.[4] He argues that 'the connection between the movement of the body, the traveller's gaze, and the acquisition of knowledge ... was a cornerstone of Greek thought'.[5] The experience of architecture was, therefore, crucial in the organization of paintings within the Roman Villa. In the context of later European art, Frances Gage has discussed the therapeutic role that princely collections of the sixteenth and seventeenth centuries were believed to play. She singles out the Sienese physician Giulio Mancini whose advice to collectors stressed the curative powers of viewing art.[6] The beneficial effects derived not only from the calming and cheering aspects of the art works themselves, but from the physical exercise derived from walking through the collections, most particularly through the long hallways known as galleries.[7] Helen Leahy has discussed more generally the embodied viewer, who not only looks, but is found 'walking, standing, talking, listening, reading, writing, sitting and, occasionally, touching' primarily in the arena of British museums.[8] This chapter expands these inquiries into the contrast between the experience of private and public spaces of art in nineteenth-century Paris by investigating accounts of the experience of the Louvre and of private collections. I also show that the pleasure that came from the experience of the private collection began to be made more public as art marketers not only mimicked private collection installation practices, but as auctioneers began staging home viewing to entice their clientele with tactile fantasies of ownership.

The experience of the museum

According to Constance Classen, the experience of art within museum spaces across Europe became progressively limited during the nineteenth century.[9] She attributes this to several factors. On the one hand, an increasing number of visitors made earlier practices cumbersome and dangerous, and on the other, the greater numbers of lower-class visitors contributed to social unease on the part of museum curators and benefactors. So while Oxford's Ashmolean Museum had routinely allowed handling and touching in its early history, by the mid-nineteenth century there were clear rules against even touching sculpture, that most tactile of arts.[10] The Louvre also limited the freedom of visitors, forcing them to leave their umbrellas and walking sticks at the door.[11] These limits on the experience of art within an institutional setting were contrasted with the freedom of private collecting.[12]

The didactic mission of the nineteenth-century Louvre began to emphasize art history as chronology, and the architecture of the 'gallery', narrow and straight, visually supported this with the perspectival 'vanishing point'.[13] Nineteenth-century paintings, engravings, and photographs of the Louvre stress the perspectival movement of the eye enacting, spatially, a teleological view of history: its architecture embodied the idea that there should be a neat historical ending to the progress of art.[14] This unfolding narrative was mocked in new wave filmmaker Jean-Luc Godard's *Bande à part* (1964) with a comic scene in which the characters break the record for travelling through the Louvre, previously set by an American from San Francisco, by running through the museum in nine minutes forty-three seconds. Critics of the fast-walking museum visitor in the nineteenth century included the poet and critic Charles Baudelaire.[15]

The gallery as a room had its origins in the fifteenth century as a connecting structure between different buildings.[16] Experientially, the gallery evolved as a place to walk, with pictures being hung to enhance the journey, as was the case for the Louvre.[17] Twenty-eight feet wide and fourteen hundred-feet long, architectural historian Anthony Blunt described it as 'in fact no more than a long corridor'.[18] First built by Henry IV to connect to the Palais des Tuileries, he planned to decorate it with views of various towns. These were not installed and Louis XIII recalled Nicholas Poussin from Rome to design a new decorative project. This also was never finished and what remained was destroyed in the eighteenth century to make way for the new museum. Once the museum opened, following the revolution of 1789, the Grande Galerie was modernized with new skylights and hung densely with pictures. A visitor in 1820, Thomas Jessup, experienced being overwhelmed, writing that 'the eye is lost in the vast and original perspective; the sense is bewildered amid the vast combinations of art'.[19] What had been invigorating for the seventeenth-century gentleman walking in his gallery had now become tiring.

Bewilderment and fatigue only increased as the century wore on. As we saw, Henry James was impressed with the Galerie d'Apollon, with its 'tremendous, glorious hall'. It was not only the architecture, however, that overwhelmed the visitors to the Louvre. James's as well as others' experience of the museum and its art was informed by a guidebook. James opened his novel *The American* (1877) with the main character, Christopher Newman, in the Salon Carré:

> He had looked at all the pictures to which an asterisk was affixed in those formidable pages of fine print in his Bädeker: his attention had been strained and his eyes dazzled and he had sat down with an aesthetic headache.[20]

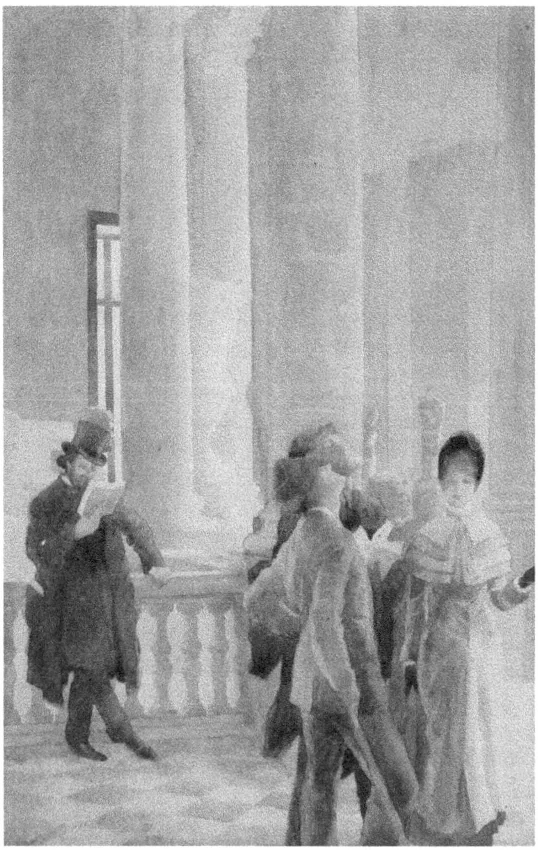

FIGURE 5.1 *James Tissot,* Foreign Visitors at the Louvre (Visiteurs étrangers au Louvre), *c. 1882, Watercolour over graphite on paper, 71.8 × 49.5 cm, Eskenazi Museum of Art, Indiana University, 80.30. Photograph by Kevin Montague.*

The artworks he had seen were related to each other by their shared asterisks in the guidebook, and the walk through the museum culminated at the gallery's great circular divan. The experience of the nineteenth-century museum was, often, a long walk down a gallery, accompanied by a perusal of a museum guidebook, and occasional rests on the few benches available.

As an aid to finding one's way through the grand architecture of the museum, as well as to enforcing a focused attention on the history of art, guidebooks were important.[21] By the end of the nineteenth century, even in the sculpture galleries of the Louvre, guidebooks were an essential accessory, as shown in French artist James Tissot's 1882 *Foreign Visitors at the Louvre* (Figure 5.1). In this depiction, the artworks are eclipsed by the surrounding architecture, and two of the figures hold guidebooks. The balustrade seems to indicate a stairwell, and we have the impression that this space is but a small part of the larger institution. Certainly, the figure at the left, absorbed in his guidebook, leans back to rest against the railing. The immense scale of the space dwarfs the figures. Only the woman looks straight ahead, seemingly unperturbed by her environment. The two central men who gaze up might be experiencing the kind of dizziness described by the poet Paul Valéry whose visit to the Louvre culminated in 'extreme fatigue'.[22] While these visitors are presumably visiting together, they are not interacting with each other. The overwhelming architecture of the national museum, the isolating and wearying experience of the Louvre prompted critics throughout the nineteenth century, from art theorist Quatremère de Quincy at the start through the Goncourt brothers, both novelists and memoirists in the later part of the century, to fault the museum for its deadening effect.[23]

The experience of the private collection

The end of the nineteenth century was a heady time for collectors. Prosperity, groundbreaking new painting styles, and a newly chronologically organized museum framed the gathering of artworks in one's home.[24] Whereas in the past, collecting had been largely confined to the aristocracy, the crown, and the church, industrializing France admitted ever greater numbers to the ranks of those able to afford artworks.[25] Galleries, which for so long had languidly presented out-of-date works discarded by the rich, were overflowing with contemporary artists, such as Monet and Renoir, who belonged to the first generation of painters to depend on the dealership system for sales. The auction houses encouraged fierce bidding. The 1889 Secrétan sale, for example, stimulated a campaign to keep France's celebrated painting, Millet's *Angelus*, from being purchased by Americans.[26]

To a great extent, Paris's new private collections were a response to a heated art market and a growing industrial class. While some collectors such as Count James-Alexandre Pourtalès aimed to build homes that were reminiscent of the public museums of Paris, others sought to produce more intimate spaces.[27] Many reacted with vehemence to what they saw as the impersonal and commercial effect of the public exhibition, and particularly museum spaces. The novelist Edmund de Goncourt's approach was hostile to the traditional museum experience. Unlike Pourtalès, he built what he called the 'House of the Artist', which he documented in a book of the same name, personalizing each room with a diverse range of objects and artworks.[28] When the time came to plan for the future of his collection after his death, he decided not to keep his collection together, instead auctioning it off, proclaiming how,

> My desire is that my drawings, my prints, my bibelots, my books, in short all the artworks that have been the happiness of my life don't suffer the cold tomb of a museum and the stupid gaze of an indifferent passer-by. [29]

In contrast to the 'cold tomb of the museum', the private collection was theorized and experienced as an invigorating space.[30] This vibrancy was conceived of in three ways. The collection was described as something that could speak on the behalf of a collector. In turn, this involved a tactile and sensual relationship with the collection. Finally, movement through the collection was not preordained, as in a museum, but variable.

Sales catalogues for private collections, after the collector died or decided to sell, often portrayed complex relations between collectors and their collections in their prefaces. The inclusion of narratives of previous owners suggests an intimacy that was fundamental to the whole idea of collecting. It implies an appetite on behalf of new buyers to learn not only about the provenance of pieces they purchased, for authenticating purposes perhaps, but about their emotional significance to the previous owner. Paul Mantz, an art historian and director of the Ecole des Beaux Arts in 1881–2, wrote in the preface to the sales catalogue for the collection of the diplomat Gustave Rothan, 'to those who live by intellectual work, art works give consolation and sometimes, advice. Gustave Rothan knew how to give a superb frame to his serious work as historian. He worked in a museum. It was in the middle of these riches that he lived.'[31] The crucial role in both the emotional and intellectual life of the collector was stressed in the last sentence: 'these excellent paintings that during so many years gave joy to our friend and which were almost his collaborators'.[32] Therefore, simply looking at the paintings was not at issue, nor learning about them in a guidebook. Rather, the collector was described as loving them. Colonel Merlin, an important military man in France whose collection sold in 1900, also viewed his collection as a friend. He was described in the preface to the sales catalogue by 'A.D.' thus:

> Little concerned with the caprices of fashion in the fine arts, he loved and admired paintings exclusively for themselves, going only to those towards which he felt personally drawn. Also, once admitted into his collection, he considered them and treated them as his friends.[33]

Both Merlin's initial choice of artworks, and his extended relationship with his collection, were based on his feelings, which appeared to transform the paintings into sentient beings, comparable to friends. The insistence on the emotion that a work of art gave a collector, rather than its historical value or artistic merit, was often repeated in auction catalogues.

Novels, sales catalogues, and articles in such journals as the *Gazette des Beaux Arts*, which ran a regular feature on collectors, also highlighted the often erotic nature of collecting, with collectors frequently referred to as 'amateurs'; the etymological derivation of this being *amour*.[34] The language of seduction in texts describing the private collection varied from the friendly to the passionate. There was a kind of rhapsodic quality in the way pleasure was presented in the prefaces of sales catalogues. For example, one explained how

> the count Daupias did not obey the objectives of a methodical historian; he wanted above all to satisfy his need for elevated pleasure; he wanted to make everything around him explode with the joy of seeing.[35]

This sense of pleasure and enjoyment was typical of the attitude towards amateur collections. Joy and pleasure, along with desire and jealousy, were the sentiments critic Léon Roger-Milès ascribed to architect Alfred Feydeau's attitude towards his collection, which was chosen with enlightened care:

> He had kept them [his art works] near him with a tender jealousy: they represented what his taste for art told him to love, and he never looked at them without an emotion in which was mixed an aesthetic joy which included never jaded memories of the great battle of the school of 1830 in which he had taken part.[36]

This closeness of taste, love, and life was sometimes expressed as specifically romantic, even if not sexual. Auguste Rousseau, a collector who concentrated on landscape painters, including Bonvin, Corot, and Daubigny, had an intensely private relationship with his collection:

> He knows the adorable joy of resting his eyes on the works that he loves and which only he has the right to love. … He created his own voluptuousness, jealous and silent: every day he came back to his little wonders of which he is the guardian, full of solicitude, and each day, for forty years, he found qualities that he not suspected that day before, insights that had hitherto escaped him, subtle illuminations of which his eye had not yet guessed the caress.[37]

In this passage the eye is a preface to 'a caress'. Such language was often repeated in connection with the collector sometimes spelled out in romanticized accounts of tender possessiveness.

M. Paulin, member of the Societé des bibliophiles français, described the passionate relationship which Alphonse Firmin-Didot, publisher, had with his collection, in this case characterized as feminine. Firmin-Didot's passion was comparable to one 'inspired by an adored mistress'; this was to such an extent that when

> he became the happy owner of one of his rare volumes that he had long coveted, he separated himself from it neither day nor night. A place was found for it under his pillow ... a new rival arriving was in turn welcomed with the same tender effusion.[38]

This loving attitude hearkens back in some ways to the premodern reverence and adoration of icons that Constance Classen traces in her *Cultural History of Touch*.[39]

This tactile prerogative is evident in Attillio Simonetti's watercolour *The Amateur*, which depicts a private collection. Here we see not only the close examination of a small painting, but also the variety of textures, colours, and materials that comprised the collection (Figure 5.2). This blending of categories both in terms of media and of era, sculpture, tapestry, furniture, classical, medieval, and baroque, was typical of private collectors who rejected museum categories by installing artworks from different periods in close juxtaposition. This colourful and intimate space, and actively engaged viewer, is a far cry from the stony grandeur of the Louvre and the lassitude of the visitors as seen in Tissot's painting (Figure 5.1). The twist of the body, the circular composition, the extraordinarily painterly clothing, and the peripheral colours all point to an embodied viewer whose knowledge, memories, and emotions are simultaneously engaged. Simonetti's painting, which seems to depict an eighteenth-century figure, can also be seen as self-referential as the artist himself became a renowned collector and antiques dealer.[40]

Movement in the private collection also differed from that of the museum. Rather than the controlled, guidebook-determined walk which museums promoted for their visitors, the private collection often employed a circuitous path.[41] Art historian and curator André Michel described his visit to the collection of Jean Dollfus, the textile magnate and early collector of the Impressionists, where the host guided Michel discretely, leaving him the pleasure of discovery.[42] Critic Pascal Forthuny made this sense of the unexpected explicit in his preface to the private collection of the violinist M. Beriot, which consisted of many landscape paintings.[43] Forthuny likened his visit to a leisurely walk: 'For the entire promenade, I was never tired nor constrained in any way, and from canvas to panel, rarely has a voyage been as agreeable nor as restful.'[44] He described the quality of this journey, reflecting on,

> what a complicated and sinuous route, what a vagabond path of poets it was necessary that I follow! What infinite variety in the aspects of nature ... what comforting bath of fresh air, fertile prairies, limpid rivers.[45]

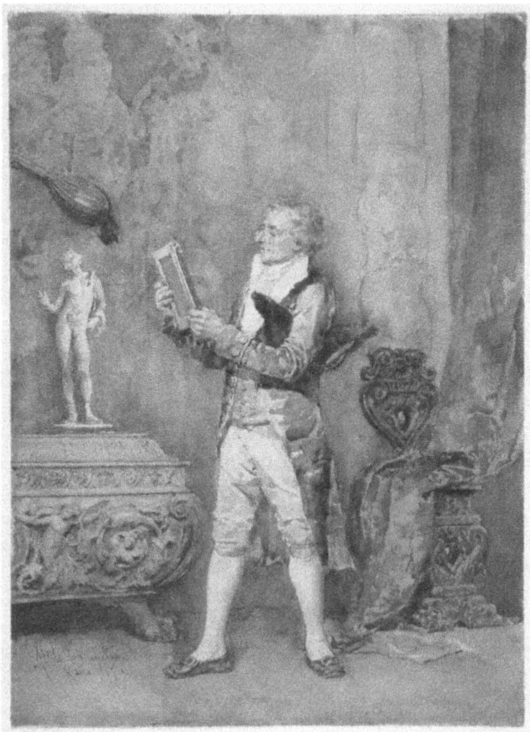

FIGURE 5.2 *Attillio Simonetti,* The Amateur, *watercolour, 35.4 × 25.3 cm, 1872, Metropolitan Museum of Art, 87.15.72, Public Domain* https://creativecommons.org/publicdomain/zero/1.0/

The contrast of these two experiences, one a walk through a linear museum gallery and the other a private relaxing stroll, corresponded to two distinct modes of viewing.[46] The museum elicited a desire to know more, supplementing the path with a guidebook or museum labels, which stressed the assimilation of specialist art history.

Commercial spaces: Bridging the divide between public and private

As Martha Ward has shown, private galleries such as those of Durand-Ruel and Georges Petit began in the 1880s to fill their spaces with comfortable furniture and plants in an effort to duplicate the intimacy of the home.[47] Their aim also was to create a non-commercial ambiance that spoke to the social ambitions of their prospective clients. Auction houses also began staging viewing hours at the homes of those whose collections were being auctioned. Eager to sell to private collectors, the auctioneers understood the appeal of intimacy, along with the freedom to touch, and imaginative pathways, and therefore promoted these aspects in both sales catalogues and by allowing prospective buyers to visit the collections in collectors' houses. For example, for the sale of the collection of Valtesse de la Bigne, an important courtesan, her grand hotel particulier was opened to visitors.[48]

Valtesse's salon, as can be seen from the photograph in her sales catalogue, was sumptuous and splendid (Figure 5.3). Decorated in a somewhat rococo style, it exuded luxury and sensuous indulgence. Many of the paintings listed in the catalogue were by either Gervex or Détaille, but she also owned works by many other artists including Courbet, Ingres, Forain, Raffaelli, and Roybet. Prominently displayed in the salon was Gervex's full-length portrait of her. However, what the catalogue dealt with rather more than her fine art collection was the apartment itself as a luxurious setting for the objects within:

> The amateurs who come on the exhibition days at the hôtel on Boulevard Malesherbes, will have lots to satisfy their curiosity. ... It is an infinity of

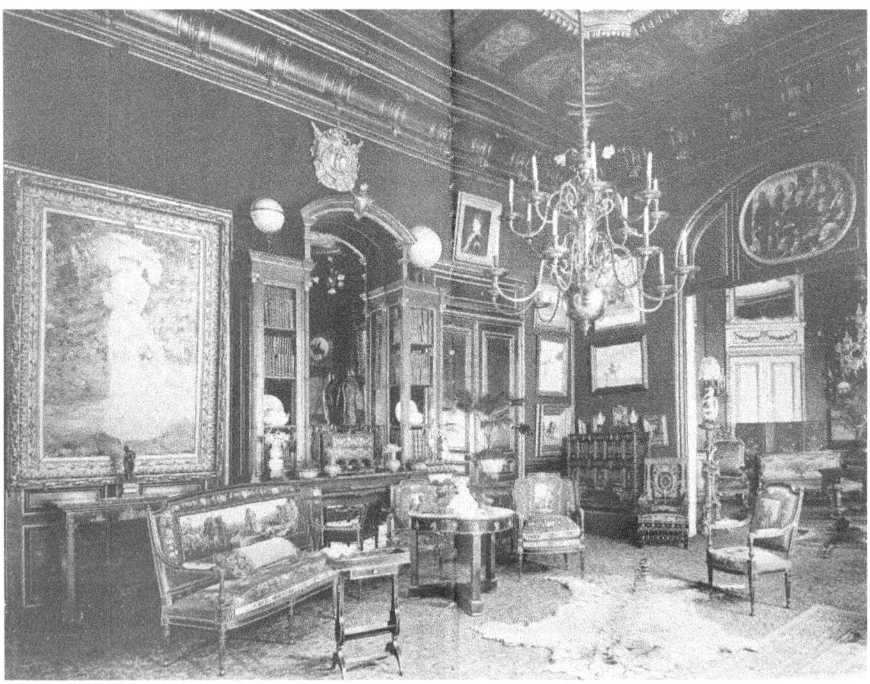

FIGURE 5.3 *Living rooms of the ground floor (Salons du rez de chaussée),* Collection de Valtesse de la Bigne *(Paris, 1902), Collection of Valerie Mendelson; Photograph by Valerie Mendelson.*

> artworks and of things of high taste that offer themselves in a luxurious setting, where the hand, most expert at elegances, pleased itself in bringing them together, in grouping them, in harmonizing them, if I can express myself in this way, for the pleasure of the eye.[49]

'The hand, most expert at elegance' is figured as presenting that which is a pleasure for the visitor's eye, as if Valtesse had decorated – grouping and harmonizing – expressly for the benefit of the prospective buyers. Here, the salesmen of the auction house refigured the early-museum experience of handling objects and examining them closely as a sales strategy. The interior was an arena of performance: a place to seduce art collectors.

The practice of visiting collections on sale in situ was well established by the late nineteenth century. Notably, the Russian Prince Demidoff's collection was sold in 1880 at the Palais de San Donato in Florence.[50] Invitations for viewing were mailed out to potential clients, although the collection was also open to the public for several days. The palace itself was enormous: the floor plans of both first and second floor were printed in the sales catalogue, allowing even those readers unable to visit Florence to imagine walking through the palace, although of course the aim was for the collection to be viewed 'catalogue in hand'.[51] Included in the sale were the wood panelling and decorative items of the palace, such as 'garnitures de fenêtres', which were much more easily displayed within the building itself. Widely reported on, including in New York's *Art Amateur*, this celebrated sale had wide international success.[52] The experience of a private collection, so much more varied, unexpected, and exclusive than the public museum, appealed to prospective buyers

Even more modest sales advertised visiting the home of the seller. For example, in a sale of drawings by Forain and Constantin Guys, among others, from the collection of one M. Ragault, interested parties were invited to see the collection in his home in Paris even though the eventual sale would take place at Drouot.[53] Similarly, an anonymous 'Seller 48', Avenue du Bois-du-Boulogne, advertised a sale of important furniture on Monday 12 May 1890 with viewing times from 1 pm until 6 pm on the preceding Saturday and Sunday.[54]

Often a catalogue would list a collection according to the layout of the house. The sixty paintings and furniture of the collection of M. Tuite, identified as artiste-peintre, located at 8 rue de Miroménil, were listed in the order of a potential visit: antechamber, room serving as a studio (including three easels), living room, dining room, bedroom, and second bedroom. In this way, even without visiting, there was a document suggesting an architectural space of private collection rather than simply an inventory. Similarly, for the sale of the collection of M le Comte D'Armaillé, the catalogue was organized by room.[55] This sale included furniture, sculptures, silver, drawings and paintings, tapestries, and 'wood panelling from the XVIIIth century'. The sale as well as the viewing took place in his home at 48 rue La Boétie on the 5th and 6th June, 1890.[56] The collection was significant enough that a simultaneous sale, focused on paintings, took place at the Gallery Sedelmeyer.[57] The room-by-room organizational structure is found in quite a few sales catalogues. Mme la baronne Hauzeur de Ciply's collection was open for viewing at her hotel 53 rue Ampère.[58] Her bedroom furnishings were listed and described in great detail although with less innuendo than in the preface to the Valtesse collection.

Sometimes the sales were held outside of Paris.[59] In several cases, railway timetables were included in the sales catalogues for convenience. Mme de Grandville's collection was viewable in her chateau at Yveteaux in the Orne and for the sale of Mme Roslin's collection, provisions were made for an 'omnibus' to ferry visitors from the station at Écouen to the place de l'Église.[60] In most cases not only paintings, but heavy furniture as well as lace and books, and even kitchen equipment, were for sale, underlining the point that prospective buyers would encounter objects from all aspects of life. This personal component of selling art was so strong, and the interrelationship between the architectural spaces and the objects within them proved so enticing that auction houses encouraged in situ visits, even outside of Paris.

Conclusion

This chapter has contrasted the experience of the Louvre at the end of the nineteenth century, with that of the private collection. Where the first tended to be tiring, both because of the guidebooks and long hallways that induced a sense of bewilderment and fatigue, encounters with private spaces of art were described as enlivening. The appeal of the latter was fully exploited by commercial galleries and auction houses, and led in turn to the proliferation of such hybrid sites: public galleries that aimed to recreate private space. This chapter has considered the way that different kinds of architecture promoted a different kind of sociability, a different kind of attention, and perhaps a different kind of individual. While the Louvre aimed to teach each visitor with guidebooks and chronological installations, the private collections sought to appeal to all the senses. One aimed to form educated citizens, the other to release the imagination. Through these different architectural experiences, museum professionals, private collectors, and auctioneers fashioned very different experiences of Paris's rich and varied artworks.

PART THREE

Designing experience

CHAPTER SIX

New York's Harvard House and the origins of an alumni culture in America

H. Horatio Joyce

In 1909 a journalist from *The Outing Magazine* could hardly contain his enthusiasm for the new university clubs taking hold in midtown Manhattan in an article on 'how they ease the tasks of young men in city'.[1] Organized by alumni for alumni, with commodious clubhouses, they offered most, if not all, of the conveniences and amenities of older, more established gentlemen's clubs in the city. Their appeal was that they were cheaper – much cheaper – and far less exclusive. As long as a graduate met the basic criteria for membership (usually as simple as having earned a degree at the respective university), he could usually expect admission. Some clubs, including Brown and Pennsylvania, rented rooms in a hotel or apartment building. Others, such as Princeton (1899) and Columbia (1901), occupied converted houses, while Yale (1897) and Harvard (1894) owned purpose-built clubhouses. The great value of such places, the journalist explained, was in helping young alumni transition into life in the big metropolis. Many of them evoked campus architecture and contained plenty of college memorabilia – a bit of the familiar in the midst of the unfamiliar.

As the dates above begin to suggest, it was Harvard graduates who first developed the alumni clubhouse idea and it is the aim of this chapter to investigate their reasons for doing so. The fact that all of the alumni associations mentioned above continue to maintain clubhouses today and, moreover, that the alumni clubhouse idea has since spread to a large number of other cities around the United States makes this development of interest to a variety of historians: architectural, urban, educational, as well as social.

This study is particularly geared towards the last two fields, though I also hope to show how architectural historians can use the design process behind buildings to elucidate social agendas that are otherwise difficult to discern. This is certainly the case for the Harvard Club, I argue, which innovated the clubhouse idea with the intention of establishing higher education as an integral part of an upper-class male identity. This, however, was never explicitly set out by alumni, in large part because it developed slowly, the product of an accumulation of ideas, constantly adapted by a variety of different alumni as well as university administrators. But by focusing on the Harvard alumni experience in New York, both before the clubhouse and through the clubhouse building process, it is possible to trace the emergence of an American alumni culture that helped transform the nature of the American elite.[2]

Towards a clubhouse

Acquiring permanent quarters was a radical departure for the Harvard Club of New York. In the years between its founding in 1865 and its first clubhouse in 1887, a rented brownstone house near Madison Square, the Harvard Club was all but indistinguishable from the dozen or so other alumni groups in the city, including those of Princeton and Yale.[3] It held monthly meetings and annual dinners in restaurants or rented rooms, and membership climbed only modestly from year to year, reaching 200 in the late 1870s and 300 by the early 1880s.[4] Like most Harvard students in the nineteenth century, the majority of the club's founding members were born in New England and came from prominent families in the region, among them the Ordways, Purringtons, and Beamans. In New York, they worked mostly as lawyers for large banks and corporations.[5] The club's motivation for signing the lease on the first clubhouse, and ultimately building its own premises a few years later, had to do with the extraordinary changes taking place hundreds of miles away at their alma mater in Cambridge, Massachusetts. Harvard was effectively reinventing itself from a small New England college into the country's first truly national university. Underlining this transformation was a clearly articulated agenda by Harvard's leaders to create an American leadership class. In moving into its own home, the Harvard Club set out to contribute to that project from their base in New York.

At the forefront of Harvard's changes was university president Charles W. Eliot (1834–1926). Shortly before his election as president in 1869, Eliot declared in the *Atlantic Monthly*, 'The American people are fighting a wilderness, physical and moral, on the one hand, and on the other are struggling to work out the awful problem of self-government. For this fight they must be trained and armed.' Over his four decades in office, Eliot set out to produce 'commissioned officers in the army of industry', Harvard-trained architects, chemists, engineers, and manufacturers, who would meet America's new organizational and technological demands and solve its 'awful problem of self-government'.[6] In an effort to make Harvard 'useful' and its curriculum 'practical', Elliot dramatically increased the number of professional schools and eliminated nearly all prescribed courses for undergraduates by instituting an elective system of courses – probably Eliot's most radical reform.[7] The rationale was to encourage young men to identify their interests and to develop their passions, so that by the time they graduated they would be well placed to think about what type of commissioned officer they wanted to be.

Harvard alumni in New York were generally enthusiastic about Eliot's reforms. They praised the elective system in particular as a necessary 'revolution' to adjust higher learning in America 'to the spirit and the needs of the time and the country in which we live'.[8] Unlike Eliot, however, they believed the university also had an important role to play beyond graduation, beyond the campus, and into the adult lives of its former students. While Eliot saw Harvard as a vehicle for delivering organizational and technical expertise, Harvard alumni were convinced of the value of maintaining college friendships and a connection with the college itself. Based on personal experience in the country's most booming metropolis, New York's Harvard alumni resolved that their alma mater would have to do more for its graduates if Eliot's leadership class agenda was to succeed. Cities were too big, too uncertain, and too full of corrupting influences for young men to navigate alone. The university needed to somehow extend its influence out from Cambridge to protect young Harvard men and to help them on their professional paths.

This was the thinking that contributed the clubhouse idea. It did not, however, develop all at once, nor did it unfold from the mind of a single individual. Rather it developed gradually, and collectively, the result of alumni experience in New York, first without a clubhouse, and then through their experimentation with various types of clubhouses. The seed of the clubhouse movement can be traced to the club's campaign to win representation on the university's Board of Overseers in the late 1870s.[9] This pitted New York alumni against Eliot and other university leaders, who favoured the status quo, which restricted the overseers to alumni living in Massachusetts. Forced to justify their position, club members began to cultivate arguments centred on the apparently alienating effects of living in a large city like New York. They felt unanchored, overwhelmed, fragmented by 'the great rush of life' taking place around them. The club's objective 'with reference to this Overseer question', as one of the club's vice presidents explained to Eliot, 'has been to renew and strengthen our friendship for each other, and especially to maintain the circuit of close connection with the University'.[10] These same arguments would be used again by the club as it began exploring the question of a clubhouse in the 1880s.

Before we can consider how the club approached this question, we need to take a closer look at the rise of club life in New York. In the same years that Eliot was implementing his educational reforms at Harvard, New York was emerging as the capital of a newly integrated and increasingly corporate American economy.[11] The behemoth companies that took shape in this period, like Standard Oil and Carnegie Steel, flocked to New York for, among other things, its abundance of professional service firms, not least the blue-chip law offices of Harvard alumni who mediated the complex relationship between big business and the state. As a consequence of this, the number of wealthy New Yorkers mushroomed, making elite society more conscious than ever of the need to actively create and maintain class identity and culture. Towards this end, they developed a number of strategies, among them gentlemen's clubs. This type of institution, originally British, lent itself particularly well to the business of class formation, thanks to its Old World aristocratic associations. Clubs, moreover, had the added attraction of being fairly flexible: they could be organized around almost anything and indeed a great variety were, including ones that emphasized culture, wealth, as well as ethnicity, whilst still subscribing to the same aristocratic ideal of leisure. In retrospect, then, it was not all that surprising that Harvard alumni should also experiment with the club idea.

Within a year of declaring itself in resounding support of Eliot's revolutionary elective system of courses, the Harvard Club of New York set off on its own radical path by leasing a brownstone premise at 11 West 22nd Street in 1887 (Figure 6.1).[12] The four-story building was located in the fashionable neighbourhood around Madison Square. An article in the *New York Times* described how

> When all is complete the first floor will be used for the restaurant, and in it also the monthly meetings will be held. The Second floor will contain a singing room, parlour, library, and reading and card rooms. The third will have a billiard room and several bedrooms for the accommodation of members, and the fourth will be wholly occupied by bedrooms. ... A beginning has been made toward the library, and the reading room is well supplied. It is intended to have in the reading room a full collection of all documents relating to Harvard.[13]

Of note were the bedrooms, not yet the norm in clubhouses, but an excellent amenity for fulfilling the club's desire of drawing itself closer to the university. No less interesting was the club's intention to stock the reading room with 'a full collection of all documents relating to Harvard'. The club's secretary, as early as 1881, had written to 'all of the surviving secretaries of past college classes ... requesting copies of their class reports'.[14] With quarters, the impulse to collect only grew. The club now appealed to members 'for anything and everything relating to Harvard' and were rewarded with a variety of memorabilia, including college photographs, 'badges, keys, and pins; and invitations, dance cards, posters, programs, and tickets to Commencement exercises, Hasty Pudding shows and the like'.[15]

Despite their best efforts to personalize 11 West 22nd Street, however, club members never quite felt at home in the building. Two factors were

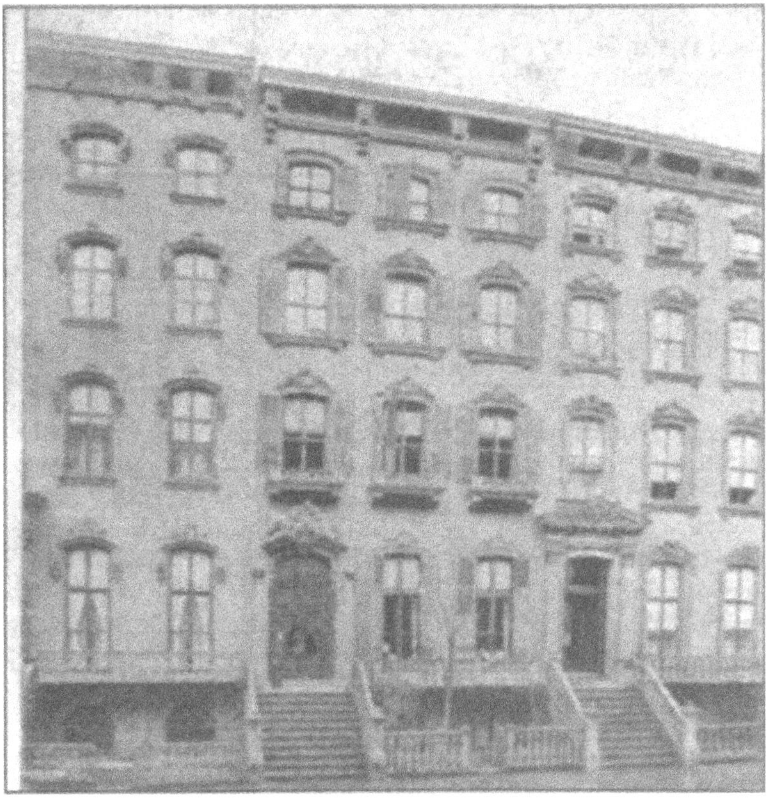

FIGURE 6.1 *The Harvard Club of New York's first quarters at 11 West 22nd Street, which it occupied between 1887 and 1894* (King's Handbook of New York City, *1893*).

mainly to blame for this and both influenced the club's later resolve to own outright any future clubhouse and to have it purpose built. One was the club's arrangement with its landlord, Nathan Clark, a former restaurateur and small hotelier. Clark managed the property, including the club's restaurant, bedrooms, and servants. If at first this arrangement struck alumni as attractive, for it allowed them speedily to set up and occupy the house, it soon became evident that it undermined their ability to foster a sense of place. Disagreements inevitably arose between landlord and club. The fact that Clark's own house on West 23rd Street backed on to the club made the situation even more difficult.[16] Second, the building itself was poorly suited for the club's purposes. One member recalled 11 West 22nd Street as 'rather mean and dismal [in] character, the rooms being ill ventilated, badly lighted, and worse heated'.[17] Built as a single-family residence with a side hall plan, likely only three rooms deep, the standard twenty-five-foot width brownstone presented challenges for the circulation of air, light, and members, of which there were now 531.[18] In fact, the building proved 'so inadequate' that, after just a few years, the club questioned whether it should 'abandon housekeeping altogether'.[19]

That the club ultimately persisted was due to its president Edward King (1833–1908), elected in 1890. King's great contribution to the clubhouse experiment was to link it more fully to Eliot's leadership class project in Cambridge, something he was particularly well positioned to do as an influential banker with a family pedigree that was equally distinguished in New York and New England.[20] Eliot described him as someone who 'typified the "Harvard Force" in its best manifestation in business life', someone upon whom the country relied in emergency, and who was worthy of this reliance'.[21] King, in Eliot's mind, represented the very best of America's Harvard-educated leaders in the world of modern business. Although both men shared a similar outlook about the social order, it was King who first argued that the university needed to play a role in the adult lives of the leaders it educated. Unlike Eliot, King lived in New York and his ideas about the club were – on some level – personal. Tellingly, his decision first to join the club and then seek election as president coincided with the matriculation of his two sons at Harvard in 1884 and 1890.

In his second year as president, as he was debating what to do about 11 West 22nd Street, King attended the annual dinners of the New York alumni clubs of Columbia, Princeton, and Yale. His stump speech at these events amounted to a manifesto about the function of alumni clubs for the new social order, a project in which Columbia, Princeton, and Yale were also increasingly invested.[22] In January, King delivered the most developed version of that speech to more than 200 Princeton alumni at the Hotel Brunswick.[23] 'The dinner was the usual formal informality,' quipped a reporter from the *New York Times*, who quoted at least one or two lines from most of the speeches that night, particularly the jokes.[24] King's speech went unnoted, however; his was serious, dry, ponderous, and philosophical – out of step with the night's festivities. But the speech, previously unpublished, hints at King's views about what role a clubhouse might play in the making of an educated elite:

> In a busy city like this, the hours of business, the quick succession of stirring sounds, the kaleidoscopic changes that pass over social life all lend to obliterate the past and to relegate college training and college culture to the misty jargon of memory. It is an absolute benefit therefore to bring a man to a gathering like this where the vigil of old classmates, the sound of old songs and the whole magnetic influence of the scene dispels the cobwebs that have dimmed the bright memories of old days at the university. And more than this – revive the interest in the things that those days brought. In the march of science, the course of literature, the ever new steps in the progress of modern culture. What we all need is just some such stimulus to remind us that the objects of life are not confined to success in business or the rewards of professional ambition, but that

> there are intellectual pleasures which like ripe fruit hang ready for the hand that is untroubled to pluck them.[25]

Thus King elaborated on the club's earlier arguments about the alienating effects of urban life that had taken shape during its campaign to win representation on the university's Board of Overseers. He introduced the idea that this urban life, when combined with the corrupting influence of wealth and ambition, had the potential to undermine the ability of the new social order to govern well. They were in danger, he argued, of forgetting that their real purpose in New York, whatever their occupation, was to steward American civilization. This is why, in his view, alumni annual dinners were important, along with college nostalgia more generally. How King might have translated this philosophy of alumni life into a programme for a new clubhouse is not difficult to imagine.

Harvard House

In 1894, after almost three decades, the Harvard Club of New York moved into its very own home at 27 West 44th Street, known officially as Harvard House (Figure 6.2). It was designed in the colonial revival style by Charles F. McKim of the firm Mckim, Mead & White. The architect, who had briefly studied at Harvard before moving to the École des Beaux-Arts in Paris, was a member of the club and gave his professional services as gift. For the façade, McKim used Indiana limestone and 'Harvard Brick', a patina after the bricks in Harvard Hall in Cambridge. McKim had especially developed the brick to use in the design of Johnston Gate (1890), one of the main entrances to Harvard Yard and his first commission from the university.[26] The relationship between the university and the clubhouse was made explicit in other ways as well. The three-storey clubhouse was surmounted by the Harvard arms with the dates 1636, 1865, and 1893, respectively the dates of the university, the club, and the house. The message, if it is not already apparent, was that these institutions had evolved organically one from the other, forming a harmonious trinity in the life of the modern American university.

The front door, under a simple Doric portico, opened onto a small vestibule, beyond which lay an entrance hall, two small reception rooms, and a grille room at the rear, overlooking a garden (Figure 6.3). The ground floor rooms opened widely onto each other, lending a sense of spaciousness to a plan which was, in fact, stage-like in its dimensions, 100 by 25 feet. Economy of space also account for the position of the staircase in a rear corner of the building, though the superbly carved balusters and heavy mahogany rail made it one of the few showy details in an otherwise plain interior. Even the club's grandest room, the high-ceilinged library, which occupied the full front of the first floor, contained only the simplest

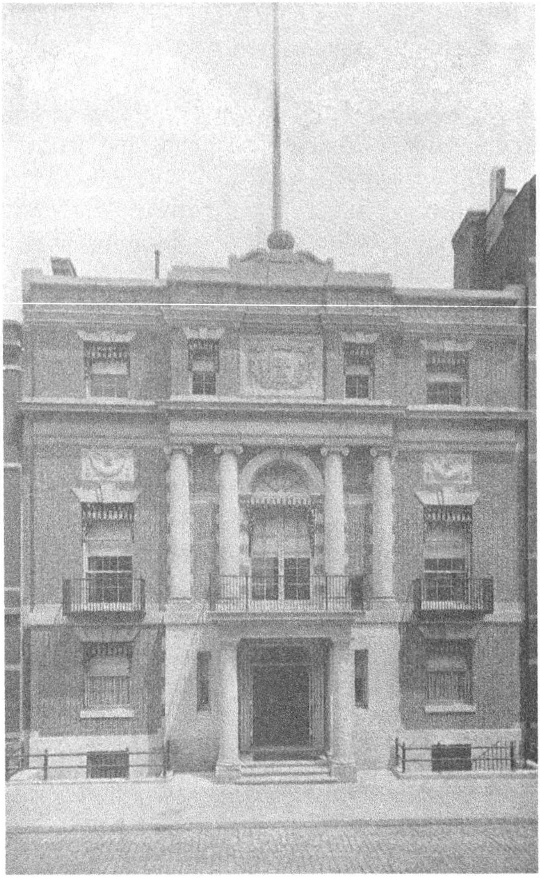

FIGURE 6.2 *Harvard House on West 44th Street in 1894, designed by Charles F. McKim. The university's crest in the attic, along with the use of 'Harvard Brick', helped distinguish the building* (Harvard Graduates' Magazine, *Vol. III, No. 9, September, 1894*).

mouldings (Figure 6.4). It was separated from the second room on this floor, the supper room, by a simple curtain. The attic above contained modest rooms for billiards (just three tables), cards, and committee meetings. There were no bedrooms, unlike 11 West 22nd Street, and only a small kitchen in the basement for occasional catering. The rooms were decorated, as the exterior was embellished, in the colonial revival style. And as McKim had done for the plans, the interiors – furniture, paintings, and bric-a-brac – had been donated by various members.[27]

There was never any question about the person responsible for bringing this little piece of eighteenth-century New England to midtown Manhattan. 'The work of Edward King!' exclaimed the chairman of the Building Committee

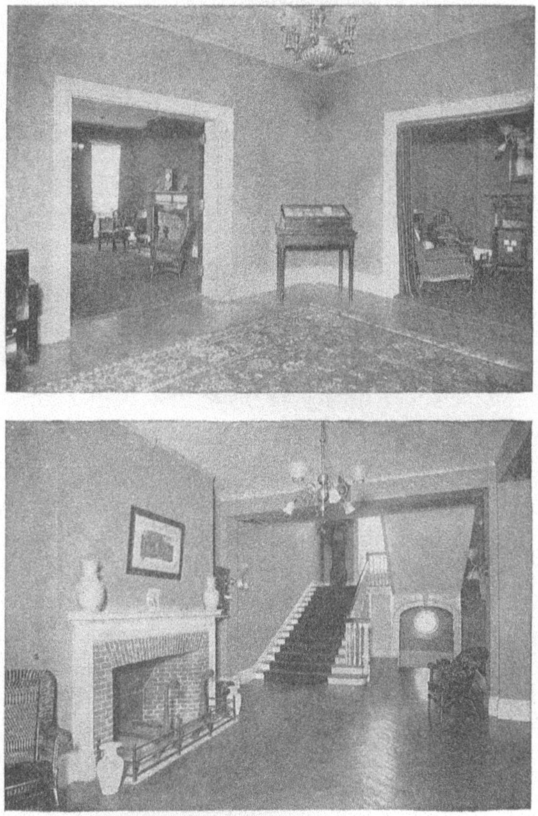

FIGURE 6.3 *Harvard House interior photographs, taken in 1894, including the reception room and staircase. Much of the decoration and furniture was donated by club members and their wives* (Harvard Graduates' Magazine, *Vol. III, No. 9, September, 1894*).

at the formal opening of clubhouse.[28] The *Harvard Graduates' Magazine* concurred, explaining to alumni readers around the country, 'Most of all, the conception and the fulfilment of the vision of Harvard House were due to the optimism, energy, and sagacity of President King.'[29] In the end, then, King had managed to mould architecture around his theories about the benefits of urban alumni communities to their members. 'It is essentially a place of reunion, comfortable and homelike. It will be the scene of many periodical jollifications and formal meetings,' the *Graduates' Magazine* explained, echoing the ideas first laid out by King at the Brunswick Hotel, 'but, above all, its chief value will be the calm and repose, and the reminiscence of the scholastic life, it will offer to those who are tired of the battle and cannot go all the way to Mecca for new inspiration'.[30] Thus Harvard House was

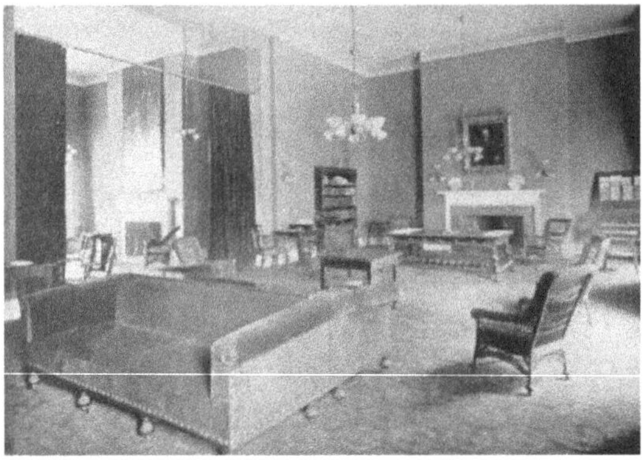

FIGURE 6.4 *Harvard House library in 1894* (Harvard Graduates' Magazine, *Vol. III, No. 9, September, 1894*).

to serve as a sort of permanent 'stimulus', for reminding elite businessmen that the progress of American culture was their actual purpose in the city, not wealth and ambition. King's work in this respect was, however, only achievable because of the architect's willingness to accommodate his ideas in the design. The nature of their partnership is suggested by a missive from McKim to the club president as the project neared completion, relating 'how much pleasure' he had had in working with the club president 'in the construction of the building whose plan was yours!'[31]

That McKim gifted the architectural plans to the club, foregoing his usual 5 per cent fee, was also of great significance for the development of the alumni clubhouse idea. It became the symbolic centrepiece for a programme of donations that helped alumni to conceptualize their building as a 'home' and themselves as a 'family'. Unlike most other clubhouses in New York, whose interiors absorbed most of the architects' time and the client's budget, Harvard Club members assumed responsibility for their interiors themselves and prided themselves on financial restraint. 'The question of furnishing', the chairman of the Building Committee Arthur M. Sherwood announced on opening night, 'was a most difficult one, for the treasury was almost empty and the club had but $6,500 to spare for that purpose.' Their fears were relieved, however, 'by the most liberal voluntary assistance from the graduates' who donated nearly every object, just as they had generously subscribed to cover the construction costs, including tables, chairs, andirons, mantels, candelabra, and clocks.[32] As for wall decoration, members donated an 'archive' to adorn them, comprising 'everything which may have bearing upon illustrating the life of a student at Harvard in the past'.[33] Items included event tickets, sports kit, and even unpaid tuition bills. More serious, but along similar lines, were the donated portraits of distinguished alumni. The total effect was something quite different to that of the typical custom-designed furniture and handpicked European antiques of clubhouse interiors, or 11

West 22nd Street, which never felt like home. Harvard House, as its name suggested, was more house than clubhouse.

The domestic aspect of the project was enhanced by the involvement of members' wives. Sherwood acknowledged the gifts of several wives in his opening night speech, including an embroidered fireguard and the Harvard flag flown from the roof. King's wife personally donated a piece of family furniture, grandly known as the Glastonbury Cathedral chair, which she hoped would be used by her husband and his successors as the president's chair.[34] In a speech many years later, King recalled how there were, in fact, two clubhouse openings, one for members 'and also a reception for ladies to whom we owed much in the way of encouragement and actual contributions towards furniture and ornaments'.[35] This was perhaps belated acknowledgement that members' wives played a more extensive role in decorating the interiors, that they also helped to organize the donations and set them out in the rooms. On any level, the collective effort of Harvard Club members and the participation of their families not only worked within King's ideas about the need to moderate the influence of wealth, but also introduced a new element: a link between the club and home, alumni and family. As the *Harvard Graduates' Magazine* described opening night: 'It was more like a home-coming after a long family separation than a house-warming; and the consciousness was on us all that it was the beginning of an epoch of Harvard life in New York of the greatest interest and importance.'[36]

The clubhouse library was another major area of donations and a central component of King's ambitions for the club. While it was not unusual for clubs to collect heavily in narrow areas of interest (the New York Athletic Club became a voracious collector of printed matter relating to the subject of court games), the Harvard Club fashioned its library as something like an extension of the university library in Cambridge. Founding club member Thomas F. Brownell initiated the collection in the late 1880s, as the club prepared to move to its first quarters at 11 West 22nd Street. Brownell had been the secretary of his Harvard class and brought a similar fastidiousness to his work as the club's first chairman of the Committee on Art and Literature. He began by writing to every club, department, institute, and school of the university, requesting copies of their printed collections. He was not always successful. 'We have literally no "literature"', replied the dean of the dental department.[37] And the secretary of the Theta Delta Chi observed, 'As the Society is Secret I am unable to send you By Laws, Constitutions, etc'.[38] But on the whole the efforts of Brownell and his successors were more successful. As Harvard House neared completion, the club broadened its collecting still further, requesting Eliot's help in obtaining copies of books whose authors were even marginally associated with the university.[39] Thus the completed clubhouse grew into a substantial repository for Harvard material, perhaps the largest outside Cambridge. In other words, just the sort of place to help alumni ward off the corrupting influence of business.

This function was augmented by regular lectures from visiting Harvard professors. Eliot's secretary supplied the club with a list of more than two dozen faculty members who might be asked to speak. He noted their fields, and perhaps just as helpfully, their ability to provide an 'enjoyable general talk' for members.[40] The club, in return, supplied the president's office with admission tickets for professors and lecturers wishing to use the clubhouse on trips to the city.[41] By bringing a little piece of Harvard to midtown Manhattan, Harvard House realized King's ideas about the value of alumni associations. Here graduates were offered a 'stimulus to remind' them 'that the objects of life are not confined to success in business or the rewards of professional ambition', as he had told Princeton alumni, but rather 'in the march of service ... literature ... in the progress of modern culture'.[42] King had plucked the 'ripe fruit' of culture that 'hang ready' and placed it in the hands of members.

Conclusion

By 1910, the alumni associations of nearly every Ivy League university in New York had acquired quarters in the city. Following the Harvard Club's example was logical given the growing ambitions of their own alma maters to become, like Charles W. Eliot's Harvard, training grounds for a new national elite. But whereas Eliot and other educational reformers had been concerned with finding a balance between social order and democracy, the new alumni clubhouse culture helped ensure that it was ultimately merit as opposed to any notion of social hierarchy that defined this class. Merit was not a driving concern in the development of Harvard House, however. It was about rulership, plain and simple.

The elitist nature of this history has only come into focus through close attention in this chapter to the alumni experience in New York. At no point in the development of New York's Harvard House did anyone announce the club's intention to contribute to Eliot's leadership class project. The closest it ever came to this was Edward King's philosophical ruminations at the annual alumni dinners of Princeton, Columbia, and Yale. Even here, however, we have had to carefully consider other points in the organization's history in order to appreciate the speech's significance. The club's campaign to win representation on the university's Board of Overseers, its years at 11 West 22nd Street, and its work with Charles F. McKim to design a suitable purpose-built clubhouse were all integral to the story. Indeed, architecture and the design process itself were instrumental. It was in building Harvard House, after all, that club members began to cultivate a language for a new type of alumni community. The house and the family were traditional sources of ruling-class power in the Old World and, in this respect at least, the American leadership class was scarcely any different.

CHAPTER SEVEN

Architectural acoustics: Thomas Roger Smith and the science of hearing buildings in nineteenth-century Britain

Graeme Gooday

> *It is unfortunate that so few of the philosophers who have devoted their time to this study [of acoustics] have paid any attention to the most practical of all its possible applications, and that consequently an idea has become prevalent that nothing at all is known to men of science which would be of value to the architect.*[1]
>
> —THOMAS ROGER SMITH, *A RUDIMENTARY TREATISE ON THE ACOUSTICS OF PUBLIC BUILDINGS*, (1861).

Who was responsible for optimizing the aural experience of Victorian buildings? The Sheffield-born architect Thomas Roger Smith (1830–1903) lamented that physicists who wrote treatises on sound offered no practical advice on how their wisdom could benefit building design. Managing the many practical facets of acoustic science was, after all, a complex topic that the architectural profession could not obviously claim as its own sole prerogative. By contrast, architects were indubitably responsible for the external and internal *appearance* of buildings. Indeed writing as University College London's Professor of Architecture in the 1880s, Smith wrote histories of classical and Gothic architecture that more conventionally prioritized instead the visual engagement of the 'spectator' as the principal sensory mode of experiencing a building. As the editors of this volume would surely emphasize, however, the congregations in medieval cathedrals discussed in Smith's historical writings were not art critics, but gathered instead to *hear* the liturgical rites of the Roman Church.[2] Importantly, Smith's writings on acoustics from 1860 to 1895 not only discussed how developments in church architecture supported various soundscapes of religious participation but also showed more generally how architects could draw upon both acoustical theory and lessons from extant buildings to shape the aural qualities of future constructions of both religious and secular kinds.

This chapter sets out to contextualize Smith's acoustic expertise within the politics of Victorian Britain's architectural profession, as well as within contemporary public debates, and more recent historiography of acoustics.[3] Avoiding a purely biographical approach, the first part of this chapter puts into broader social context the kinds of debates among architects that prompted Smith's (intermittent) efforts to define the professional responsibility of architects in this area. In later parts, I explore how Smith's expertise was eventually eclipsed by the quantitative fin-de-siècle laboratory researches of American physicist, Wallace Sabine (1868–1919). As is well known Sabine's famous eponymous equation of 1900 for predicting and adjusting resonance periods was embraced as a new 'scientific' canon by many architects in the twentieth century.[4] To complement this, I show how Smith's critical *qualitative* approach to the aural ecology of buildings was the major reference standard among British architects for at least three decades since 1860 in ways previously unrecognized by architectural historians.

I thus reshape the interpretation of Smith's writings in Emily Thompson's study on American soundscapes which documents the ascendancy of Sabine's approach. She notes the conclusions drawn in 1895 by the 'Science Standing Committee' of the Royal Institute of British Architects (RIBA), that architectural acoustics was still an 'obscure' topic, and that Smith told this committee that it was still somewhat a matter of 'instinct' (i.e. based on personal intuition and thus not fully articulable). While Thompson infers from this that Smith had contributed little of long-term value to architectural acoustics, I show how Smith's various writings explicitly showed how to apply knowledge of 'the laws of sound' in ways that were based on much more than pure 'instinct'.[5] Overall I argue that understanding Smith's hitherto little-studied writings requires us to examine not only what was already known about building acoustics before Sabine's arrival, but also to take more seriously than historians have previously done Smith's alternative *experiential* approach to the 'science of architecture'.

The problem of acoustics in Victorian public buildings

The challenges facing the growing architectural profession in the nineteenth century were numerous: aesthetics, cost, hygiene, safety, utility, and acoustics, to name but a few. Architects had published lore to guide them in building centuries-old genres such as the theatre: generations of architects had brought their expertise to bear to ensure the acoustic success of plays and operas to paying audiences in enclosed metropolitan theatres.[6] Of course, acoustical considerations to ensure the clear projection of a human voice to all present in the building were by no means paramount in all larger-scale architectural endeavours of the Victorian period. It was not necessary in the design of hundreds of railway stations, factories, and libraries; and for the discreet commercial transactions of elegant new Corn exchanges, the priority was instead for localized transactional conversations that were not transmitted across the entire building.[7] Yet other new kinds of grandiose project brought unprecedented challenges for acoustics, specifically new civic edifices serving the public function of oratorical spaces or as concert halls. For such cases there was a cultural premium attached to architects accomplishing a soundscape in which human utterances could be heard and understood without distracting repetitive echo or the deadening dullness of un-resonant sound.[8]

The issue of acoustics was a particular problem for the swathe of town halls built across England from the 1820s as civic sites for all classes to attend public concerts, lectures, and assemblies of myriad other kinds. Smith himself noted in 1861 that large school-rooms, lecture halls, assembly rooms, and indeed the majority of moderate-sized halls built since then were 'very liable to acoustic defects'. Two factors in architectural practice were typically the source of problems: ill-judged building proportions and inopportune surface finishes. The former of these involved large empty spaces above or behind a performer: these could either dissipate sound into inaudibility or produce persistent echoes that distorted speech's clarity and/or intelligibility. As for the latter, while sound scattered by highly decorated surfaces avoided direct echoes, a performer directly facing plain flat surfaces would typically encounter unhelpful reverberations that compromised the audience's appreciation of words said or sung.[9]

Smith's early writings tactfully focused on successful exemplars of town hall acoustics produced by fellow architects. As a model specimen he recommended in particular the Manchester Free Trade Hall completed in 1856, while passing in silence over the problems at the Town Hall in nearby Stalybridge. Rachel Milestone notes that the latter, built in 1831, was so prone to both acoustic and aesthetic defects, that it had fast become a laughing stock. So much so, in fact, that when the town's Mechanics

Institute was opened in 1862, all musical events in Stalybridge were abruptly transferred to that new venue. After remedial building work some concerts returned to the Town Hall eight years later. Yet the acoustics were not sufficiently improved to impress a reviewer from the *Ashton Reporter* in 1876 who discerned that 'defective acoustic properties of the hall were rather painfully apparent', with multifarious echoes preventing 'thorough blending' of the vocal and instrumental parts.[10]

This Pennine town was evidently not the only one to suffer so.[11] In the month immediately following Smith's 1861 publication of his *Rudimentary Treatise on the Acoustics of Public Buildings*, the topic was discussed in *The Builder*, a weekly periodical designed to appeal to architects, builders, and all fellow professionals engaged in associated processes. One correspondent, 'T.B.', wrote in July 1861 deploring the discovery that the recently constructed Town Halls of Blackburn and Leeds, and of St George's Hall in Liverpool were 'sadly defective' as regards their acoustics. T.B. contended that most readers of *The Builder* would admit that architects had a special responsibility in ensuring the 'edification and pleasure' of audiences in such buildings. Few were unaware of

> the difficulty we experience in hearing clearly and correctly public speakers, preacher and singers, in most of our churches; and particularly in our great public buildings, especially in some parts of the buildings. This does not so much arise from the deficiency of the speaker or singer as from the peculiar size, dimensions or proportions of the buildings.

Although various remedies had been tried, T.B. contended that up until that point no attempted mitigation of acoustic difficulties had been found that could completely 'remedy the evil complained of'. In his view the only architectural space in Britain which approached 'perfection' was the Cheltenham Pump-room in the spa town of Harrogate; this had been erected with Doric columns in the neoclassical style from the designs of 'Mr. Clark of Leeds' in 1833.[12] Laying out the dimensions of this building, the writer surmised that the architect might have 'happily', and probably fortuitously, hit upon the best proportions for a building to have optimal acoustics. T.B. conceded that while his judgements for the ideal dimensions of this room did not conform to the guidance in Roger Smith's recently published *Treatise*, Harrogate's Pump-room was nevertheless, 'an example of a good room to be heard in'.[13]

As a final example of acoustically troublesome architecture, the Royal Albert Hall, constructed in South Kensington from 1867 to 1871, was evidently not built to the recommendations of either Smith or 'T.B.'. Designed to surpass in sheer grandeur any other building of its kind in Britain dedicated to the arts and sciences and in keeping with Queen Victoria's wishes for her late-lamented Prince Consort, this gigantic tribute was the work of two Royal Engineers: Captain Francis Fowke and Major-General Henry Scott.

To commemorate the prince's huge cultural legacy, the eponymous hall was modelled on classical amphitheatres: Rome's elliptical open-air Colosseum was one apparent model. Nevertheless, the addition of a high-domed glazed roof of wrought iron to mitigate the inclement weather of Northern Europe was both entirely un-classical in credentials but also brought a long legacy of acoustic problems to this grandiose edifice. Following the completion of the Hall on Christmas Day 1870, these problems soon became apparent. Noting the unprecedented size of this construction, an editorial published in *The Times* on the day of its official opening (29 March 1870), alerted readers to anticipated difficulties:

> There are misgivings that the Hall exceeds the scale fixed by the conditions of humanity, inasmuch as it is about twice as large as the largest building yet found to answer its purpose. But there are many possible appliances to assist the sight and hearing, and as yet we are but tiros [*sic*] in the science of acoustics. The Hall can hardly be worse for seeing or for hearing than the position of St Paul's under the vast and lofty dome. … All this remains to be ascertained, and corrected if necessary.[14]

To some deferential journalists at least the Prince of Wales' speech at the opening ceremony was audible; and John Tyndall, professor at the Royal Institution, was evidently lucky enough to be situated in seats where no disturbance was apparent. Yet journalists seated elsewhere in the Hall reported problems of a persistent echo, and the ensuing concert revealed the more general acoustic problems engendered by imposition of the high-domed roof. Fowke and Scott initially sought to manage the problem by hanging a large canvas 'velarium' below it to lessen the effective height of the hall and thereby shorten the duration of its echo.[15] Even so, Scott felt obliged to write to apologize to the audience via the correspondence column of *The Times* for the acoustic infelicities that more than a few had experienced. Correspondents in the *Building News* were also unsympathetic to the apparent disparity of experience among those occupying the 8,000 seats. One 'CE' (perhaps Civil Engineer?) dismissed the Albert Hall as 'nothing more than a bad concert-room, quite unsuited for International Exhibitions or scientific lectures of any description'. The canvas awning was the only appreciable acoustic improvement included in the Albert Hall for nearly eighty years; thus critics noted wryly of the Hall's echo that it was the only concert venue in Britain in which composers would be guaranteed to hear their new composition twice.[16]

So significant were the problems encountered with the Albert Hall that this building was one of the very few recent constructions to which Smith felt obliged to comment critically in the lightly updated (1895) edition of his treatise on acoustics. In contrast to the variety of ceiling shapes that had proven to be conducive to high-quality sound transmission, he judged the Albert Hall's ad hoc arrangement to be unsuccessful. Some parts of the hall still experienced unavoidably compromised acoustics, a point which he attributed to the coving which joined ceiling to walls:

> In the Albert Hall this cove – running round an elliptical building – appears to be injurious rather than helpful, as it throws down an echo from such loud sounds as are able to pierce the canvas velarium, and concentrates the echo upon individual parts of the auditorium, where it becomes unpleasantly perceptible.[17]

Indeed it was mainly the identification of acoustic defects of buildings erected in the thirty-four years since the book's first publication that Smith devoted attention in material added for this second edition. Let us now turn to Smith's career to understand how he acquired such expertise in architectural acoustics.

Thomas Roger Smith and the emergence of architectural acoustics in Britain

A fellow of the RIBA from 1863 and professor of architecture at University College London from 1880 until his death in 1903, Thomas Roger Smith was a well-known public figure in the Victorian profession. His reputation stemmed both from the buildings he designed in England and India, and the many public services he performed in Britain and its empire. Yet historical scholarship on him has focused either on his aesthetic reservations about the Gothic Revival, or somewhat conservative (anti-nativist) views on the architecture appropriate for imperial India.[18] More recently, attention has focused on Smith's role in the RIBA's Standing Committee for Science.[19] Started in 1886, this technical committee addressed broader civic concerns among the architectural profession about the proper management of air, light, and hygiene via the most recent scientific research. What is not acknowledged, however, in any extant account is that Smith's career in architecture had a long association with science that dated back to his early writings on acoustics in the 1860s.

After private education in Sheffield, Smith was a pupil of London architect Philip Hardwick, and after a year's travel set up an independent London practice in 1855. As Paul Waterhouse has stressed, Smith was a dedicated public lecturer, especially for the Architectural Association, which he joined in 1851 and for which he lectured on acoustics for the first time, in November 1858. He delivered his most substantial lecture on the topic at the age of thirty, to the RIBA in December 1860, effectively marking his arrival in the architectural establishment. While papers on the acoustics of architecture had occasionally been published in *The Builder* since 1846, Smith's lecture was judged to be of such importance that both *Building News* and *The Builder* published it in extenso.[20]

In assembling this lecture, Smith undertook a substantial amount of personal research, weaving personal acquaintance of the acoustic properties of buildings encountered in his travels together with wisdom gleaned from the few standard writings of British, French, and German architects that discussed acoustics.[21] As much time had elapsed since the RIBA had received a paper on this subject, and because so many sources on acoustics were inaccurate, he searched 'very thoroughly' for all pertinent information. He thus summarized the research of major scientific authorities on acoustics: John Herschel's treatise 'Sound' in the *Encyclopaedia Metropolitana*; Mary Somerville's *On the Connexion of the Physical Sciences*, and the writings of internationally renowned specialists such as Ernst Chladni.[22] Armed with this extensive knowledge of how much an architect could do to enhance building acoustics, Smith appealed to fellow architects now to embrace this topic as one of their core responsibilities. It was not enough, he declared for professional architects to produce buildings that were aesthetically pleasing, well-ventilated, useful or hygienic:

> The proper construction of buildings intended for music or public speaking is a point of vital interest to every architect, as under this category may be comprehended all the more important works that come into our hands; and such buildings (however excellent in other respects) cannot certainly be said to have fulfilled the design with which they were erected, unless they had been made favourable to the easy transmission of sound.[23]

His analysis began with seven abstract principles of the propagation of sound as a vibration through a medium, and of the constitution of sound in frequencies of vibration, as demonstrated by the use of turning forks. Subsequently, he looked at the means available to the architect for influencing the transmission of sound, especially around obstacles and its movement to an audience. His models for this were the mirror (for reflected sound), the speaking trumpet used as a megaphone (for amplified sound), and the violin (for maximized resonance). For the first two of these, he observed that where sound underwent significant amounts of reflection around a room, some would hear speech or music at a different time or different volume to those situated elsewhere, often with echoes marring the sound. Conversely, a speaker with a very high ceiling above them would experience the effect of a speaking trumpet in a large empty space: much of the sound would be lost travelling upwards, making the hearing of words more difficult. Thirdly, Smith advised architects to treat the violin as the epitome of how judicious configuration of resonating wooden components could naturally amplify sound without creating disturbing echoes; this technique was particularly valuable for aiding speech communication in larger buildings. Overall in Smith's view, combining these three elements to optimize acoustics was the architect's main creative challenge.

In this respect, religious buildings presented some of the greatest challenges to an architectural acoustician. In older stone edifices, such as Canterbury cathedral, the resilient resonance enhanced the sonority of music performed there, yet greatly impeded the comprehensibility of speech uttered by the clergy – unless the cathedral's resonance was dampened by the blessing of a large congregation.[24] Smith pointed out that in some other cathedrals, columns of stone were located so as to break up such uncongenial resonances, as could complex decorated vaultings. Yet these lessons had evidently not been embodied in the architecture of more recently built churches. This was somewhat ironic given the priority that Protestant theology placed (unlike the enjoyment of exquisite sonorities of sung liturgy in the Roman tradition) on ensuring that congregations heard each and every one of the clergy's words of salvation. Tall undecorated ceilings and plain reflective walls were indeed endemic in the 'low church' tradition in ways unconducive to well-communicated sermons. Smith thus reported an invention some decades earlier by Rev. Michael Blackburn to mitigate the echo-prone effects of his high-roofed church at Attercliffe near Sheffield. The Rev. Blackburn's installation of a parabolic pine wood reflective sounding board directly above his pulpit was essential to render his sermons properly audible to his congregation. This innovative way of refocusing speech from the pulpit towards the congregation can still be seen in numerous churches around Britain.[25]

From analysis of this successful technique for ameliorating acoustic difficulties in tall churches, Smith moved to investigate how to overcome the chief acoustic problems experienced in secular buildings: echoes, (excess) reverberation, obstacles, and 'unshapeliness, or bad proportions' (implying echoes). To avoid echoes, Smith advised that speakers or musicians should not be placed facing a flat wall directly opposite them, nor have any high empty space above them. Smith concluded that the Free Trade Hall in Manchester and the Philharmonic Hall in Liverpool met all of these requirements, which explained why the acoustic experiences in these buildings were judged to be so effective by audiences.[26] Indeed much of Smith's acoustic expertise had come from talking not to the architects of buildings that he visited, but to those who had direct and extensive experience of the sound world within them: 'In forming an opinion upon the success or failure of any public room or building, by far the surest guide is the account given of it by the persons who speak or sing in it.'[27]

This unusual level of empiricism in audience research evidently caught the attention of one publisher, as Smith's lecture was immediately approached by Crosby, Lockwood & Co. to secure a monograph version for its 'Rudimentary Scientific Series'. At the time (1860) this Series comprised over three hundred books targeted at engineers, architects, builders, artisans, and students. It was in this specific context that Crosby, Lockwood & Co. published an expanded and retitled version of Smith's lecture as *A Rudimentary Treatise on the Acoustics of Public Buildings; or, the Principles of the Science of Sound*

Applied to the Purposes of the Architect and Builder (1861). This volume not only contained more detailed analysis of the above points, but also discussed the publications by civil engineer and naval architect John Scott Russell (1808–82) on the new topic of 'isoacoustics'. This was the principle of design deployed to accomplish equal hearing and visibility for all auditors seated in concert halls and lecture theatres. Such an analysis enabled Smith to explain the acoustic success of the Royal Institution's Lecture Theatre in Albemarle Street, which not only used suitably resonant wood and spaces of air in the traditional model of theatres, but epitomized 'isoacoustic' lines of sight and sound in its upwardly curving seating patterns.[28]

This *Treatise* received warm reviews. For example, *The Builder* in 1861 remarked that it was an 'ably written' volume, albeit on a topic that was 'not yet thoroughly understood'. Although Smith purported merely to have collected together the writings of others into a convenient form, *The Builder* considered it to be more than just a compilation: 'It is a professional view of acoustics as applied to the science of architecture and the art of building and well merits a perusal by others than mere tyros in professional practice'. *The Builder* in fact endorsed Smith's judgement of buildings 'successfully' constituted for acoustic success, and reprinted for its readers the relevant sections concerning the Manchester Free Trade Hall *in extenso*.[29] Unsurprisingly then, this book was the standard volume on the topic for the following three decades, with an additional edition (c. 1878) in which an index was added. Finally, a slight revised and updated version in 1895 added material on both the new electrical modes of amplification and sound transmission (the telephone, microphone, and phonograph) as well as highlighting the continuing acoustic defects of the Royal Albert Hall.

Sabine versus Smith: Algorithmic and experiential sciences of architectural acoustics

In Emily Thompson's historical accounts of architectural acoustics Smith's writings are acknowledged briefly, albeit as the putatively pre-scientific ancién regime. This is understandable since when Smith republished the new edition of his acoustics volume in 1895, his authority was clearly waning. In March that year, an associate member of RIBA, H. W. Burrows presented to a RIBA meeting a review paper on the status of acoustics as recently commissioned by its Science Committee. Noting the foundational status of Smith's RIBA paper of 1860 and his 'excellent' treatise the following year, Burrows nevertheless went on to highlight the many discrepancies in advice now apparent in the architectural literature about how to optimize building acoustics: 'the inherent difficulties of the subject are great, and they are by no means lessened, but amplified, by the strange divergence of opinion at times expressed upon one and the same point'. Significantly he acknowledged the rising authority of physics in this area: unlike Smith's confident deployment of acoustical theory, Burrows apologized for being 'merely an architect, not a physicist' and thus 'not fully competent' to deal with the science of acoustics in its 'abstruse bearings'. In the ensuing discussion Smith agreed that a new programme of systematic experimental research was needed to explain these discrepancies. Yet in focusing particularly on the recent discovery that atmospheric conditions could significantly affect a room's acoustic properties, Smith did not defer to physicists to produce the desired unanimity in architectural acoustics.[30]

As Thompson emphasizes, in that same year, one physicist began work that would, at least for some architects, bring about just such a unified approach. Wallace Sabine's use of experimental laboratory methods at Harvard produced a classic acoustics research paper which appeared serially under the title 'Reverberation' in *American Architect and Building News* between April and June 1900.[31] This publication contained the later eponymous 'Sabine Equation' which enabled quantitative predictions to be made of the echo period of a room even before it had been constructed. From knowing the effective volume (V) and surface area (A) of that room, and the average absorption coefficient of its surfaces (a), the reverberation time (T) could be calculated in feet as $T = 0.049\ V/Sa$ or alternatively in metres as $T = 0.161\ V/Sa$.

Smith and his co-workers produced this entirely empirical algorithm from investigating the troublesome reverberation in Harvard University's Fogg Lecture Hall: as originally completed in 1895 from designs by the pre-eminent US architect Richard Morris Hunt (1827–95) this room had a 5.5 second echo. This contrasted starkly with the echo time of just 1 second in Harvard University's Sanders Theatre, completed in 1876, and considered thereafter acoustically ideal for speech transmission.[32] After detailed comparative investigations between the Fogg and Sanders theatres, Sabine and his team of student assistants formulated the universal equation mentioned above for calculating echo times in both locations. Moreover, Sabine formulated further advice on how to reduce excessive echo by deploying new sound-absorbent materials. Having solved Harvard's practical acoustic problem, this episode made Sabine's academic career as a university physicist, and enabled him to launch a successful side business as a consultant acoustician and manufacturer of sound-absorbent materials.[33]

Arriving as it did in a professional world of architecture marked by frustration at previous discordance among localized results in acoustic matters, it is easy to see why Sabine's locally produced but universally applicable equation would have had appeal. And in a mood of increased deference to the disciplinary remit of physics in the early twentieth century, a number of British architects eventually embraced Sabine's acoustic science as a new canon for their field.[34] Yet this outcome was not immediately obvious at the time of Sabine's first publications. One architectural commentator reported critically in 1906 that his equation made no allowance for the well-known phenomenon that an audience-filled concert hall or lecture theatre would have a shorter reverberation time than an empty one.[35] Thus in 1911 an editorial in the *Journal of the Society of Architects* argued that the acoustics of buildings remained a 'difficult problem' without any clear authority able to resolve the key contentious matters. Instead this writer emphasized the value of Smith-ian qualitative wisdom in acoustic planning, for example, that soundboards over lecterns and pulpits should be parabolic in shape.[36]

Nevertheless after his early death in 1919, Sabine's reputation as the new scientific authority on acoustics was given a considerable boost by the posthumous publication of his collected papers in 1921–2.[37] The leading British advocate of Sabine was Hope Bagenal (1888–1979), who had trained as an engineer at the University of Leeds before corresponding with, and then studying with, Sabine in 1914. In reviewing Sabine's papers six years later, Bagenal was moved to describe Sabine hyperbolically as the 'Isaac Newton' of architecture.[38] Similarly positive was Alexander Wood (1879–1950), the Cambridge University physicist at Emmanuel College: 'here at last is the greatest individual contribution to the subject of architectural acoustics made accessible to all'.[39] The advocacy of Bagenal and Wood, perhaps go some way to explaining how far Sabine's writing eventually became canonical in the interwar Britain as it was already in the United States.

Given such endorsements by leading acousticians such as Bagenal and Wood, it is easy to see why Emily Thompson's historical account emphasizes Sabine's explicit and quantitative claims to originality over Thomas Roger Smith's synoptic and mostly qualitative account. Beyond that we can also see in the early twentieth century a more conspicuous role emerging for mathematical equations in public scientific authority as epitomized in Albert Einstein's iconic equation $e = mc^2$ that correlated the energy of matter (e) to its mass (m) and the speed of light (c).[40] In a similar vein, Sabine's simple but powerful equation captured very clearly his authority as an architectural acoustician who seemed to have mastered a platonic abstract truth underlying the untidy contingencies of quotidian architectural acoustics. This particular valorization of Sabine was also, I would argue, a sign of the professionalizing imperialism of twentieth-century physics: taking over problems in architectural acoustics, appropriating them to their disciplinary canon as if primarily the prerogative of acoustical physicists.

Yet we do not have to accept at face value that peculiarly twentieth-century representation of architectural science as an equation-based project of abstraction. As far as 'architecture as a science' was concerned, that was not obviously the archetype of what a science was in the second half of the nineteenth century when Thomas Roger Smith was writing on architectural acoustics. Indeed, Smith explicitly refused the idea that the subject was the algorithmic application of general abstract principles to particular cases. Instead he saw architectural acoustics much more as a sensitive discretionary craft which required great prior experience to be viable. The model he used in fact was that of the architect as a form of physician rather than a mathematician, with instincts informed by experiential practice, not platonic revelation:

> Practical architectural acoustics will always be in a position very much analogous to the practice of medicine. The physician, after he has gained all the knowledge of disease and of medicines which books can afford, is still quite unfit for actual practice unless he have the skill and intelligence to know how to vary his mode of treatment, and to suit his application of laws and principles to the different circumstances of each case, and the different constitution of each patient.[41]

It was in this respect, Smith argued, that acoustical work in architecture required a kind of instinct over and above any algorithmic rules, so that such rules could be applied most effectually to accomplish good effects:

> The most successful architects will tell you that their judgment of the probable acoustic effect of this or that arrangement is as much, or more, the result of a sort of instinct – a kind of internal perception of what will do, or what will not do.[42]

We can therefore revisit Emily Thompson's discussion of how Smith presented the status of his endeavours in 1895 before the RIBA Science Standing Committee as based on 'instinct'. Thompson implies that the absence of quantitative science explains why Smith could not dissuade the RIBA committee from viewing architectural acoustics as still an 'obscure topic'.[43] In fact each edition of Smith's book on architectural acoustics opened with an exegesis on the 'science of acoustics' citing no fewer than seven propositions from contemporary physics on the nature of sound and its propagation. Indeed, in the wake of that RIBA discussion his 1895 publication of a third edition of the *Treatise* reiterated his approach thus premised on the science of acoustics which required discretionary application shaped by well-honed instincts. It was as if to remind the RIBA that his studies of architectural acoustics showed that this subject was neither obscure nor based solely on instinct.[44]

Also notable, in characterizing Sabine's putatively more 'scientific' practice, Thompson shows how his successful management of architectural acoustics was dependent not only on Sabine's equation but also on his development of special surface materials to suit each architectural case.[45] That latter development was not, however, exclusively Sabine's innovation since architects had long relied on bespoke material finishes to manage the acoustic properties of particular rooms. Smith had himself noted in 1861 how effectively specialist new material coverings on built surfaces could help to dampen or eliminate unwanted reverberations. He gave the specific example of the newly erected British Museum: to quell the echoes from the many polished surfaces, all chairs and desks were covered in leather, while the museum's floors were covered in 'kamptulicon', an artificial material of powdered cork in natural rubber.[46] Half a century later Sabine implemented a similar strategy but with the key difference that he did so with materials which he had himself patented. Since he did so as a physicist specializing in architecture rather than an all-round architect, posterity has paid rather more attention to Sabine than to Smith as the progenitor of architectural acoustics.

Conclusion

Upon Thomas Roger Smith's death in 1903, *The Times'* obituary of him recorded his writings on acoustics as just one of many among his impressive accomplishments as a leading professional architect in Britain. Alongside his teaching and scholarly obligations as a UCL Professor, he had been a successful public lecturer, professional consultant, designer of numerous building including the Post Office at Bombay (Mumbai), and wrote two histories of architecture and much else besides. Yet in an era that looked increasingly to sub-disciplinary experts rather than seasoned all-rounders to produce the key innovations, by 1903 Smith's characteristically Victorian breadth of accomplishment in architectural acoustics was no longer the (sole) basis of authority for what was becoming a new technical *specialism* in the disciplinary domain of laboratory physics.[47] Yet to focus on why Smith was posthumously remembered for other achievements than his acoustical writings is to miss the point of this chapter.

I suggest that Smith's acoustic writings from 1860 to 1895 set a benchmark for his architectural contemporaries in the latter part of the nineteenth century. Unlike some, he did not treat the aural properties of buildings as irreducibly idiosyncratic, unfathomably mysterious, or simply not the architect's problem to resolve. Instead, his well-travelled practice embodied an understanding of architectural acoustics as an experiential science that necessarily combined the established principles of sound transmission with the lessons of past architectural ventures and the testimony of those who had performed in the public buildings he discussed. Given the comprehensive nature of his study, and his openness about freely sharing professional knowledge of various acoustical problems and their resolution, there was apparently little to add to his wide-ranging *oeuvre* for three decades. Accordingly, while he persuaded at least some architects to embrace professional responsibility for acoustic quality, he did not build a research school in the area as did Wallace Sabine from 1895. And it would seem that the extent and scope of architects' responsibility for acoustic matters has never been fully resolved.

Nevertheless, from a survey of Smith's writings, historians of nineteenth-century architecture can get a clearer sense of how far the lived experience of Victorian buildings was from just being a visual (or even voyeuristic) encounter with decorated bricks and plaster. In many respects, to live and work in a building was to use it to communicate via its sound properties. This was rarely a trivial matter, and in an era before electronic amplification, it was (whether recognized or not) part of the architects' remit to minimize the problems of echo and diffusion that arose when building designs deviated from past precedents. Only by studying both positive and negative auditory experiences, whether through the ears of Smith or of his clients and confidantes, can we hope to recover a sense of everyday public life in Victorian Britain. In particular we might thereby understand better why some venues such as the Royal Institution in Albemarle Street were so successful for speech-based communication, and why others, such as the Royal Albert Hall, were not. Finally, the story of how architectural acoustics as a science developed by Smith as an architect for fellow architects (before appropriation by physicists) raises the broader question of how far we can see architects as active agents in shaping useful technical knowledge for their profession, not just passive recipients of science imported from the physics laboratory.

CHAPTER EIGHT

Powers of politics, scientific measurement and perception:

Evaluating the performance of the Houses of Commons' first environmental system, 1852–4

Henrik Schoenefeldt

Speaking to the Select Committee of the House of Commons in 1844, the Scottish physician David Boswell Reid (1805–63) explained his scheme for the ventilation of the two debating chambers of the new Palace of Westminster, the seat of the British Parliament in London.[1] In his statement he stressed that one of his main objectives was to accomplish a sophisticated system of climatic control that was responsive to the members of Parliament's personal experience of the air quality and climate conditions inside the chambers. This system, as laid out in his statement, was implemented inside the House of Commons between 1847 and 1852, and its performance became the subject of empirical observations by scientific and engineering authorities for a period lasting over two years, in which the personal experience of occupants was the primary focus. While scientific instruments were used to measure the physical conditions to which MPs were exposed during sittings, insights into more subjective factors, such as a thermal comfort or perceived air quality, could only be gained through self-reported feedback from occupants. Experience itself became the subject of scientific investigations, aiming to acquire a deeper and more objective understanding of the causes of thermal discomfort experienced within the debating chamber.

This chapter explores the role of the user experience in the design development and evaluation of Reid's ventilation system, focusing on the period between 1835 and 1854. Eyewitness accounts from members, which were recorded in Hansard reports, parliamentary papers, and newspapers, as well as scientific reports and the engineers' monitoring logbooks, which contained notes on members' self-reported feedback, provide critical insights into the internal environmental conditions and how members experienced them. This chapter also retraces how insufficient success in satisfying the MPs' expectations drove the House of Commons to commission various scientific inquiries into the system and contributed to the premature decommissioning of Reid's system after only two years. Inquiries into the experience of occupants in buildings, however, were not unique to the Houses of Parliament. They represent a major strand within the history of building science in the nineteenth and twentieth centuries, and still form an important part in modern methods of Building Performance Evaluations.[2] As such, the inquiries inside the House of Commons offer some insights into early-nineteenth-century practices of environmental design.

Origins and evolution: From scientific research to occupant-responsive systems

The methodology used to engage MPs in the design of the ventilation system has its origins in earlier scientific studies that Reid had conducted in Edinburgh and Westminster in the 1830s. Detailed accounts of these studies were published in two books, *Illustrations of the Theory and Practice of Ventilation* (1844) and *Ventilation in American Dwellings* (1858), as well as in several lectures.[3] His inquiries into ventilation began with fundamental physiological research into the effect of air purity and climates, which Reid had undertaken, first while being employed as a lecturer of practical chemistry at the University of Edinburgh, and after 1832 in his private chemistry laboratory in the same city.[4] In these studies, volunteers, after having been exposed to atmospheres of varying air quality and different climatic conditions, were interviewed to determine how they had affected concentration, appetite, and physical well-being.[5] Aiming to provide design with a stronger empirical foundation, Reid used similar methods to evaluate and refine the design and management of ventilation from an occupant perspective. In his lectures, *Progress of Architecture* (1856) and *The Revision of Architecture in Connection with the Useful Arts* (1855), Reid reported of experimental rooms that he had erected in his laboratory to test ways of diffusing air currents, using different configurations of perforated walls, floors, and ceilings.[6] Volunteers were placed inside these rooms to provide feedback on the thermal sensations produced by the incoming air currents and how these were affected by changes in the direction, temperature, humidity, or velocity. These studies of maintaining thermal comfort and adequate ventilation were not examined in isolation, but were treated as highly interrelated issues.

It should be noted that these inquiries largely focused on the human and environmental rather the mechanical engineering aspects of ventilation and central heating. This was a reflection of Reid's background in the fields of medicine and chemistry. They were also a demonstration of his belief that the natural sciences, and practical chemistry in particular, could provide new methodologies for the design and evaluation of ventilation systems, which were distinct from both engineering and architecture. In several of his textbooks, such as *Rudiments of Chemistry: With Illustrations of the Chemical Phenomena of Daily Life* (1836) and *Elements of Practical Chemistry* (1830), Reid offered an introduction to the science of ventilation and demonstrations of how it could be studied experimentally within the laboratory.[7]

His experimental approach was first used in conjunction with inquiries into the ventilation of the Palace of Westminster in Spring 1836. Reid erected a large model of a debating chamber at his private teaching laboratory in Edinburgh to demonstrate the viability of a concept he had presented to the 'Select Committee on Ventilation and Warming the new Houses of Parliament' in the summer of 1835.[8] The House of Commons had appointed this inquiry to investigate modern methods of heating, lighting, and ventilation and their potential application in the design for the new Houses of Parliament.[9] Reid's model House of Commons was used to explore how adequate ventilation and comfortable climate conditions could be achieved inside a sealed room, in particular when crowded and at night when the chamber was illuminated with gas lighting. As with his earlier experimental inquiries, this was evaluated based on the self-reported experience of volunteers.[10] Tests were continued, but this time under real-life conditions and involving MPs and Lords instead of volunteers, inside the temporary House of Commons (in use between 1836 and 1851) and the temporary House of Lords (1838–47). The architect Robert Smirke (1780–1867) had erected the temporary Houses of Parliament by early 1835, a few months after a fire had destroyed the original medieval Palace of Westminster, to provide the British Parliament with provisional accommodation.[11] Reid was commissioned to remodel the ventilation of the temporary chambers based on his principles and he was also employed to supervise the day-to-day management of the systems, enabling him to empirically evaluate and refine the technological arrangements over several years. Lords and MPs were directly involved in this process, which yielded critical new insights that underpinned the development of a more sophisticated system for the Palace of Westminster after 1840.

The post-occupancy history of the temporary House of Commons shows that the challenge of satisfying MPs' perceived thermal comfort acted as the main driving force behind the refinement of the environmental system.[12] MPs were not passive observers, but active agents, in the development of Reid's system. To gain tighter control over a wider range of climatic factors that affected the MPs' perceived comfort, the ventilation evolved from a basic into a highly complex system. It resulted in the introduction of an early form of air conditioning that incorporated facilities for cooling, humidification, heating, and air filtration. It also yielded a sophisticated method of environmental monitoring. This enabled the systematic gathering of subjective feedback from MPs, alongside the recording of measurements. The attendants working the ventilation engaged directly with MPs, acquiring an intimate understanding of the members' response to various environmental stimuli. Being a psychological state, thermal comfort was not directly measurable through scientific instruments, but required qualitative methods. MPs were themselves 'instruments' for measuring perception. Reid noted that this experimental approach provided 'information as to the ever-changing feelings of Members, of which no one can possibly judge but themselves'.[13]

Demonstrating a methodology by which the experienced interior atmosphere could be continually 'metered' alongside the measuring of physical stimuli, this monitoring system could be interpreted as an early example of psychophysical principles being applied to architecture. Reid's perspective resembles very closely what the German experimental psychologist Gustav Fechner, fifteen years later, would describe as *äussere psychophysik* (outer psychophysics). In his book *Elemente der Psychophysik*, which was published in 1860, Fechner described outer psychophysics as a scientific field concerned with the correlation between physical stimuli (*äusserer reiz*) within the environment and the sensations (*innere empfindung*) they produce.[14] Although his approach was more informal and less systematic than Fechner's later method, Reid reviewed self-reported experience to determine how people's perception of thermal comfort was affected by climatic conditions. Analysing several years of user-responses and measured data collected inside the temporary Houses of Commons, Reid attempted to determine the climatic conditions at which the majority of MPs felt comfortable. Reid discovered that 'as far as I have been able to observe, a temperature of 65 °F, with an atmosphere moving in a very gentle stream, so as not to be perceptible, is the most agreeable in rooms that are not overcrowded'.[15] He expanded on this in 1852, reporting that 'when there is a difference between 5 °F between the dry thermometer and wet-bulb thermometer next to it, I have the least number of complaints'.[16] Managing a climate based on feedback was a difficult process and required the Serjeant-at-Arms, whose main responsibility was maintaining security and order in the House, to take on the role of moderator, who reviewed the often conflicting responses received from individual members directly, or via a messenger. In 1839 Sir William Gosset, Serjeant-at-Arms, reported that

> sometimes Members come to me, and say the House is very hot, or very cold; I look at the thermometer, and see if so, for different people have

> different feelings with regard to temperature. People come in very hot, and say, 'How cold the House strikes'; and another man says 'I have been sitting here half an hour, and I am in fever': and if I see the thermometers are too high or too low, I give directions accordingly.[17]

Indeed, Reid understood that it was impossible to meet the expectations of every individual within the chamber. In chapter eight of *Illustrations*, entitled 'Causes of modifying the supply of the air required for ventilation', Reid provided a detailed examination of the nature of thermal comfort.[18] In this chapter he illustrated that thermal comfort was not only affected by environmental conditions, over which he could exercise some control through technology, but also personal factors, such as clothing, state of health, level of physical activity, or body weight. He reported that there was 'scarcely a meeting of the House at which there are not some Members who would like the temperature to be at 55 °F degrees and others at 70 °F or 72 °F'.[19] In this process he was also confronted with the problem of feedback being largely negative, and as some of the responses were also published in prominent newspapers, including *The Times*, Reid became increasingly anxious about his reputation being damaged. In 1837 he became pro-active in gathering positive responses from members that were subsequently published in newspapers, journals, and two pamphlets, entitled *Narrative of Facts as to the New Houses of Parliament* and *Extract from Official Documents, Reports and Papers*.[20]

In 1839 Reid received the commission to remodel the ventilation in the temporary debating chamber of the House of Lords, which is the upper house of the British Parliament. The Lords had been discontent with their temporary facilities from the beginning. Only a few months after the chamber had been opened, the Lords began voicing their dissatisfaction, arguing that it did not provide sufficient space and ventilation. In 1835 it appointed a Select Committee to inquire into the possibility of erecting a new temporary chamber that provided more space and adequate ventilation.[21] Proposals for a new chamber were discarded due to concerns about the cost and instead the Lords asked the architect Robert Smirke to improve the design of the existing chamber. Reid was engaged to introduce a new ventilation system following similar principles to those deployed in the House of Commons. He used this as an opportunity to test an alternative approach to climate control. Instead of immersing several members within one uniform climate, he tested how far user-satisfaction could be increased by providing microclimates in different parts of the chamber. Crowded areas, being more likely to experience overheating, were supplied with cooler air than more sparsely populated areas. The temperature in one section could be as low as 52°F and as high as 75°F in another. In the House of Commons, Reid and the Serjeant-at-Arms reported that it was difficult to achieve a consensus among MPs when the climate was uniform, making climate control a political struggle. Continuous attempts were made to manage the shared climate according to the preference of the majority, while dealing with the few individuals who were vocal about their dissatisfaction.

Responses from the Lords collected between 1843 and 1846, however, reveal that the new approach did not increase satisfaction.[22] The Lords voiced their dissatisfaction during several sittings. The Peers had various debates about the indoor climate, revealing how they had perceived the internal conditions. Lord Campbell wrote that the system was successful in maintaining a good air quality, but felt that the main problem was insufficient control over the temperature and currents. During a debate in February 1843 he complained that the 'alternate heat and cold of the place made it at one time a cold bath, and at another a vapour bath'.[23] On 24 April 1846 Lord Brougham observed that the 'Lords were sometimes broiling and sometimes freezing'.[24] The level of dissatisfaction was particularly high during important debates, such as the debate of Maynooth College Bill at the beginning of June 1845, during which between 200 and 400 Lords were sitting inside the chamber.[25] On 5 June 1845 Lord Brougham complained about the wretched state of the atmosphere, while Campbell reported that some Peers 'suffered so severely last night from the imperfect ventilation, and the sudden draughts of hot and cold air'.[26]

Notwithstanding these difficulties, Reid continued developing his experiment-led ventilation system in his plans for the permanent Houses of Commons and Lords. Reid refused to see the problems encountered inside the temporary House of Lords as evidence against the general viability of his concept. The implementation of his scheme had been compromised, he argued, by a tight budget as well as the physical constraints imposed by the existing fabric. For the new House of Commons, Reid was provided with a considerably larger budget, enabling him to implement more substantial physical changes to the chamber, and he subsequently received additional funding for technical improvements. Furthermore, he noted, its effectiveness was compromised by insufficient cooperation from the Lords in providing his attendants with the quantity of regular feedback required to respond to their experiences of the atmosphere.[27] In a statement given to a Select Committee in July 1842 Reid claimed 'that individuals have stated that they have remained for a whole evening uncomfortable, without even telling us, though there was a person constantly stationed in the House for this purpose'.[28] Reid described his plans for applying the new scheme to the permanent Houses in a series of interviews with select committees in 1844 and 1846. His proposal was to further increase the comfort of the Lords by introducing a more complex system that allowed the climate and air supply around each bench to be adjusted individually. In his statement to the Select Committee in 1844, Reid noted that

> our only alternative has frequently been to make a local change under the benches occupied by them [certain individuals] or suit their convenience at the expense of incommoding the House generally, unless they were left

> subject to an amount of annoyance of which they bitterly complained, for the state of the air being more congenial to those around them than to themselves.[29]

The working drawings, produced between 1847 and 1851, illustrate how the scheme was implemented inside the permanent House of Commons.[30] The temperature and humidity of the fresh air was monitored and adjusted inside an air chamber under the main floor of the House and finally admitted through perforated cast-iron floor plates along the back of the benches. Every bench, as well as the chairs for the speaker of the House and Serjeant-at-Arms, were provided with a separate air supply duct, which were both equipped with individual sliding vales. The attendants working inside the air

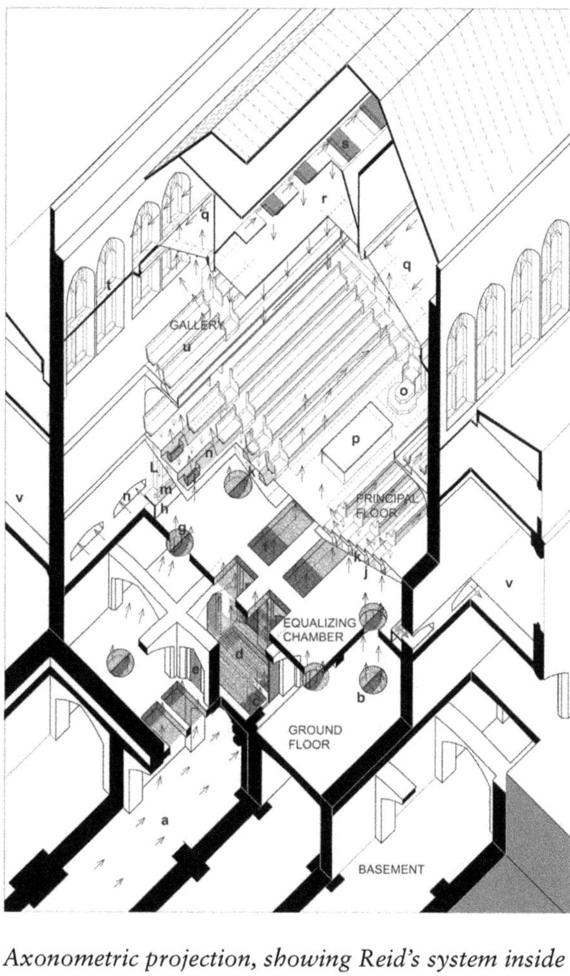

FIGURE 8.1 *Axonometric projection, showing Reid's system inside the Permanent House of Commons (author's own drawing).*

chamber below had to manually operate over sixty sliding valves to achieve this level of control (Figure 8.1).[31]

Key for figure 8.1: (a) Fresh air passage linking inlet shafts to central air chamber; (b) Valves for conveying air from basement into cool air chamber (Circular valves with shutters, shown in open position); (c) Valves for conveying air from basement to central heating chamber (rectangular valves with adjustable curtains below grating, shown partially opened); (d) Pipes of hot water apparatus in heating chamber; (e) Vertical door valves for conveying hot air into cool air chamber; (f) Rectangular curtain valve for admitting hot air into equalizing chamber; (g) Circular shutter valves to admit unheated air from cool air chamber into equalizing chamber; (h) Horizontal duct in which vitiated air extracted through perforated floor was collected before it was exhausted via the boiler smoke shafts in north-west turrets of Central Tower; (i) Sliding valves for supply of individual benches; (j) Sliding valves for supply through treads inside the gangways; (k) Vitiated air chamber under perforated iron floor (extract); (l) Vertical ducts connecting vitiated air chamber with horizontal ducts; (m) Steam and hot water pipes (heating and humidification); (n) Valves conveying air to fresh air chamber under the perforated floor of the Division Lobbies; (o) Speaker's chair; (p) Table; (q) Vitiated air chamber above sloping side panels, extract of ceiling system; (r) Fresh air chamber used to supply tempered fresh air through central ceiling panels (ceiling system); (s) Sliding valves for regulating air supply to ceiling; (t) Line of acoustic ceiling retrofitted in 1851, covering half of Barry's original window; (u) Gallery with air supply through floor; and (v) Division Lobbies.

The feedback mechanism: Accounting for the measured and perceived

In the permanent House of Commons, Reid anticipated an interactive system that was capable of responding to the environment and occupants. The system was designed to react to external conditions, fluctuations in the number of MPs attending, and personal feedback from those sitting. For this purpose, detailed environmental data was collected in logbooks. These logbooks had large pages with columns for numerical data on temperature, humidity, and air speed, but also had margins for written notes referring to operational procedures, feedback from members, and instructions from the Speaker and Serjeant-at-Arms.[32] Figure 8.2 shows a page from the logbook kept inside the main ventilation office to consolidate data collected in different areas of the House (Figure 8.2).

There were two paths by which feedback on the environmental conditions was transmitted to the attendants: one for quantitative data, and another for the qualitative feedback (Figure 8.3). The personal messenger of the Serjeant-at-Arms logged readings inside the debating chamber at hourly intervals and submitted them to the ventilator's office in the south-west

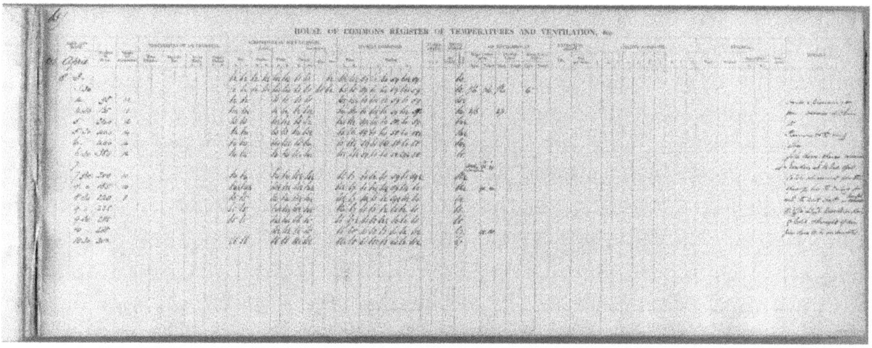

FIGURE 8.2 *Sample of page (8 April 1853) from the original logbook used to record measured data, observations, and oral feedback from Members inside the permanent House of Commons (Parliamentary Archives, OOW/5).*

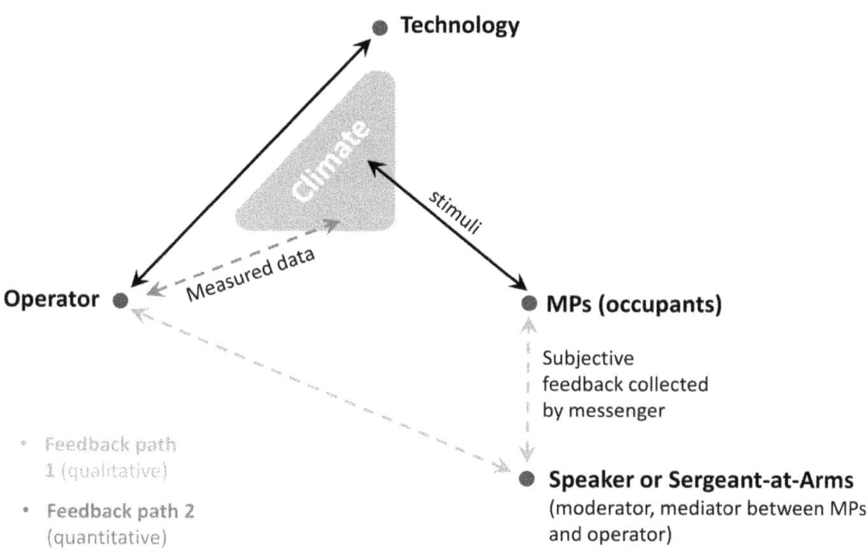

FIGURE 8.3 *Diagram of mechanism used to collect and process qualitative and quantitative data on the internal atmospheric conditions (author's own drawing).*

corner of the Member's Lobby.[33] The log-sheet contained columns for readings from four thermometers on the main floor. These were located near the Speaker's chair, bar end, and the two blocks of benches, one on the government and another on the opposition side. Additional columns were provided for thermometers located inside the galleries. Humidity was only measured within the ventilation chamber below the floor, before the fresh air was admitted into the House, but not within the debating chamber itself. The attendants in charge of the day-to-day operation of the system, which

Reid supervised, recorded the readings inside the different air chambers below and above the House. Registers with temperatures were sent to the main ventilator's office, where it was transcribed into a central logbook and analysed. These measurements were taken to provide the superintending engineers with feedback on the conditions inside the House which they required to keep them under tight control.

According to Charles Barry, the team working under Reid's management comprised of one sub-engineer, two firemen, two labourers, and one boy.[34] Reid acted as superintending engineer for the House of Commons from February until November 1852, before the Office of Woods and Forests terminated his employment and transferred his responsibility to Alfred Meeson, an engineer who had worked within Barry's office and who had, since 1847, been managing the ventilation in the House of Lords.[35] The superintending engineer had a small private office in the south-west corner of the Member's Lobby, which ensured that he was in close proximity to MPs and messengers[36] (Figure 8.4). His attendants, who were responsible for the technical operations, did not interact with members. They were stationed inside the air chambers. The main ventilation office, which was used for coordinating these operations, was situated on the ground floor.[37] It was linked to Reid's private office by a stair case.

Key for figure 8.4: (1) Concealed door and stair leading from bar lobby on principal floor to air chamber below the debating chamber; (2) Office of Superintending engineer; (3) Stair leading to main office of ventilation department at ground floor level; (4) Main office of ventilation department; and (5) Air chamber below debating chamber.

The attendants acquired additional feedback through direct observations and personal responses from MPs. The messenger also collected feedback from individual MPs, but in contrast to the measured data, the MPs' self-reported experiences were carefully reviewed by Serjeant-at-Arms, Lord Charles Russell, before any orders were sent to the attendants. Reid's team used these instructions to make ad hoc adjustments to the internal climate conditions. Russell reported that he was the 'usual medium of communication, as regards the ventilation, between Dr. Reid and the Members', though he was not a passive mediator of information, but actively moderated the subjective feedback process, engaging with the often conflicting perceptions of individual members.[38] The logbook entries give some insight into the instructions and feedback passed to the ventilator's office. On 31 March 1854, for instance, the attendants noted that the 'Speaker said the House [was] too warm', and then on 7 April 1854, 'J. C. Russell wished the House a little cooler'. During several debates held in April 1853, the Serjeant-at-Arms repeatedly notified the attendants about draughts and low temperatures. For example, on 22 April 1853 the attendants recorded a 'Cold gusty wind with air penetrating through every opening. 'Complaints of cold by Lord Charles Russell', while the entry for 7 pm on 3 April 1853 observed 'Complaints of draughts from the table and by Members at the bar'.[39]

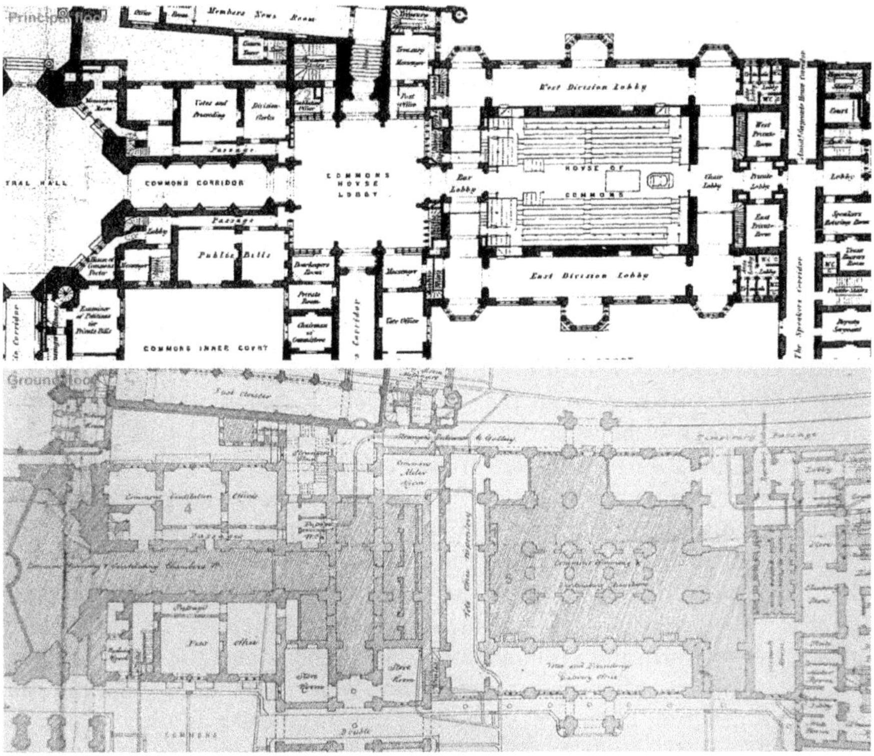

FIGURE 8.4 *Plan of principal and ground floor, 1852, showing position of ventilation chamber, offices, and access routes (Historic England Archive, Swindon).*

Deepening insights: Independent re-examinations

In addition to the day-to-day monitoring procedures, further insights into members' experience were gained through a series of empirical studies undertaken by external scientific advisors. These were commissioned by several Select Committees and Office of Woods and Forests between 1852 and 1854 as part of measures taken to improve the performance of the system.[40] Throughout February and March 1852 Reid and his team of attendants received continual complaints from members about the climate inside the chamber being uncomfortable; an issue that also became the subject of several debates.[41] On 4 February 1852, for instance, Joseph Hume, radical MP for Montrose Burghs, noted that he had to leave the chamber as he could not bear the heat and asked for measures to 'keep the place moderately cool'.[42] Captain Fitzroy mentioned that MPs were exposed 'to puffs of alternate hot and cold air'. During the debate on 10 February, the atmosphere was again criticized for feeling too hot, and MPs complained about being exposed to 'tremendous draughts of cold air'. The gallery was perceived as particularly hot as the air temperature in the upper part of the chamber was not only higher, but members were also exposed to the strong radiant heat emitted from the gas chandeliers.[43] According to Denham Jephson-Norreys, MP for Mallow, the chandeliers produced 'a burning sensation, such as if I were exposed to a red hot iron'.[44] The physician Goldsworthy Gurney took spot measurements during the sitting on 19 March and confirmed the observed temperature difference. The temperature on the main floor could get as low as 61.5 °F (16 °C), but rose to 68 °F (20 °C) on the gallery floor and 73 °F (23 °C) above the seats.[45] The data recorded in the logbook show that the temperature on the main floor was between 62 °F and 70 °F, and in the gallery ranged it from 63 °F (17 °C) to 73 °F.[46] It was constantly 2 °F–6 °F higher than below. Maximum temperatures of 73 °F do not appear exceptionally high, but eyewitness accounts show that air temperature readings alone were not sufficient to fully understand the causes of perceived discomfort. The MPs' perception was affected by the heavy clothing worn during debates and also by other environmental factors, such as humidity, air movement, surface temperature, and radiant heat.[47] The logbooks for the years 1852–4 show that factors other than temperature were not routinely monitored inside the debating chamber. Humidity, for instance, was only regularly recorded from December 1853. The Clerk of the House of Commons and the Serjeant-at-Arms reported problems with the air being too dry, which, by irritating throats and lungs, caused MPs to cough.[48] On 24 March the Speaker reported how he

> sent once or twice to Dr. Reid to beg that he would make some change in the state of the air, for it was so dry that it caused an irritation in the throat, and I could hear the Members coughing all around.[49]

Physicians Neil Arnott and John Leslie, who had examined the monitoring system on behalf of the Select Committee in 1852, highlighted that the scope of the physical measurements was too narrow. It did not provide attendants with feedback on the physical sensations members were experiencing, and thereby remained dependent on qualitative feedback from members.[50] Leslie noted that 'thermometers tell one tale, the body another'. This was critical as the cooling sensations produced by strong air currents contributed significantly to the perceived discomfort which members reported between 1852 and 1854. In response to this dissatisfaction, a Select Committee was appointed in March 1852, and Gurney was commissioned to examine the internal conditions. The Committee conducted interviews with the Speaker, Serjeant-at-Arms, and several MPs on their experiences. To examine the physical conditions that MPs were describing more objectively, using quantitative methods, Gurney and engineers James Mather, James Hann, and John Hutchinson took additional measurements, involving anemometers (air speed), barometers (atmospheric pressure), and wet-bulb thermometers (humidity).[51] These measurements revealed that internal currents were caused by difficulties in managing the atmospheric pressure within the chamber. The pressure inside the chamber became lower when the volume of hot air extracted through the ventilation shaft was not matched by the quantity of fresh air delivered through the floor. This resulted in air being forced into the chamber through doors, anytime they were opened, and through unsealed air valves below the floor and above the ceiling.[52]

Between April and May 1852, Reid made a series of technical alterations in an attempt to improve comfort.[53] To reduce the temperature inside the galleries of the House of Commons chamber, he introduced a new lighting system and also reorganized the ventilation arrangements above the ceiling to allow cool air to be supplied directly into galleries. The measured data suggest that the maximum temperature difference between the floor and gallery had only been reduced marginally (6 °F to 3 °F).[54] A steam-driven fan, which increased the air supply, was installed to counteract the low air pressure. According to commentaries in the logbooks and eyewitness accounts covering the years 1853 and 1854, however, currents remained an issue, largely due to difficulties in synchronizing the fan-powered supply with the stack-driven extract.

In November 1852, the responsibility for managing the day-to-day operations was transferred from Reid to the engineer Alfred Meeson, who, similar to Reid, was continually confronted with complaints from MPs that felt dissatisfied with the internal conditions.[55] To protect MPs from vertical currents, he sealed large parts of the perforated iron floor and, after Easter 1853, ran trials with different methods of raising the humidity.[56] At the same time, another lighting arrangement, in which the gas burners were concealed behind glazed ceiling panels to protect the interior from the heat, was tested.[57]

These modifications, however, did not succeed in yielding more agreeable climate conditions. MPs continue to voice their discontent during several debates between May 1853 and March 1854.[58] This led to another, and final, evaluation of Reid's system, undertaken under the direction of separate select committees, which the House of Commons and Lords appointed, respectively.[59] In April 1854 Reid's ventilation system was remodelled based on the findings of Gurney's early study in 1852. Attendants were ordered to maintain temperatures between 63 °F and 64 °F (17 °C–18 °C) and internal currents were monitored using down feathers that were attached to strings suspended across the chamber.[60] MPs were interviewed before and after the alterations to determine how far Gurney's alternative system had improved thermal comfort.[61] Gurney's main objective was to achieve a less volatile atmosphere.[62]

The logbooks did not contain measurements for the period following the alterations, but anecdotal evidence provided through interviews with MPs between May and July 1854 suggest that the climate had significantly improved. The Serjeant-at-Arms reported that the temperatures were more tightly managed and draughts markedly reduced.[63] According to Robert Smith, MP for Northampton, the atmosphere was fresher and did not become oppressively hot. The MP for North Riding noted that draughts only occurred occasionally, and Edward Bouverie, MP for Kilmarnock Burghs, found that the attendants were able to adjust the temperature more quickly. In its second report, dated 26 May, the House of Commons Committee formally concluded that the members' responses were sufficient evidence to confirm that Gurney's interventions had succeeded in improving thermal comfort and recommended that his system should be permanently adopted.[64]

The power of perception

This chapter has shown that the involvement of politicians in evaluating the performance of environmental technologies was an important strand in the development of David Boswell Reid's ventilation and central heating system for the House of Commons. Both intentionally and unintentionally, members played a significant role in assessing its performance. MPs were fully embedded in the day-to-day operation, and contributed to the refinement of technical solutions and managerial procedures. This process of user-engagement was only partially driven by scientific interest, building on earlier laboratory-based studies on air quality and thermal comfort within enclosed spaces. This focus on the user experience resulted in the process of performance evaluation becoming highly subjective. It made Reid vulnerable to scrutiny from building users, in this case users who had the power not only to voice their views but also to enforce physical and operational changes, which included the decision in 1854 to discard and remodel Reid's system. Reid, Meeson, and later Gurney were confronted with the unresolvable challenge of devising a system that satisfied MPs' expectations. The perceived, rather than the measurable, became the primary performance indicator and its interpretation was in the hands of politicians.

Reid's inquiries inside the Houses of Parliament, however, cannot be fully understood in isolation from wider developments within the field of building services engineering. The interest in experience was neither confined to Westminster nor was Reid the first to investigate the climatic and personal factors affecting thermal comfort. In *Principles of Warming and Ventilating Public Buildings*, published in 1824, the engineer Thomas Tredgold (1788–1829) dedicated a whole chapter to the subject, and in 1825 the physician William Heberden (1767–1845) experimented with methods for measuring 'sensible cold', taking into account the combined effect of air temperature and currents.[65] This wider interest was intimately connected with the emergence of new central heating and ventilation technologies in the early nineteenth century. Allowing occupants to be completely immersed in artificial climates, these technologies drove engineers and scientists to define standards for such climates. Thomas Bedford, situated Reid's work within an early phase in the development of thermal comfort studies as a particular branch within the field of building science, stressing that he had taken into account, environmental, physiological, and behavioural factors.[66]

PART FOUR

Audiences and experience

CHAPTER NINE

Publicity and exclusivity: The experience of the public rooms of the London 'grand hotel' at the end of the nineteenth century

Emma Anderson

At the end of the nineteenth century, visitors to London, the 'modern Babylon' at the heart of the Empire, were able to enjoy an experience of hotels which had not been possible fifty years before.[1] As long as they possessed sufficient financial capital, guests could avail themselves of new standards of luxury, which combined distinction, cosmopolitanism, and modernity. In an article of 1898 entitled 'Modern Hotels', *The Hotel World* described the public rooms of a large London establishment:

> A fairy scene of luxury and wealth, of light and glitter and colour, of palms and flowers, of mirrors and pictures and statuary: and as one passes out from the splendid vestibule he finds a large gathering of men and women of various nationalities lounging in cushioned chairs around little tables, ... quietly chatting, watching arrivals and departures, smoking cigarettes and cigars and sipping tea and coffee and listening to the delicious strains of the hotel band.[2]

This account, describing the sights, sounds, and scents of this new building type, the luxurious metropolitan hotel, encapsulated its attractions. These grand hotels developed in the second half of the nineteenth century as a response to an expanding social elite, increasingly rapid forms of transportation, and fast population growth.[3] They not only provided resting places for male and female travellers, but also were aspirational venues: in a society where the visible performance of consumption endowed status, luxury hotels were sites of significance.[4]

However, these venues were potentially contradictory. Such buildings needed to attract thousands of guests per annum to be commercially successful, while also remaining exclusive. In response, hoteliers fashioned a careful image, which disseminated the attractions of the hotel to a wide audience through advertising and press reports. This image combined an emulation of the aristocratic home, including the comfort, luxurious materials, and personal service which this entailed, with the promise of a glittering fairyland, all sustained by up-to-date technology. Grand hotels offered not only a place to rest one's head, but an experience of luxury available to all, at a price.

Yet this publicity could be at odds with the offer of exclusivity. To maintain their status as a luxury venue, the public rooms of hotels were designed both to impress, but also ostensibly to limit access to a select, socially appropriate clientele. This entailed a building plan which provided physical exclusion in the form of tangible thresholds, or gateways, through which the visitor had to pass. Access to the interior could be halted at the outer doorway, at the reception desk or in the lobby. In addition, the architectural style of the building, the opulence of the historicist interiors, and the appearance and behaviour of the staff formed intangible barriers of taste and experience, which only those with the appropriate social cachet might comfortably negotiate.[5]

The experiences in such buildings – intended for women, whose role as both consumer and commodity was vital, as much as men – were designed to amaze the senses. Enabled by developing construction technologies, the very size of many of these spaces overwhelmed. Music, muted by deep carpets and opulent drapery, served to distract from the sounds of the city outside. Foreign voices, of staff and guests, confirmed a hotel's cosmopolitan status. In restaurants, both fashionable elites and aspirational Londoners could experience the tastes and smells of new dishes, which French chefs prepared and European waiters served. These *salles à mangers*, and the heterosocial lounges and palm courts which developed towards the end of the century, were designed for the performance of taste, wealth, and social connection. Guests, as both actor and audience, participated in an experience intended to enhance social connections and prestige.

'The pressing public want of the age': The arrival of the grand hotel

In the middle of the nineteenth century, the provision of better-quality hotel accommodation in London was limited, and what did exist was of a questionable standard and value. Correspondence in *The Times* during 1853–5 and Albert Smith's *The English Hotel Nuisance* (1855) had identified the problem of poor-quality, dirty hotels, with high prices and uncivil landlords, a 'fortress system of discomfort', which was the 'terror of tourists in England'.[6] Charles Dickens and Anthony Trollope both observed the deficiencies of London hotels compared to those in Europe and America.[7] At the same time, the travelling public was both increasing quantitatively and diversifying qualitatively. New railway terminus hotels met some of this demand, but for a longer sojourn, closer to social, retail, and leisure attractions, another type of hotel was desirable. Indeed, for the author of an 1863 article which demanded a 'new hotel system', so severe was the lack of first-class hotels that it was considered 'the pressing public want of the age'.[8]

Often constructed on sites made available during metropolitan improvements, the large, purpose-built hotel developed initially in the 1850s and 1860s. Following the Limited Liability Act (1855) and the Joint Stock Companies Act (1856), companies, formed by groups of investors, or which raised capital through the sale of shares, rapidly entered the hotel market in large numbers.[9] Visitors were directed in their choice of establishment partially by personal recommendation, but also by advice literature. Guidebooks such as John Murray's *Modern London* (1879) categorized these new constructions into several distinct classes. For Murray, these included '*Grand Hotels,* generally managed by companies; *Family Hotels* patronised by the English and Foreign nobility and gentry who have no town residence of their own, ... [as well as those] frequented by bachelors and sportsmen, [or] owned and patronized by foreigners'.[10] This differentiation between hotels was based not so much on services and price, as on social distinction.

Guidebooks defined the categories of hotels by identifying their principal features and benefits. Grand hotels were conveniently located, close to shops or other attractions. Rather than being adaptations of domestic buildings, they were designed specifically for their purpose, with public, private, and service areas, and were generally five or six storeys high, with attic and basement. They were also often modelled on American or European examples. This emulation of fashionable foreign competitors was, in part, an acknowledgement of the international source of some of the most desirable guests. It was also evidence of the desire for certain luxuries of comfort, service, and decoration hitherto available only to the most wealthy of travellers. Hotels aimed to offer the best aspects of three hotel-keeping traditions, combining English comfort with French elegance and American organization.[11] This created a hotel experience rooted in cosmopolitan service and style. In addition, extortionate prices and unexpected hotel bills had been a concern for correspondents with *The Times* in the early 1850s, so, even in the best hotels, the publication of fixed tariffs was advocated. Minimum charges for rooms and meals tended to be published in general guides, or the hotel's own guidebook.[12] *The Langham Hotel Guide*, for example, listed starting prices for sitting and bedrooms, depending on size and floor, along with rates for the provision of various extras from children's cots to cups of tea.[13]

These new buildings also deliberately provided for the comfort of both male and female guests. Catering for the physical and social requirements of respectable women increased business for hotels in several ways. Male clients were lured from dining in their clubs, as female companions were encouraged in hotel restaurants. In addition, women consumers formed an important part of the metropolitan retail and leisure economy, with department stores, cafes, and theatres increasingly designed to attract and accommodate them.[14] In the earlier hotels, this meant the provision of some spaces predominantly for women, in line with the 'separate spheres' advocated for well-to-do domestic settings, and both shared and separate public reception rooms were often planned. At the Langham (1865), female guests could enjoy both a drawing room and a music room, as well as a separate refreshment room. At the Grand (1880), the large drawing room for ladies was on the first floor, away from the dining rooms, and the male-dominated smoking and billiard rooms on the ground floor.[15] As the century passed, however, women and men were encouraged to socialize together, not only in hotel restaurants, but also in novel, less formal, public rooms.[16]

'Bitter competition in the London hotel world': The problem of publicity

By 1889, the number of hotels listed in *Baedeker*'s *London and its Environs* totalled 119, of which 10 were railway terminus hotels, with the same number being other large, company-owned establishments. Although the total number of hotels recorded in *Baedeker* remained relatively static until at least 1905, the quantity of bedrooms in grand hotels increased significantly during this period.[17] Some smaller venues closed, but were replaced in the guidebook by new luxury hotels such as the Cecil (1896) on the Embankment, and the Carlton (1899) on the corner of Haymarket and Pall Mall. Some existing establishments, such as the Savoy (1889), were extended, and others, such as the Coburg (1896), which was subsequently renamed the Connaught, and Claridge's (1898), were completely reconstructed. In 1898, *The Hotel World* commented on the bitter competition in the luxury hotel market, with a number of establishments struggling for survival.[18] Such rivalry meant that venues needed to attract not just the wealthiest and most aspirational of clients, but almost any guest who could both pay the bill and behave appropriately. Consequently, the narrative of hotel publicity depended upon a delicate balance between appearing both exclusive and accessible to a broad clientele.

Traditionally, the experience of luxury was permitted only for the social elite, and was inseparable from the idea of restricted supply. The quantity of fine objects was limited, due to difficulties of production or inherent rarity, both of which added to the cost, and endowed status upon the user.[19] In grand hotels, however, as supply grew, luxury could not be defined by rarity alone. London hotels had hundreds of thousands of room-nights to sell each year. The largest, the Cecil with 700 bedrooms, had potentially over a quarter of a million to fill per annum.[20] In addition, during the 1880s and 1890s, the fashion for 'conspicuous consumption' was increasingly evident in hotel public rooms.[21] The attraction of residing in a grand hotel, dining in the restaurant, or dancing in the ballroom was as much about performance and display, as the experience alone. Luxury consumption in these establishments, therefore, was not defined by scarcity, but by a '*virtual rarity*: the feeling of privilege and of exclusivity'.[22] Hotel publicity was designed to stimulate this interpretation of luxury, and to broadcast it to a wide audience.

For both guests and contemporary commentators, such publicity presented an account of luxury, inspired by aristocratic style and elite connections. Improved sanitation and up-to-date technology, without which large establishments could not function, fed into a narrative of novelty and ease, and cultivated the reputation for quality. The Metropole Hotel (1885) offered residents 'every possible convenience and comfort'.[23] At the Savoy, the advertising campaign for the hotel's opening spoke of the 'perfection of luxury and comfort'. The venue's delights included electric lighting and hydraulic lifts, both day and night, and 67 bathrooms for the 400 or so rooms – an exceptionally high number for the time. Even the corridors were heated in cold weather.[24] The hotel's first brochure, *The Savoy Souvenir*, highlighted the company with whom a guest might mingle. 'During the Season', the booklet noted, 'there is almost a club-like character about the place, so esteemed is it of the wisest fashionables of our day and generation'. In the hotel, any guest was certain to see well-known artists and authors, as well as the social elite. The Coburg, according to its publicity, was luxurious and refined, and ideally located for all the best county families and Members of Parliament.[25] According to the image-makers, the luxury hotel was available to all, bestowing refinement, social cachet, and connections upon any guest.

However, the actual experience of these hotels was often somewhat less ideal than the advertising suggested. Hotel guests were not members of a club, and although the newly wealthy might be able to pay their bills, but they did not necessarily have equal social standing. Rather, as *The Queen*, a magazine for the social elite established in 1861, noted, they were 'drawn from all parts of the world and all social grades – like big fish and little taken in a drag net'.[26] In profit-driven premises of this size, the real luxuries of discretion and good taste were inevitably subject to compromise. For grand hotels, therefore, the challenge was to manage the tensions between the promises of luxury for all, as made in the publicity, and maintaining the impression of exclusivity. This was achieved through the hotels' organization, design, and service, and through the management of the guests' experience.

'A wealthy man's private mansion': The assurance of exclusivity

Like 'a wealthy man's private mansion', upon arrival, the grand hotel was designed to impress.[27] In style, the earlier grand hotels tended to adopt a form of French neoclassicism, which had been used at the Great Western Hotel (1854) at Paddington. Later establishments were often more eclectic. Of particular note were the neo-Gothic Midland Grand (1873–6) by Sir George Gilbert Scott, and the 'café au lait' terracotta Russell Hotel (1898), in Russell Square, by Charles Fitzroy Doll.[28] However, for both guests and commentators, architectural design and ornamentation were generally secondary to the hotels' remarkable scale. At the Grosvenor (1862), Andrew Wynter, a doctor who frequently wrote for general and literary periodicals, observed that 'no object in the metropolis strikes the provincial Englishman with more astonishment than the first sight of this huge building'.[29] Others used similar superlatives. Hotels were described as mammoth or monster. The Langham was 'colossal in size and palatial in appearance'. The Metropole had a frontage of 320 feet onto Northumberland Avenue and could seat 1,000 for dinner in a single day.[30]

At the entrance, the porters safeguarded the door. Performing the role of both aristocratic footman and military guard, and dressed accordingly, these staff ostentatiously expressed the style of their hotel. One of the earliest restaurant critics, Lieutenant Colonel Newnham-Davis, wrote of the porters at the Cecil, describing them as 'three gentlemen in gorgeous uniforms, and with as much gold lace round their caps as a field marshal wears'.[31] A well-cut uniform, it was acknowledged, gave porters the correct and military bearing, which was necessary to their position.[32] Such uniforms intentionally established status for a hotel, guarded privacy, and maintained exclusivity.

Once past this threshold, the guest entered the lobby or hall. This boundary between the street outside and the privileged hotel interior was designed to be a holding space, a 'semi-public gateway to private places', in which a number of activities might occur.[33] Some visitors, particularly previous guests, those who had booked in advance, or who had been introduced to the hotel by a known contact, could arrive at the reception desk to be greeted warmly by the clerk, and transformed into a resident. Others, it was reported, were made to feel less welcome, evaluated by the judgemental reception staff, in the manner of 'a hardened offender', or at the very least, 'a person who is not by any means to be encouraged'.[34]

Lobbies were also spaces in which guests would wait, providing an opportunity to both observe and be observed.[35] Such pauses encouraged the appreciation of the size of the interior. Scale celebrated technological innovation, with iron and steel frames providing the structural core for large public rooms.[36] At the Langham, the principal hall was 50 square feet, and the *salle à manger* was 100 by 40 feet.[37] Such enormous spaces were intended to overwhelm the senses, both amazing and, potentially, intimidating. Often the plan of the lobby and interconnecting public rooms was designed both to amplify scale, and to entice the guest onwards. Narrow doorways led to open spaces beyond, and darker halls gave onto well-lit reception rooms. This management of sensory experience and of movement was a technique adopted in aristocratic or royal palaces, where status was indicated by the level of intimate access granted.[38] At Claridge's, Mrs Humphry, a widely published social commentator, was impressed by 'the vista of great spaces that dazzles the visitor on entering'.[39] The size and view created immediate impact, and drew the eye to more protected interiors. At the Cecil, the hall's remarkable size was enhanced by a view which rose up the majestic staircase to the floors above (Figure 9.1). Executed in carefully chosen marbles, the hall radiated all the prestige of an Italian Renaissance palace, tempered by soft carpets and exotic palms.[40] The resemblance to the entrance at Vuillamy's Dorchester House was striking, and an observer could have no doubt about the standard of comfort and luxury that the hotel promised.

This legible, symbolic language of wealth was employed throughout the public rooms.[41] Elaborate, historicist interiors, with sumptuous materials were customary. Gleaming marble, evoking high-status aristocratic and religious buildings, offered a wide choice of colours and patterns. Expensive fabrics, tapestries, and carpets dressed windows and floors, impressing with their generosity, while muffling noise, to provide a quiet sanctuary within the busy metropolis. Glittering gas and, eventually, electric light twinkled from gilding and mirrors, enhancing visibility and creating the experience of a magical fairyland.

Observers in both the trade and general press often commented upon the décor and impact of such interiors. The opulent dining room at the Grand was decorated with marble walls and white scagliola columns with gilded capitals, tall Venetian mirrors on borders of maroon satin and gold, black walnut furniture engraved in gold, and crimson carpets.[42] At the Metropole, the entrance hall was paved with mosaic, and adorned with columns of coloured marble from the same quarries as those employed for *Les Invalides* in Paris. The lower portion of the walls in the *salle à manger* was in dark green marble. The large bevelled glass mirrors above amplified size and light, and facilitated visibility within the room.[43] At the Cecil, the decorations were considered exquisite and the interiors furnished with fine marbles, tapestry, and silken hangings. In the drawing room, an opulent *Louis Seize* scheme was adopted by the decorator, S. J. Warings (Figure 9.2). Above the picture rail, a deep frieze illustrating a procession of dancing maidens in Grecian robes was recognizably redolent of aristocratic London townhouses. The panelled walls were covered in patterned silk, or with pale, painted panels. Fashionable palms decorated tables. Silk upholstered chairs, sofas, and stools were arranged in informal groups to encourage conversation. A grand piano was available for the enjoyment of the guests.[44]

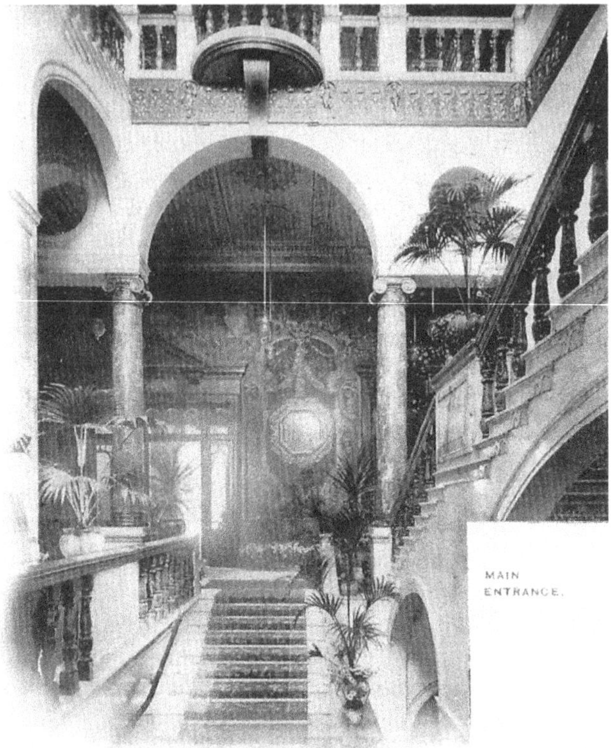

FIGURE 9.1 *Decorated in the manner of a Renaissance palace, the Hotel Cecil's main entrance staircase. Source: Hotel Cecil, London (London: 1906), 9.*

Music in hotels was desirable for several reasons. Playing the piano in the drawing room echoed the private performances given in the homes of the middle and upper classes. In lounges and restaurants, music could both mask the voices of other guests, and also fill any 'oppressive silence', which, according to the influential hotelier, César Ritz (1850–1918), 'sometimes seemed to hang like a pall over an English dining table'.[45] Music encouraged diners to linger, which tended to increase their expenditure. Also, initially this was a fashionable, cosmopolitan practice more often seen abroad, and when adopted by London venues appealed to British and foreign guests alike.[46]

However, this very cosmopolitanism was potentially risqué, and both hotels and the licensing authorities sought to manage any concerns. At the Savoy, the hotel defended their practice of providing a small band to play music to guests spending their Sunday evenings 'in inoffensively dining' in the restaurant. An application for a London County Council entertainment

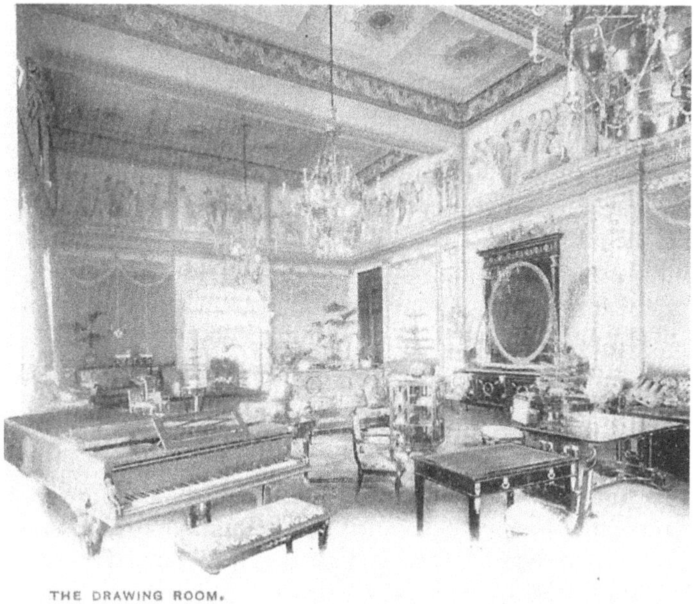

FIGURE 9.2 *The Drawing Room of the Hotel Cecil, complete with grand piano, fine furnishings, and a deep painted frieze. Source: Hotel Cecil, London (London: 1906), 15.*

licence on behalf of the Cecil confirmed that music was only required during meals in the dining room and 'not for the purposes of performances to which the general public would be promiscuously admitted'.[47] By such controls, respectability was maintained and the exclusivity of the hotel protected from that deemed socially inappropriate.

The 'spirit of the time': Cosmopolitanism and heterosociability

The production of 'fashionable cosmopolitan hotel', a phrase used by the *Illustrated London News* to describe the Langham, was more than merely the adoption of practices which were common abroad.[48] Rather, for these buildings, cosmopolitanism was an amalgamation of design with cultural and social indicators, which inferred the adventure and sophistication of international culture, but within a carefully managed environment. It also incorporated the benefits of modern technologies, such as lifts and electric bell systems, which were first developed overseas, often, but not exclusively, in the United States. The term 'caravanserai', originally a large, quadrangular, Eastern inn, was commonly used to refer to grand hotels, at home and abroad, and was a means of communicating impressions of lavish scale, combined with this safe cosmopolitanism.[49] The Hotel du Louvre in Paris, the Savoy and Claridge's were all pronounced huge or palatial *caravanserais*.[50] In these buildings, publicity surrounding the arrivals and departures of glamorous guests from the Empire, America and Europe, who might include the Sultan of Zanzibar or the royal houses of China, Persia, and Japan contributed to the desirability of a venue where luxury and notions of exotic rarity were bound together.[51] Cosmopolitanism, in the form of strange foreigners, or novel practices, might hold dangers, but if controlled carefully, by the licensing authorities and hotel management, it could suggest excitement, novelty, and distinctiveness.

In grand hotel restaurants, interpretations of cosmopolitanism filtered into interior decoration, consumption, staff, and behaviour. Reflecting other new metropolitan spaces where women fulfilled a role as both spectacle and spectator, these interiors were designed as a favourable backdrop for female guests.[52] To avoid unflattering glare, César Ritz advocated the use of indirect lighting.[53] At the Carlton, the *Daily Telegraph* asserted that the *salle à manger*, which was decorated in cream and pink, used 'no ostentatious and assertive colours ... to "kill" the delicacy of the ladies' toilette'.[54] Although French was the dominant culture in hotel dining rooms, with well-known chefs predominantly from France, and French the *lingua franca* of the kitchen, 'gastro-cosmopolitanism' combined a broader experience of food on the diner's plate with the service provided.[55] Waiters in the smartest hotels were often German, or from other European countries.[56] Foreign specialists were employed to prepare particular national dishes, and restaurants made a point of catering for a diverse range of tastes. The menu for a dinner celebrating Queen Victoria's Diamond Jubilee at the Savoy included French *nymphes a la meunière* (frogs' legs), a traditional Russian borscht, American-style turtle timbales, and pink champagne sorbet. 'The cuisine is cosmopolitan', boasted the hotel publicity, 'the foods of almost all nations and their special methods of preparation [are] at your command'.[57]

In the last decades of the century, this heterosocial cosmopolitanism spread from hotel restaurants into a new type of public room. Palm courts, winter gardens and, where space allowed, open-air courtyards were planned to facilitate informal, highly visible, fashionable socializing between men and women. 'Everything that segregates the sexes is contrary to the tendency of nature and the spirit of the time', wrote the *Pall Mall Gazette* in 1887.[58] Spacious lobbies and halls, where guests had been encouraged to wait and observe, became places to 'lounge'.[59] The nightly 'passing show' of stylish residents and diners moving through these interconnected rooms, as celebrated in the Savoy's brochure, *Home of the Passing Show* (1900), was as much part of the entertainment as the hotel band.[60] Older hotels adapted areas of the ground floor to create these new public rooms. The

Langham's central courtyard was covered in 1871 at a cost of £13,000, and became a smoking lounge for both men and women to take coffee after dinner.[61] In new hotels, where the traditional courtyard plan was employed, the central 'cortile' was covered, and used for circulation and informal relaxation. At Claridge's the central quadrangle was covered with a domed stained-glass roof, and furnished with palms and upholstered chairs.[62] At the Hotel Russell, the provision of the glazed winter garden and lounge was considered by the *Builders' Journal* to be a recognition of the 'importance of the social side of hotel life'.[63] The glass-roofed Palm Court at the Carlton formed a fashionable and luxurious lounge, which was considered the centrepiece of the hotel's immediate social and financial success.[64] Top-lit by a glazed roof, or illuminated by sparkling electric light, and decorated in the pale, fashionable styles of the French eighteenth century, these novel spaces were designed to encourage the heterosociability so desirable, as Mrs Hardy, the social critic wrote in *The Queen*, in 'the better class modern hotels'.[65]

Conclusion

In 1902, the author, Robert Machray (1857–1946) described his visit to a grand hotel in London:

> Your footsteps are inaudible on the thick carpets – the whole atmosphere of the place is one of luxury. Here are serenity, peace, repose. The air is perfumed with the scent of flowers. The room is full, but not too full, of small tables, and on the tables are softly glowing shaded lights. And the men and women who are dining or about to dine, are well dressed, well bred – at least, some of them. They are of all nationalities under the sun.[66]

Established as a response to the lack of high-quality accommodation at a time when expectations and demand were growing, grand hotels created a novel interpretation of luxury, which sought to combine distinction, cosmopolitanism, and modernity. The men and women who entered the halls, lobbies, and drawing rooms of these buildings were, like Machray, presented with experiences designed to stimulate the senses, to impress and to amaze. In order to maintain their position as luxury venues, the public rooms evolved throughout the century. Hotel restaurants, and later, lounges, winter gardens, and palm courts provided for a new, fashionable, and highly visible heterosociability.

To attract the thousands of guests required to ensure their commercial success, hotel publicity disseminated a narrative which indicated that these experiences were available to all who could afford them. At the same time, to maintain the impression of rarity and status, so crucial to assertions of luxury, the public rooms were required to retain a certain exclusivity.

As Machray recognized, and as this chapter has shown, the competing demands of publicity and exclusivity created inherent contradictions. How could a hotel's status and respectability be ensured, if anyone could enter, regardless of social class, from anywhere 'under the sun'? Hotels managed these potentially troublesome paradoxes through the use of space, design, materials, and the behaviour of their staff, influencing and directing the response of the guests. Through these experiences, the grand hotel promised, the ordinary man or woman could be transformed into a member of the elite.

CHAPTER TEN

'The fullest fountain of advancing civilization': Experiencing Anthony Trollope's House of Commons, 1852–82

Edward Gillin

The country is governed from between the walls of that House. ... From thence flow the waters of the world's progress, – the fullest fountain of advancing civilization.[1]

MR BOTT, *CAN YOU FORGIVE HER?* (1864)

With this, Anthony Trollope's (1815–82) fictional Liberal Member of Parliament (MP), Mr Bott, proclaimed the significance of the House of Commons not just for Britain, but for the world. Completed in 1852, Charles Barry's new debating chamber was, in 1864, still a new building. In Chapter 1 of this volume, William Whyte observed that in the nineteenth century there was a growing consensus that architecture was not passive, but something that humans actively experienced.[2] Buildings do not hold inherent meaning; they are not disinterested unchanging scenes, but are emotionally charged. Like writers such as Marcel Proust and John Ruskin, Trollope recognized this, observing that the House of Commons required time to acquire the hallowed sacredness that it deserved as the nation's political heart. In this chapter, I use Anthony Trollope's literary portrayals of the House of Commons to explore how literature might be of value to architectural historians. When explaining how audiences experienced architecture, we need to take care to define who these audiences were. The Palace of Westminster's architecture has been a common historical subject, but what is often overlooked is how limited and privileged the audiences were who witnessed the building.[3] Beyond MPs, journalists, and a select few, hardly any Victorians directly experienced the House of Commons. So if we are to understand what the House of Commons meant to Victorian society, we need to look to the cultural representations of the debating chamber. Obviously this includes newspaper reports and artworks, but also literature.[4] How Trollope depicted the House of Commons is therefore important in assessing how broad society experienced the chamber.

Why then choose Trollope? Of all Victorian authors, Parliament featured more centrally in his works than any other and, as Elaine Hadley has argued, Trollope provided the most engaged literature directly addressing mid-Victorian liberal politics. As Hadley puts it, Trollope worked to make politics appear mundane.[5] He went to great lengths to ensure his account of the House of Commons, and the debates within it were represented as accurately as possible. He understood the importance of this, recalling how, in preparing to write *Phineas Finn*, 'as I could not take my seat on those benches … I had humbly to crave … permission for a seat in the gallery, so that I might thus become conversant with the ways and doings of the House'.[6] Trollope emphasized the value of being a reliable reporter in works of literature. Accuracy and detail were central to becoming a 'trustworthy' authority whom audiences could rely on. As he puts it, there 'are two kinds of confidence which a reader may have in his author. … There is a confidence in facts and a confidence in vision. The one man tells you accurately what has been. The other suggests to you what may, or perhaps what must have been'.[7] On the importance of accurate detail in describing customs and institutions, Trollope felt that the 'poor fictionist very frequently finds himself to have been wrong in his description of things in general. … He catches salmon in October; or shoots his partridges in March … [he] makes Parliament sit on a Wednesday evening'.[8] Trollope constructed his accounts to appear as reports. Contemporaries regularly acknowledged this detailed accuracy. In an 1869 review of *Phineas Finn*, *The Dublin Review* praised Trollope's 'realistic' political portrayal, noting that his authority was as if 'he had sat through half a dozen Parliaments'. In the 1880s, the same journal celebrated Trollope as a 'faithful painter' who wrote as if he had sat for years in the chamber.[9] The *Edinburgh Review*, in 1877, considered him a 'trustworthy guide' and advised foreigners to study his novels to learn of British politics.[10] Historians and literary critics have noted this quality, with James Kincaid suggesting that the language of Trollope's political works appeared to have no literary style and Ayelet Ben-Yishai arguing that the use of elaborate detail built confidence with readers, establishing Trollope as an authority who could be trusted.[11]

Who then, exactly, were Trollope's audiences? Trollope was very careful in his choice of publisher and publication type. He found releasing his novels through popular journals to be highly lucrative, and of his thirty-four novels between 1862 and 1882, twenty-five were serialized, with just three initially produced as books. Trollope favoured this method as it ensured a wide circulation and cheap production before his works were subsequently printed as stand-alone novels.[12] *Can You Forgive Her?*, for instance, first appeared between 1864 and 1865 in thirty-two 6p parts. In terms of the type of reader, *Phineas Finn* appeared in *St Paul's Magazine* between 1867 and 1868, which had an educated middle-class to upper-class readership of about 25,000. In contrast, Trollope chose the *Fortnightly Review* for *The Eustace Diamonds*, whose circulation was about 2,500 in 1871, comprised mostly of middle- and upper-class readers of a liberal to radical political disposition. Similarly, Trollope serialized *The Duke's Children* during 1879 in the middle-class *All The Year Round*, which was Liberal in politics and religiously broad, with a circulation of up to 300,000 at Christmas. Trollope took something of an experiment in 1873, choosing to publish *Phineas Redux* in *The Graphic*, an illustrated newspaper positioned to compete with the *Illustrated London News* and of somewhat lower literary standards than Trollope's usual place of publication.[13] These places of publication not only show us the extent of Trollope's readership, but help us garner some idea of the politics and social background of his audiences.

While the majority of Britain's population could not vote, many of Trollope's readers were experiencing electoral participation for the first time. With the exception of *Can You Forgive Her?*, each of Trollope's political novels appeared following the 1867 Reform Act, which dramatically changed the British electoral system. This legislation granted the vote to all male householders in boroughs, as well as lodgers who paid more than £10 p.a., and it reduced the property threshold in counties to enfranchise agricultural landowners and tenants with small amounts of land. In real terms this meant an increase of about 1.5 million voters, effectively doubling the electorate. While in the 1865 election, 697,932 votes were cast, in the following election of 1868, this figure rose to 1,996,704, including large numbers of male working-class voters.[14] This meant that although many of Trollope's readers were still unable to vote, including all his female audiences, some were reading of a political world which, for the first time, they were exerting influence over. This post-reform-act context helps to explain some of the success and relevance of Trollope's political portrayals. Not only was the House of Commons relatively new, but so were those voting for MPs.

This chapter will provide an example of how literature can serve as a tool for architectural historians. I begin by showing how Trollope described the architecture of the Palace of Westminster and the way he presented his characters' experiences of debates within the House of Commons. Through figures such as Phineas Finn and Augustus Melmotte, Trollope provided his readers with imagined experiences of the chamber. Within these accounts, he emphasized the uniqueness of the House as a room, appearing to have an effect on the air MPs breathed and the sound of their voices. Although Trollope was never an MP, he worked to make such descriptions as detailed as possible. I then examine the significance Trollope ascribed to the chamber. In his novels, he constantly reiterated that politicians and audiences in the House experienced a unique, even sacred, structure. It was the cross-bench form of the Commons which made it so important for Trollope. The chamber physically embodied the perceived strengths of Britain's political system. The two-sided layout of the room appeared symbolic of the balance between liberal progress and conservative tradition which Trollope believed so essential to political stability. I conclude by evaluating how Trollope conceptualized the House of Commons as a theatre. This analogy reveals that Trollope portrayed the House as a masculine space. Part of the building's character, according to Trollope, was that it was a place of manly confrontation, unsuitable for feminine delicacy. Throughout this analysis I show how Trollope presented his readers with a highly politicized, often romanticized, and deeply gendered experience of the Palace of Westminster. This chapter argues that while architecture cannot be definitively read, what was read about architecture was very important to how nineteenth-century audiences experienced the buildings around them.

Experiences of Parliament

Anthony Trollope was born in London, the son of a barrister, Thomas Anthony Trollope, and the author Frances Trollope.[15] After beginning a career in the General Post Office, Trollope's first publication came in 1847 and he wrote constantly throughout the 1850s and 1860s. Increasingly interested in politics, he published *Can You Forgive Her?*, the first of six politically focused 'Palliser novels', in 1864. In November 1868 he stood unsuccessfully as the Liberal candidate for Beverley, in the East Riding of Yorkshire; although always coveting a seat in Parliament, he never stood again. Politically, Trollope described himself as 'an advanced, but still a conservative, Liberal'.[16] This 'conservative-liberalism' was the combination of Trollope's love of tradition, in particular for institutions, with his desire for social improvement, and positioned him broadly as a supporter of the Liberal Party.[17]

Denied a seat, Trollope expressed his political beliefs through his novels: notably in the five subsequent Palliser volumes, *Phineas Finn* (1867–8), *The Eustace Diamonds* (1871), *Phineas Redux* (1874), *The Prime Minister* (1876), and *The Duke's Children* (1879). These works focused heavily on the fictional careers of Plantagenet Palliser, an MP and later prime minister, and his socialite wife, Glencora. Much of the drama in Trollope's Palliser series was set in the House of Commons, where architecture played a central role. Although not published in his lifetime, Trollope considered Parliament's architecture directly in his non-fiction manuscript, *The New Zealander*. Condemning those who criticized English architecture, Trollope asserted Westminster equal to Antwerp or Milan, explaining how,

> we have erected finer buildings than are to be found in either. Now that our Houses of Parliament are nearly completed it is of course the fashion to abuse them. They are too low, too much burdened with decoration. ... The towers are, or will be, too heavy. There is no point from which to see it, and nothing worth looking at if such a point were found. Such are the judgements pronounced by architectural critics of the present age, and yet it may be doubted whether many nobler piles have ever yet been built by the hands of man.[18]

Trollope approved of Charles Barry's Gothic design, preferring it to what he regarded as the 'mechanical' styles of the Dutch and Flemish cities (Figure 10.1). It was more than suitable as the architectural seat of Britain's political representatives, and an irresistible setting for Trollope's narratives.

Trollope provided his audiences with a literary construction of what it was to architecturally experience Parliament. Within this, the detail of Parliament's building was essential. Trollope worked hard to present a realistic portrayal of the Palace to complement his account of the political endeavours of his characters. In *Can You Forgive Her?* Trollope's elaborate

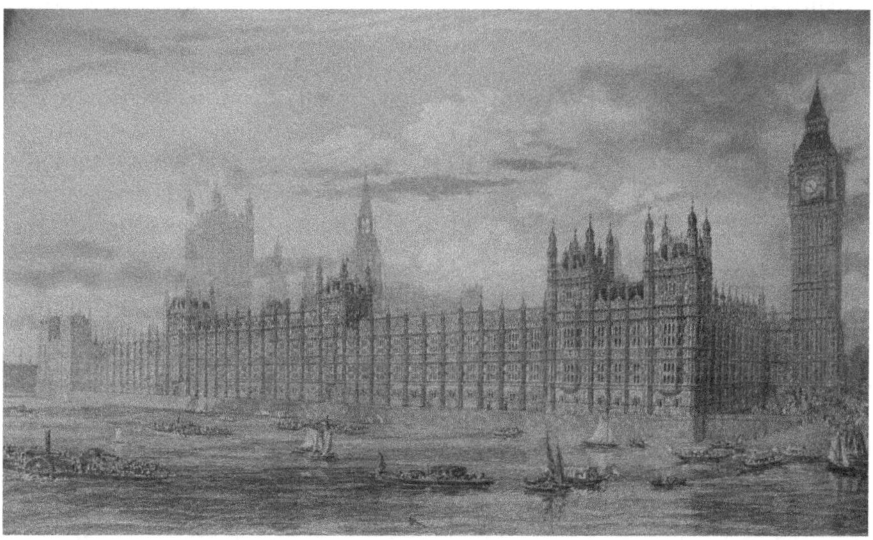

FIGURE 10.1 *Charles Barry's Gothic Palace of Westminster. From (Anon.),* The New Palace of Westminster, *(London: Warrington & Co, 1867), image in author's possession.*

description of the entrance to the House of Commons mixed rich aesthetic detail with his perceived importance of the place.

> There is on the left-hand side of our great national hall ... a pair of gilded lamps, with a door between them, near to which a privileged old dame sells her apples and her oranges. ... Between those lamps is the entrance to the House of Commons, and none but Members may go that way! It is the only gate before which I have ever stood filled with envy ... hast thou never confessed, when standing there, that Fate has been unkind to thee in denying thee the one thing that thou has wanted? I have done so; and as my slow steps have led me up that more than royal staircase, to those passages and halls which require the hallowing breath of centuries to give them the glory in British eyes which they shall one day possess, I have told myself, in anger and in grief, that to die and not to have won that right of way ... is to die and not to have done that which it most becomes an Englishman to have achieved.[19]

Readers who had never seen the inside of Parliament could thus experience the grandeur of the building. Trollope portrayed the Commons not only as an almost sacred space, but as the most privileged space in Britain. Yet this also was a young building that would become more glorious with time. Great historic scenes, Trollope believed, would enhance Parliament's standing in British society. He was keen that his readers should share in this sense of the building's historical significance.

Through the various characters of Trollope's novels, audiences could share the experiences of MPs inside the Commons. An early example was the trials of the young Irish MP, Phineas Finn. Trollope described Finn's first impressions of the Palace as an intoxicating encounter. Within a few weeks 'the taste of his palate had been already changed by the glare of the lamps in and about palatial Westminster'. Finn could not stand the thought of losing his seat, for 'the air of the House of Commons was now the very breath of his nostrils'.[20] The Commons was also intimidating, with Finn's maiden speech a traumatic occasion. While he had lost some of the initial terror inspired by 'the row of ministers, and by the unequalled importance of the place', on rising to his feet Finn's 'original awe of the House returned'. The architecture transformed the sound of Finn's words; on speaking he did not recognize 'the sound of his own voice in that room'.[21] When Finn later lost his seat and returned to Ireland, he longed to be back in the Commons; 'his very soul had sighed for the lost glories of Westminster. ... He had revelled in the gaslight, and could not lie quiet on a sunny bank'.[22] Finn's experience of Parliament's architecture was a central part of his development as an influential statesman. Trollope ascribed to Parliament's physical building a power over the senses; the air, light, sound, and atmosphere of the architecture exerted an overwhelming sensation over its members.

How characters experienced Parliament was not just literary detail, but central to the narrative of Trollope's novels. Of particular importance was what Trollope described as the 'forms' of the Commons; these manners and customs, unique to this space, shaped the passing and debating of legislation. He emphasized to his readers that these practices were crucial to the experience of Parliament. Indeed, Trollope's Liberal MP Mr Bott explained that 'no man can know what Parliament is who has never had a seat. Indeed no one can thoroughly understand the British Constitution without it. ... The forms of the House are everything'.[23] The practices of the Commons seemed to imbue members with a sense of tradition and respect; manners such as addressing fellow Commoners as 'honourable gentlemen', respecting the authority of the Speaker of the House, and removing hats when speaking. Trollope portrayed these customs as important to conditioning the legislature into a coherent body. Characters such as Finn could only succeed in politics if they mastered the forms of the chamber.[24]

Yet while readers could share in the experiences of Bott and Finn, Trollope provided a warning for those who refused to respect the unique rituals of the Commons. In his epic *The Way We Live Now* (1875) Trollope used the Commons as the location for the demise of the fraudster and financial maverick Augustus Melmotte. Trollope turned the chamber into a place of trial, marking Melmotte out as a man unsuitable for public service. Melmotte may have tricked his way into polite society, but he could not master the Commons. After becoming the Conservative MP for Westminster with promises of commercial endeavours, railways through Russia, and telegraphic submarine cables encircling the globe, Melmotte found the chamber a hard place to succeed in.[25] Trollope's Commons appeared to reduce Melmotte from greatness, undermining any confidence he assumed from his public support and revealing him as a social imposter. Unlike Finn, he lacked respect for the House and held its physical form in contempt: 'The place was very much smaller than he had thought, and much less tremendous. ... It seemed to him that they who spoke were talking much like other people in other places.'[26] Readers could share in both Finn's and Melmotte's experiences of the House of Commons, and from both, Trollope drew out moral lessons for his increasingly politically active audiences over how politicians should conduct themselves and the sort of character they should possess. Trollope was not enthusiastic over MPs who were connected to financial speculation or ungentlemanly dealings, and was keen to cultivate these sentiments with his readership.

Progressive architecture

Trollope not only provided his readers with an elaborate portrayal of the interior of Parliament, but asserted that the architectural layout of the

Commons embodied the strengths of Britain's political system. The floor plan of the Commons, with its cross-bench structure, was essential to Trollope's conception of how politicians achieved progress for the country. Through his character Palliser, Trollope asserted that a 'Liberal, if he have any fixed idea at all, must, I think, have conceived the idea of lessening distances, – of bringing the coachman and duke nearer together'.[27] The purpose of Trollope's House of Commons was to bring about social improvement through gradual reform. He believed that the clear two-sided balance in the Commons ensured that there was always a side advocating reform, and always an opposition to moderate it. For Trollope, the strength of the British political system was embodied in the very architecture of Parliament.

Trollope was not alone in associating the architecture of the House of Commons to the form of political debate carried out in Parliament. Before the destruction of the original Palace in 1834, a Parliamentary Committee, established to investigate the building's architecture and suggest ways for its improvement, interviewed several leading architects over the question of the shape of the Commons. In April 1833, the Greek revivalist Decimus Burton (1800–81) came before the committee and gave his opinions on changing the cross-benched chamber into a semicircle or oval-shaped room. He did not believe a change was appropriate as 'the mode of debating which I have observed is practised in the English House of Commons, where Members sometimes give replies across the House, on those occasions not addressing the Speaker'. For business to continue in the Commons in the English style of politics, Burton believed, required straight parallel benches. He did 'not consider a semicircular House would be suitable for this mode of debate'.[28] Architect Thomas Hopper (1776–1856) concurred with this view. When the committee asked which shape would best suit the House, he advocated a quadrangle with cross-benches. As he explained, 'In a lecture-room, where one person is to address an assembly, an amphitheatre or semicircular form is the best; but where Members have to debate with each other, it seems to me that the quadrangular form is best'. Hopper felt this important not only for the practicality of debate, but also to aid sound, although architect John Soane (1753–1837) disagreed with this judgement, preferring a circular apse.[29] Throughout the 1830s and 1840s, radical politicians were particularly displeased with the commitment shown to cross-benched debating chambers.[30]

Trollope's attention to the shape of the House of Commons was not unique, but he was a firm advocate of a cross-benched chamber. He maintained that while Liberals could advocate reform, a solid Conservative opposition checked zealous radicalism and respected tradition. An effective act of Parliament could hence be produced through thorough consideration and sustained debate. Following his failure at Beverley, he admitted that he was 'among those who desire the ascendency of our party for sheer party purposes. … Nor are we in the least ashamed of this spirit of doggish battle. We believe that without it politics cannot be carried on to a true end or useful purpose ... on the floor of the House ... there should be internecine war'.[31] The benches he portrayed as a gladiatorial arena, with questions likened to a 'broadside' of musketry.[32] In such conflict, the Conservative opposition to the lessening of distances was an important element of stability in the process of improvement. To successfully push progressive legislation, Trollope felt it necessary for those of a reforming nature to unite on the Liberal side of the House. As Palliser recognized, to do good in politics was only possible by being practical, and this encompassed a loyalty to this Liberal side.[33]

Although a member of the Liberal party, Trollope appreciated the importance of political opposition and admired its embodiment in the floor plan of the House of Commons. The confrontational nature of the two-sided House, where the party in power faced their political adversaries across the dispatch box, was vital, he believed, to progressive governance. With two sides to the debating chamber, members were encouraged to choose a side and follow a party line. This sentiment was clearly defined through the character of Barrington Erle. A Liberal advocate of party loyalty, the description of Erle in *Phineas Finn* illustrated both Trollope's aversion to parliamentary independence, and the desirability of a clear two-sided House:

> With a good Conservative opponent he could shake hands almost as readily as with a good Whig ally; but the man who was neither flesh nor fowl was odious to him. According to his theory of parliamentary government, the House of Commons should be divided by a marked line, and every member should be required to stand on one side of it or on the other.[34]

In 1977 John Halperin asserted that Erle 'represents the worst aspects of the English party system as Trollope sees it'.[35] However, given Trollope's constant emphasis on the desirability for two-sided party conflict, Halperin's assessment would seem erroneous. Trollope's approval for the House's two-sided hostilities would suggest he sympathized with Erle's sentiments. Physically, the cross-bench shape of the House established a clear line between the ideologies of liberalism and conservatism; Commons debate thus transcended personal grievances and became a contest over the reduction of social distances. Tellingly, Trollope surmised that 'you can hardly be personal to a whole bench of Conservatives'.[36] The structural layout of the Commons, for Trollope, ensured that political confrontation remained ideological rather than personal. The shape of the Commons thus appeared to embody what he perceived were the great strengths of the English Constitution.[37]

As if to reiterate the importance of this constant two-sided political system, Trollope warned of the dangers of removing the divided nature of British politics in *The Prime Minister*. Although Palliser finally ascended to the position of prime minister, it was not of a Liberal majority, but rather a

Liberal-Conservative coalition. The novel saw Palliser struggle with the role, and ultimately prove unsuitable due to his preference for absolute honesty. Trollope's account of the failure of gentlemanly morality to triumph in the political arena was accompanied with a subtler illustration of the relevance of Commons debate to progressive government. By removing the conflict of party debate, coalition politics became passive and overly comfortable for MPs.[38] With coalition government, the impetus of traditional party rivalry was removed and replaced with a familiar form of politics which undermined the production of legislation.[39]

Trollope provided an architectural dimension to this lesson on the dangers of peaceful coalition government. With Commons debate suspended, the building was made redundant. While in the first four Palliser novels the centre of Trollope's political world was inside the House, in *The Prime Minister* this changed. Instead, Gatherum Castle, the seat of Plantagenet Palliser, became the centre of political drama. On discovering her husband was to be prime minister, and realizing that with no 'sides' in the House, politics could be removed to a more peaceful environment, Glencora Palliser declared her intention to establish Gatherum as the new privileged site of politics. Within six weeks, 'all the world had begun to talk of the Prime Minister's dinners, and of the receptions given by the Prime Minister's wife'. The Commons lost its significance as a place of debate: 'for the moment ... there was to be peace ... there was so to say no opposition, and at first it seemed that one special bench in the House of Commons would remain unoccupied'. That bench was of course the front bench of the opposition. Even the leader of the traditional opposition sat 'just below the gangway'; eventually however, 'that gentleman returned to the place usually held by the Prime Minister's rival'.[40] What we see then, in *The Prime Minister*, is the political state of the nation symbolized through the physical use and structure of the House of Commons.

Trollope's portrayal of the coalition was not a happy one. Without the discomfort created by the cross-bench shape of the Commons, the government stagnated. To appease all the members of his government, Palliser found himself swayed to inactivity. Totally unable to introduce any suitably liberal policies, he watched as his wife's hospitality and his government's serenity descended into 'vulgarity'.[41] With Parliament subdued, political rule at Gatherum became unconstitutional and oligarchical. Trollope's account of Palliser's coalition offered a warning to his readers of the dangers of replacing the Commons with a completely private style of government. It illustrated the importance of the cross-benched chamber. Of course the political state reached in *The Prime Minister* was not due to the architecture of Parliament and Gatherum, but Trollope used these spaces to explain the political situation in which Palliser found himself.

In this style of government, the opposition benches appeared sadly obscure; to have surrendered political differences for peaceful government was to have sacrificed 'principles to place'. Without a direct opposition in the chamber, the government was answerable to no one; 'argumentative philosophical Radicals, – men of standing and repute, who are always in doubtful times individually flattered by Ministers', could be ignored, and there 'grew up unconsciously a feeling of security against attack which was distasteful to these gentlemen, and was in itself perhaps a little dangerous'. Without opposition, Trollope feared that more radical forms of hostility to the government might emerge. By implication, the physical shape of the House was important in maintaining stable politics. As Trollope concluded, the coalition was 'so abnormal that there could hardly be said to be any sides in the House. A stranger … would have thought that no minister had for many years commanded so large a majority'.[42]

A political theatre

What then did Trollope think of foreign, rival, legislatures? What was it that made the House of Commons at Westminster so unique? Trollope had toured the United States in 1861 and published an account in 1862. Trollope's observations on the Capitol Building in Washington, including both the Senate and the House of Representatives, provide a contrast to his views of the Palace of Westminster. Respecting the building's aesthetics, Trollope lamented that the

> entrance is made under a dome, to a large circular hall, which is hung around with surely the worst pictures by which a nation ever sought to glorify its own deeds. There are yards of paintings at Versailles which are bad enough; but there is nothing at Versailles comparable in villainy to the huge daubs which are preserved in this Hall at the Capital.[43]

Admittedly there was considerable refurbishment in progress at the time, yet Trollope described the architecture as revealing 'the tenuity' of the legislature. He described how the Representative Chamber was in a 'semicircular form, or in a broad horseshoe, and every member as he sits faces the Speaker', which although possible for a body of 240 members would, he maintained, be unsuitable for an assembly on the scale of Westminster, which had 656 seats from 1861, and 658 from 1865.

Trollope felt the American model to be efficient but lacking in 'dignity'. The Speaker of the House of Representatives had a voice 'always ringing in my ears, exactly as does the voice of the croupier at a gambling-table. … Perhaps it might be found that any great accession of dignity would impede the celerity of the work to be done'.[44] While Trollope portrayed the Commons as a dignified edifice, its American counterpart, the House of Representatives, was a place of efficient governance. In comparison to the practice of dividing into the lobbies at Westminster, in Washington, 'during the ceremony of voting the members look very much like sheep being passed into their pens'. The ritual of voting in Washington appeared to Trollope as void of any respectability at all. Instead of employing lobbies, two members of the House stood at the front of the semicircle and counted as the 'ayes' came forward, before then registering all the 'noes'. This manner of recording by having members walk between the counters was characterized by a 'rapidity' which created efficiency, but seemed chaotic and inaccurate.[45]

While Trollope confessed a curious respect for the efficiency of the Representatives, there was within his novels a sense that the British Parliament was different to other national legislatures. It was as a theatre that Trollope presented the Commons to his readers. For Melmotte, as for all of Trollope's MPs, the Commons was the setting for much drama. Trollope likened the characters of this theatre to gods, and their exchanges to scenes from a classical play: 'There is something very pleasant in the close, bosom friendship, and bitter, uncompromising animosity, of these human gods. … If Parliament were an Olympus in which Juno and Venus never kissed, the thing would not be nearly so interesting.' Those who had an interest in politics 'should not be desirous of peeping behind the scenes. No beholder at any theatre should do so.'[46] What made Parliament a theatre was that it was the site of momentous scenes. Throughout the Palliser series this sense of spectacle was consistently exhibited. Although an uninspiring act, Palliser's attempt to reform Britain's currency by introducing a five-farthing penny attracted a crowd to the chamber. To oversee the introduction of Palliser's 'stupendous measure', those individuals most interested congregated in the Commons: 'all the Directors of the Bank of England were in the gallery, and every chairman of a great banking company, and every Baring and every Rothschild'.[47] On another occasion, Trollope described the ladies gallery as 'quite full' with spectators, all drawn by the possibility of hearing Glencora Palliser's name discussed in the House. The Commons became a spectacle, as there had never been 'a matter that was so interesting to them for it was the only matter they remembered in which a woman's conduct might probably be called in question in the House of Commons'.[48]

In Trollope's novels, the Commons was the scene of the most dramatic political choices of the nation. This sense of theatre climaxed with the Conservative party's proposed disestablishment bill in *Phineas Redux*. The debating of this fictional measure to sever the links between the state and the Church of England was truly a spectacle. Trollope described how the ensuing drama filled the clubs and hotels of London with Anglican clergy. When the time of the debate arrived, the House was filled with observers:

> Ladies' places had been balloted for with desperate enthusiasm. … Two royal princes and a royal duke were accommodated. … Peers swarmed in the passages. … Men, and especially clergymen, came to the galleries loaded with sandwiches and flasks, prepared to hear all there was to be heard. … The very ventilating chambers under the House were filled

> with courteous listeners, who had all pledged themselves that under no possible provocation would they even cough during the debate.[49]

At such a crucial moment in the nation's history, the Commons acted not only as a theatre, but a stage at the very heart of British society. Men and women of all ranks wanted to be in the audience, but as few had such access, Trollope's novels offered a rare experience of such political drama.

Despite his portrayal of Parliament as a theatre, Trollope feared that the Commons could be exploited to secure political power. Trollope's satirical Conservative leader, Timothy Beeswax, was just such an opportunist; 'to him Parliament was a debating place ... in which, and by no other means, he, – or another, – might become the great man of the day'. Beeswax, based on Benjamin Disraeli (1804–1881), exploited the space of the Commons:

> The Treasury Bench on which he sat and the big box on the table before him were to him fortifications of which he knew how to use every stone. The cheers and the jeers of the House had been so measured by him that he knew the value and force of every sound.[50]

In Trollope's account of the Commons, a disreputable politician, such as Beeswax, transformed what was a sacred space into a fortress for his own advantage.

Trollope was also certain that the Commons was, essentially, a masculine space. To his readers, he portrayed the debating chamber as a manly room.[51] As the Commons was a theatre and place of insensitive debate, Trollope believed it was no place for a woman. The often brutal experience of the chamber meant that to succeed within the Commons, a man

> should ask the gods for a thick skin as a first gift. The need of this in our national assembly is greater than elsewhere ... opponents are almost in accord, as is always the case with our parliamentary gladiators, they are ever striving to give maddening little wounds through joints of the harness.[52]

The nature of parliamentary debate meant that values of toughness and resilience were demanded and these were not qualities Trollope usually ascribed to women. Plantagenet Palliser's cousin, Jeffrey, warned of the change women would bring to the chamber: 'think where we should be if we had a feminine House of Commons, with feminine debates, carried on, of course, with feminine courtesy'.[53]

Nevertheless, Trollope's novels did emphasize that the Commons was susceptible to feminine influences. Finn's promoter, Laura Standish, coveted political influence; 'it was her ambition to be brought as near to political action as was possible for a woman without surrendering any of the privileges of feminine inaction'. She lamented 'that a woman's life is only half a life, as she cannot have a seat in Parliament'.[54] Yet this feeling of feminine impotence was not endemic in Trollope's works. Other women who desired influence in the Commons often assumed it. Palliser's wife, Glencora, was in many ways a more effective political figure than her husband. In *Phineas Redux*, she actively undermined the upcoming Chancellor of the Exchequer, Mr Bonteen, in order to secure Finn a Cabinet position.[55] Through social entertainments, Glencora assumed a position of political power.[56] While she could not sit in the Commons, she could exert influence over those who did. Who sat on the front bench of the government side of the chamber was very much open to female influence.

Despite the agency Trollope accorded his female characters, the experience of the Commons itself remained exclusively masculine due to the nature of parliamentary debate. Mrs Finn summed up this sentiment succinctly:

> I should never have had patience to sit all night upon that bench in the House of Commons. How men can do it! They mustn't read. They can't think because of the speaking. It doesn't do for them to talk. I don't believe they ever listen … that can't be pleasant. I look upon the Treasury Bench in July as a sort of casual-ward, which we know to be necessary, but is almost too horrid to be contemplated.[57]

For Trollope, women had a place in political life, but that place was not in the Commons. They could shape it, but the practices of that space required what Trollope perceived to be masculine traits. Aggressive debate and resilience, endurance and toughness; these were the characteristics for success in the House and marked it as a space of masculinity. Throughout the Palliser novels, Trollope's readers experienced the Commons as a theatre and place of manly confrontation. Clearly then, he was eager to show his readers that this architecture was for men only; he was sure that it was something that women should not personally experience, unless as spectators.

Conclusion: Reading experiences

Elsewhere I have explored how MPs, journalists, and a privileged few experienced Parliament.[58] I have looked at how science shaped the way this elite group saw, breathed, and listened in Parliament. However, it is to material such as Trollope's writings that we should look if we want to understand how broader society experienced the building. Trollope's novels represent an industrious effort to convey an architectural experience of the Palace to an otherwise excluded audience. What can we conclude from all this? I would argue that when addressing the question of how nineteenth-century architecture was experienced, it is crucial to make explicit who the audiences were. With a space as exclusive as the Commons, it is clear who experienced the chamber, but it is unclear what wider audiences thought. Furthermore, I would argue that literature can be useful in addressing this problem. Trollope provides a great example of literature's value to architectural histories concerned with experience. We should appreciate this value and make use of it, but never lose sight of the fact that such literature is not objective and impartial, but an interpretation. Nevertheless, this should not detract from the resource that literature presents to architectural historians. If anything, literary accounts of buildings such as the Commons remind us that architecture is not passive and singular, but loaded with meaning and capable of diverse interpretation. If buildings have no inherent worth that can be simply read, then this enhances the worth of reading literature depicting architecture. Literature provides a tool with which to explore the ways society and architecture were engaged in the nineteenth century. When we study architecture in literature, we not only explore how an individual experienced a building, but the broader experiences of a society.

CHAPTER ELEVEN

Building student bodies: College gymnasia and women's health in nineteenth-century America

Caitlin DeClercq

This chapter examines the architecture constructed between 1865 and 1889 to develop healthy student bodies at Vassar College, established in 1861 as the first women's college in the United States. Specifically, I focus on three buildings in which the relationship between health and education was most apparent, namely, Main Hall (1865), the Calisthenium (1866), and Alumnae Hall (1889). Each of these buildings contained space for physical exercise, a central component of nineteenth-century higher education and the focus of this chapter.[1] The founding (and study) of Vassar College and its architecture illuminates the inherent contradictions of educating women at the time. Unlike many of his contemporaries, Matthew Vassar (1792–1868), founder and benefactor of Vassar College, believed that men and women were essentially similar in intellectual capacity. He therefore sought to ensure that women could obtain the same collegiate education men enjoyed: an endeavour described by John Raymond (1814–78), the second president of Vassar College, as 'an experiment of liberal education for that sex to which liberal education has ... been hitherto denied'.[2] Yet, echoing and responding to popular anxieties about the bodily effects of women's education, Vassar insisted on a regime of physical education as part of the college's curriculum.[3] Vassar College then, was, and is, an important precedent for women's colleges because its founders articulated a vision for this new type of educational institution and, in so doing, confronted prevailing ideas about gender, social roles, and public health, all of which were tied up with the popular debate surrounding women's education in the late 1800s.

Nineteenth-century higher education

Historian Rebecca Edwards suggests that the ideological roots of the push for women's education in the United States lay in the Enlightenment and American Revolution, the latter of which 'sought to give concrete political form to Enlightenment ideas'. Indeed, opportunities for women's higher education existed long before the founding of Vassar College. Female seminaries and academies (e.g. Emma Willard's Troy Female Seminary, 1821, and Mary Lyon's Mount Holyoke Seminary, 1837) led the effort to offer an education to women that rivalled opportunities long enjoyed by college men. Yet, Edwards notes, these schools emphasized different subjects than those taught in institutions for men, and curricula varied according to social class. While schools that catered to wealthy students emphasized subjects that reinforced traditionally feminine roles and 'domestic arts', women of more modest means at Mount Holyoke were prepared for teaching professions and engaged in domestic work strictly as a means of financial support.[4] Later, co-educational colleges (e.g. Oberlin, 1837), women's colleges, and coordinate colleges offered women further access to liberal and professional education. Still, as feminist scholar Daphne Spain argues, these colleges were spatially separate and their curriculum distinct from men's colleges, and higher education remained a rarified experience for young women in the late 1800s.[5]

Nevertheless, the nineteenth-century emergence of seminaries and colleges that gave women new entry into public life profoundly disrupted the 'separate spheres' ideology of home and work that defined Victorian society and, according to legal historian Terry Kogan, echoed and fuelled other social concerns, particularly those surrounding public health.[6] Critics of women's education couched their objections in terms of inherent intellectual ability or argued that women could not endure the physical rigors of college and that, should they try, they would bear 'sickly' offspring, or none at all.[7] In this latter argument, the capacity for educational achievement, stated in biological terms, echoed Darwinian theories of evolution increasingly popular in social and physical sciences at the time.[8]

Historian Susan Cahn explains that many formally trained doctors saw in the articulation of such concerns an opportunity to claim themselves experts in women's health problems. In an effort to cement their professional status, nineteenth-century physicians offered their own theories of women's health and solutions for how to mitigate harm.[9] Educational institutions, already undergoing considerable change and questioning the direction that modern education should take, were fertile ground for medical practitioners to plant their ideas. In a widely read 1873 book, *Sex in Education, or, A Fair Chance for the Girls*, Dr Edward Hammond Clarke (1820–77) famously cautioned that if women's education was too strenuous or intellectually demanding, bodily resources would be diverted to the brain and away from the female 'reproductive apparatus'. Clarke was adamant that women's education must take a different form than men's: less taxing and with adequate supervision to ensure health, nutrition, and the proper regulation of mental work.[10] Not surprisingly, female physicians diverged from their male colleagues in how they conceived of women's health problems and their implications for higher education.[11] Dr Mary Taylor Bissell (b. 1854), for example, offered her own theories to explain the poor health of women, including the deleterious impacts of corsets and a sedentary life.[12] Recognizing an 'urgent medical need' to increase women's strength, female physicians like Bissell advocated against the sheltering of women's bodies, and instead recommended systematic exercise and physical education.[13]

Educational institutions thus were a focal point for Victorian anxieties, as well as sites for special bodily intervention. In particular, physical education was an essential aspect of the goals of nineteenth-century higher education for both men and women, and was inscribed into the charter and physical fabric of colleges.[14] Yet, as Daphne Spain argues, these efforts focused more acutely on female students, as campus administrators, health professionals, and architects united to design and implement a constellation of organizational, behavioural, and spatial tactics to protect female students and promote physical activity.[15] These efforts to ensure that women's physical health, bodily aesthetic, and reproductive powers would not be harmed by the strains of study thus tempered efforts to provide women with access to higher learning equal to that enjoyed by men.[16]

College gymnasia: Architecture and experience

College gymnasia, often among the first buildings to populate new campuses, were the focal point and architectural home of gymnastic and calisthenic educational programmes aimed at strengthening and remediating student bodies.[17] Indicative of the Victorian emphasis on 'sound minds in sound bodies', college gymnasia housed special apparatuses for physical training and postural remediation, both of which were intended to strengthen and train student bodies to withstand the rigors of scholarly life.[18] What follows is a study of the history of these spaces and practices of physical education at Vassar College, as conducted through the lens of experience. This experiential approach introduces, against a background of institutional changes (coeducation and the rise of physical education) and organizational practices (campus architecture and administrative interventions), a somatic level of analysis to show how these broad forces were projected and enacted on physical bodies. In other words, this approach illuminates how the design of campus buildings facilitated specific physiological forms and practices through a host of interventions to protect female bodies. These interventions relegated women to a 'separate sphere' within these new institutions and created, in the words of Susan Cahn, 'new forms of discipline and control for the modern female body'.[19]

Like other nineteenth-century buildings, gymnasia were designed to be experienced in a particular way. Therefore, foregrounding experience, as both envisioned and realized, fosters an emic understanding of these spaces.[20] Historian Heather Munro Prescott argues that concern for the health and fitness of female bodies influenced both the design and curriculum of co-educational and women's colleges through the development of health and physical education programmes and their requisite spaces.[21] Indeed, Matthew Vassar established health as a 'MAXIM in the college' and in so doing, positioned architecture as an active participant in the moral, intellectual, and physical education of students.[22] Specifically, Vassar's spaces of physical instruction functioned as both protectors of student bodies and a means to convey the founder's lofty vision to an ever-vigilant public. Uniting these aims, in the design of his namesake college, Vassar envisioned a specific, productive bodily experience for students. The 1865 prospectus for Vassar College, a document intended to articulate Vassar's vision to Trustees (and a public audience beyond the college), elaborated these ideas: 'Recreations, particularly in the open air, will not only be encouraged, but regulated and taught, and ... required of all the students. ... For this purpose, in-doors, the spacious and cheerful corridors of the college edifice, and, without, the beautiful college park, will afford unusual advantages'.[23] Here, we see both the design of the campus and organization of student experience taking physical movement for granted by recognizing it as an essential part of women's higher education.

Yet, while these aforementioned experiences inspired Vassar's architecture, the writings of John Raymond suggest that the college's founders wrote the prospectus tentatively, experimentally even, with the expectation that it would be modified with further experience.[24] This underscores the value of reading Vassar's buildings as architectural hypotheses, refined over time in dialogue with observed use and impact. The experiential approach employed in this chapter thus extends conventional architectural analysis by providing a methodological entrée into not only how campus buildings were designed to be inhabited, used, and experienced, but also how they were actually experienced, and how their use inspired new functions and forms.

Gymnasia were a primary component of the experience of nineteenth-century higher education. For students, gyms were a place for daily instruction, periodic bodily assessments, and both compulsory and recreational physical activity, while for staff, gymnasia were spaces for professional practice and advancement. Beyond the campus, for a watchful public, gyms were a focal point for both criticism and praise. Below, I explore how these three groups experienced Vassar's nineteenth-century gymnasia. In so doing, I demonstrate not only the ways in which the campus's numerous spaces of physical instruction were designed with a particular bodily experience in mind, but also how the actual experience of these spaces challenged or confirmed these ideals. Indeed, the same spaces and programmes borne of conservative criticisms of women's education also made room for women to participate in new social, physical, and professional experiences at educational institutions across the United States. Thus, a final implication of an experiential focus is its insistence on illuminating alternate, and at times conflicting, readings of the built environment. This includes both the ambivalence of built forms and the layered meanings of intended and actual experiences.[25] Ultimately, I argue that Vassar's gymnasia were ambivalent spaces at once innovative and conservative, and constricting and freeing of female bodies.

Vassar College: Main Hall and campus grounds (1865)

By prioritizing student health, Matthew Vassar placed under the jurisdiction of the college not only the development of student minds, but also student bodies. In particular, he sought to ensure that women would 'go forth physically well-developed, vigorous, and graceful … with enlightened views and wholesome habits as regards the use and care of their bodies'.[26] To carry out this goal, Vassar looked to the regulation of the physical and social experience practiced in women's seminaries to inform the design and administration of Vassar College.[27] In particular, Vassar's prospectus outlined a range of interventions such as 'the sanitary regulation of the college', 'the provision of healthy foods and facilities with proper ventilation', and 'regular instruction in … the laws of health'. Additionally, Vassar called for explicit times for walking and resting, as well as 'a regular medical examination' and 'regular instruction … in the arts of Riding, Flower-gardening, Swimming, Boating, Skating, and other physical accomplishments suitable for ladies … and promotive of bodily strength and grace'.[28] This regime echoes the sheltered, supervised experience which Dr Edward Hammond Clarke advocated, yet also conveys a more reforming emphasis on physical education.

Matthew Vassar chose a remote, pastoral site for the college; he lauded the campus 'grounds, with their miles of gravelled paths' and 'ample and pleasant' playgrounds, as spaces in which women could exercise 'without danger of outside intrusion'.[29] Similar to 'Pleasure Ground' parks of the era, the campus's pastoral setting offered fresh air (the 'air cure', according to historian Harvey Green), and its expansive views were, to one nineteenth-century journalist, an 'essential means for fashioning noble women out of impulsive girls'.[30] Thus, beyond mere enjoyment, Vassar's 'pleasant' environment was designed to encourage the moral and physical uplift of women.

Vassar's first building, Main Hall (1865), elaborated these ideas. Whereas nineteenth-century men's colleges were comprised of a community of buildings (e.g. Jefferson's 'academical village' at the University of Virginia), a single, impressively scaled structure contained all of Vassar's functions in order to shelter female bodies.[31] An 1873 *Scribner's Magazine* article described the immense size of Main Hall: 'The main edifice is almost five hundred feet in length ... and ... the height of the centre building from the foundation to the top of the dome is ninety-two feet'.[32] Main Hall was one of the largest structures in the United States at the time of its construction; its scale evocative of an optimistic tone regarding the value of women's education.[33] Yet Main's vast size also ensured that women were literally surrounded,

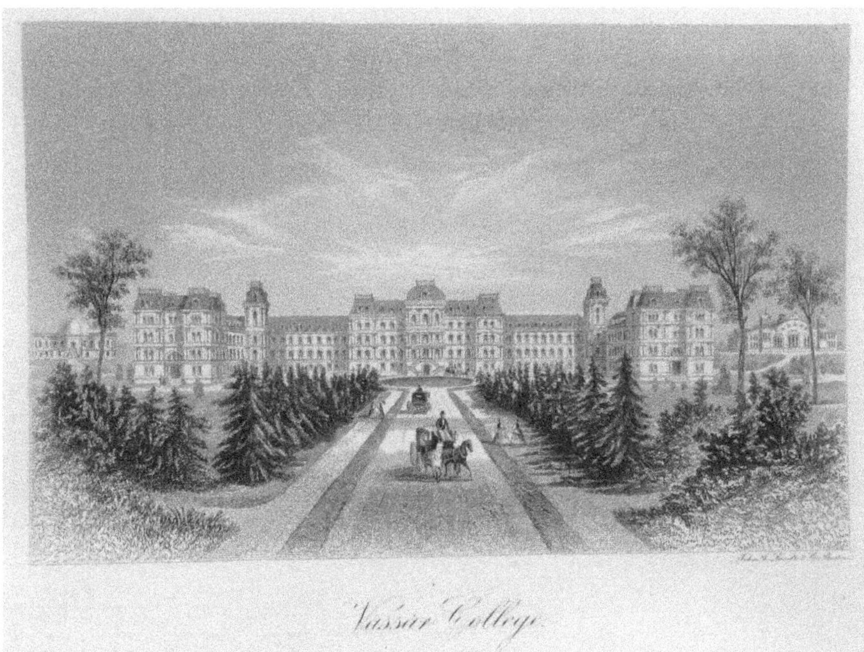

FIGURE 11.1 *Engraving of Vassar College by John A. Lowell and Co. (n.d.). Main Hall is at the centre and the Calisthenium to the right. This etching conveys an idealized pastoral setting and depicts women walking along paths. Photographs, Folder 3.4, Vassar College Archives and Special Collections, Poughkeepsie, New York.*

protected, by architecture and the building's fashionable Second Empire-style façade, modelled after the Tuileries in France, enclosed a seminary-like interior (Figure 11.1). With these architectural references, Vassar deliberately appealed to public sentiment by offering familiar forms to help spectators interpret this novel institution as viable and socially valuable.[34]

Renowned architect James Renwick, Jr. (1818–95) designed Main Hall. Renwick's impressive resume, including the design of the Smithsonian Institution Building (1847–55) in Washington, D.C., Grace Church (1843–6), and St. Patrick's Cathedral (1858–79), both in New York City, undoubtedly lent prestige to this novel institution and edifice.[35] Main housed a diverse programme: dormitories, classrooms, the library, a museum, and space for physical education. Regarding the latter, the building's corridors were particularly commodious – 'twelve feet in width and eighty-five feet in length' – for the singular purpose of housing physical activity in inclement weather.[36] Though these hallways were a less formal space for physical activity than the exercise rooms built in Vassar's subsequent gymnasia, they demonstrate nevertheless the urgency of this concern for women's health and hygiene.[37] Vassar's first gymnasium was slated to open just a year later, yet the need for daily exercise could not wait.

As a result of the need to accommodate spacious hallways in Main, however, one journalist observed that 'two out of three of the sleeping rooms' in the building's dormitories had 'no windows except into the corridors' (Figure 11.2).[38] Thus, poor ventilation was the price to pay for what Harvey

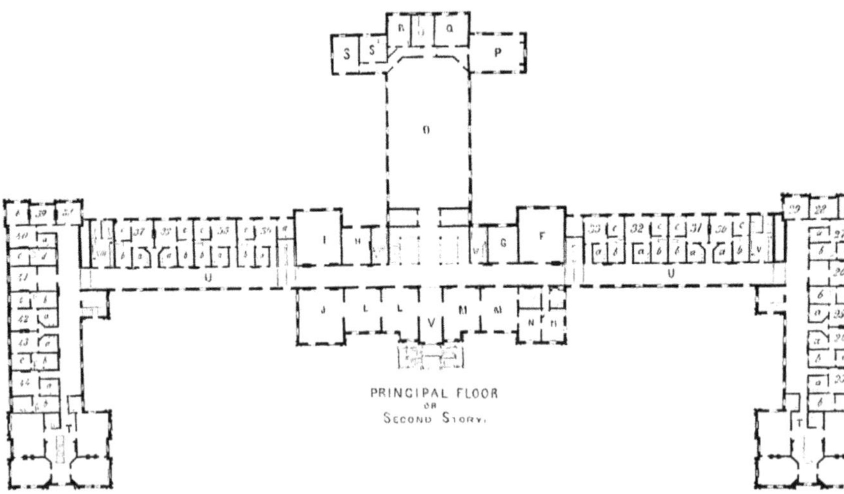

FIGURE 11.2 *Floor plan of Main Hall (1865). The bedrooms adjacent to Main's spacious corridor did not directly open to the outside. Benson J. Lossing,* Vassar College and Its Founder *(New York: C. A. Alvord, 1867), 122, https://catalog.hathitrust.org/Record/001452512. Image courtesy of HathiTrust.*

Green calls 'the movement cure', a surprising fact given Victorian beliefs of the dangers to health of 'bad air'.[39] We see in this example how competing priorities were negotiated architecturally: ultimately, the desire for women's daily exercise trumped a primary preoccupation of the era. An 1875 article in *Harper's Magazine* only mentions this point in passing; thus, we can assume that Main's design did not cause significant alarm in the eyes of the public.[40] Indeed, though outdoor exercise and the intake of fresh air were preferable at the time, designing spaces for exercise into the building likely appeased critics by ensuring that women could engage in daily physical activity, rain or shine.

The Calisthenium (1866)

The first catalogue of Vassar College reported that in addition to Main Hall, 'A still larger and more costly building is in the process of erection to contain a riding-school ... a Gymnasium Hall ... and ... the School of Physical Training'.[41] Costing approximately $46,000, Vassar's first gymnasium, the Calisthenium (1866), represented a significant investment in and more formal addition to the College's physical education programme. Vassar explained the wisdom of this investment, stating that the 'income from the pupils engaged in ... physical exercises will more than pay the interest on its cost'.[42] Local architect J. A. Wood (1837–1910) designed the Calisthenium, a building the *New York Times* praised for its unrivalled beauty.[43] The Calisthenium's intricate Lombard Romanesque façade complemented the grandeur of Main Hall, yet its interior was more revealing of student experiences and broader social ideas about proper exercises for women. The Calisthenium housed a music hall, gym hall, bowling alley, and riding school with horse stables.[44] These activities were considered 'suitable for ladies' and informed by the ambivalent desire to strengthen female bodies without risk to feminine form, fertility, and practice.[45] In this way, the Calisthenium was consistent with what Terry Kogan has observed as a broader effort to maintain in novel nineteenth-century institutions a 'separate sphere' to reinforce women's domestic role by encouraging activities that would not compromise their traditional association with the home and family.[46]

Matthew Vassar envisioned that 'the Gymnasium will be furnished with every apparatus required to make it attractive and useful, and placed under the direction of an experienced and successful Lady Instructor. The system of light gymnastics as perfected by Dio Lewis will be taught to all in the college'.[47] The choice of physical culture advocate and educator Diocletian (Dio) Lewis's regime was appropriate in that he advocated an integrated education similar to that promoted by Vassar Lewis saw calisthenics as a way to achieve both muscular strength and 'the mental and moral improvement of practitioners'; he was also an outspoken critic of women's corsets.[48] His instruction manuals recommended specific costumes for exercise and conveyed images depicting women wearing loose trousers akin to the bloomers Elizabeth Cady Stanton advocated as part of women's liberation.[49] Similarly, at Vassar, with the adoption of Lewis's calisthenic regime in 1866 came standard, 'loose-fitting', uniforms.[50] One student remarked in a letter home that 'it is a pleasant site to see so many … girls dressed in the pretty costume practicing' exercises in the gymnasium, and another wrote of a walk on the grounds for which 'we most of us wore our gymnasium suits, which added very much to our ease & comfort'.[51] These uniforms offered brief respite from corsets during exercise, yet the use of corsets persisted, as evidenced by an 1876 letter from a student who requested a pair of 'underwaists' that were 'long enough to cover my corsets'.[52] Thus, though exercise costumes were a liberating bodily experience for Vassar women, they were a limited intervention: experienced only within the context of gymnastic space and activity.

Female physical educators implemented Lewis's regime at Vassar, an example of how nineteenth-century college gymnasia were significant spaces for women's professional advancement and venues for resistance against critics. [53] In campus gymnasia, female faculty, staff, and physicians administered surveys and authored studies, informed by physical inspections and anthropometric measurements, which they used to refute popular claims about the impact of intellectual work on women's bodies. For example, an 1885 Association of Collegiate Alumnae (ACA) survey stated unambiguously that the 'admitted experience of 705 college women … proves that instead of a loss there was an absolute gain of physical strength'.[54] In a 1900 report to Vassar College president James Monroe Taylor (fl. 1886–1914), Harriet Ballintine (1865–1951), director of the gymnasium, noted similar gains. Ballintine wrote that

> the following statistics are of interest in showing the increase in strength test examinations. … 164 students examined 12 whose total strength did not improve. These twelve are students who have spinal curvature or are otherwise abnormally delicate. Average gain of 151 students who did improve … 45.1 kilos. Some improved as much as 128 kilos. … Only one 5 kilos.[55]

This data-driven approach appealed to Victorian audiences, as did ACA chairman Annie Howes's conclusion that 'a higher education for women is in harmony with the vast law of the survival of the fittest'.[56] Less equivocal were findings that college-educated women had fewer children than their uneducated counterparts. Still, advocates were quick to point out that those who did have children typically birthed healthier offspring. In this way, data both quelled and fuelled critics.

Alumnae Hall (1889)

Twenty years after the founding of the college, and armed with decades of data showing the benefits of educating women's minds and bodies, Vassar alumnae articulated the need for a new gymnasium in order to keep current with other, newly opened women's colleges (e.g. Wellesley, 1875 and Smith, 1883).[57] In 1885, the Alumnae Association began a long process to raise the $20,000 they estimated a new, state-of-the-art, gymnasium building would cost – an effort that culminated with the 1889 erection of Alumnae Hall.

To inform the design of Alumnae Hall, the Building Committee, a sub-committee of the Alumnae Association's Committee on Physical Culture, visited other gymnasia. The Committee then 'invited architects to bid on account of evidence given of their ability' and experience designing gymnasia. All bids far exceeded the Committee's $20,000 budget, so the Association revised their expectations and solicited a second proposal from architect William Tubby (1858–1944), who had contributed to the design of Pratt Gymnasium at Amherst College.[58] This process conveys the degree to which, by the 1880s, architects specialized in the design of gymnasia, and suggests a reading of Alumnae Hall as illustrative of a burgeoning architectural typology, rather than the vision of a single benefactor. Ultimately, the Committee made compromises in the building's programme and material, as well as the sum paid to the architect, but achieved nevertheless a beautiful, though modest, Richardsonian Romanesque-style building that met 'all the salient needs' of their original vision: the final sum came to $21,900.[59] Importantly, to look beyond the modesty of Alumnae's brick façade is to see the historical and social significance of a reforming nineteenth-century gymnasium funded entirely by women.[60]

In Alumnae Hall, large windows, evocative of Roman baths, ensured ample sunlight and ventilation, both components of the hygienic school construction which Dr Mary Taylor Bissell advocated.[61] Notably, the gymnasium housed a 47- by 27-foot swimming tank (a novel feature for the campus and the largest collegiate indoor pool at the time); positioned nearby were twenty-five needle baths and forty dressing rooms.[62] Also on the first floor, an exercise room accommodated individual exercise and physical examinations (Figure 11.3). A stage for dramatic productions and netting for tennis practice occupied a large room on the second floor. Though a standard practice beginning in 1884, physical examinations were not assigned a specialized space until the construction of Vassar's third gym, Kenyon Hall, in 1933.[63] Therefore, photos, student diaries, and departmental reports bring this practice to light.[64]

Though lauded at the time of its founding as an innovative building, conservatism persisted. The large windows of Alumnae Hall, positioned high on the wall, provided abundant light, but also shielded exercising bodies from public view. Further, Alumnae's dressing rooms, located

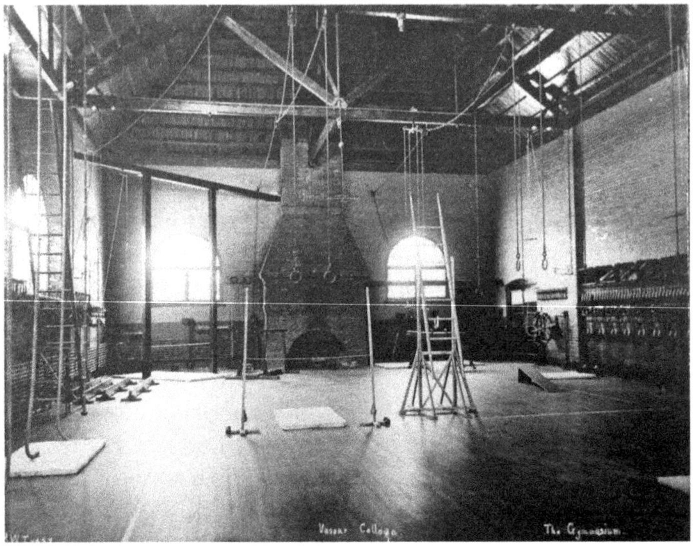

FIGURE 11.3 *Alumnae Hall (1889) exercise and examination room with large, arched windows positioned high on the wall. Photographs, Folder 2.24, Vassar College Archives and Special Collections, Poughkeepsie, New York.*

adjacent to activity areas, meant that women no longer had to walk from their residences to the gymnasium in their exercise costumes, as at the Calisthenium, a fact that had provoked concerns about health and propriety. Instead, exercise costumes and the bodies that bore them were enclosed within Alumnae Hall. Historian Roberta Park explains that in Victorian America, while men performed sport to an assumed audience of spectators, social convention kept women's sports 'cloistered' and away from public view.[65] Therefore, though it offered new experiences for women, Alumnae Hall was emblematic of a broader paradox in Victorian society: it reflected a conservative response to the very social and bodily freedoms it fostered.[66]

Women accessed unprecedented educational opportunities at Vassar. However, interventions designed to enforce a sheltered experience tempered women's entry into this novel institution. Curfews, the setting of the college, and the design of its spaces of physical instruction, ensured that the physical activities in which women could engage were limited in space and time, and kept from public view.[67] Yet student letters and diaries suggest that exercise in fact represented something more significant: it was a social as much as physical experience, with students reporting who they walked with and where.[68] Historian Janice Ross argues that nineteenth-century women had to negotiate this divide between their increasing independence and persistent beliefs about their physical frailty and unsuitability for public life.[69] Indeed, we have seen above how Vassar women, who walked and exercised in loose-fitting costumes, navigated this contradiction between conservative Victorian ideologies and their own, lived experiences.[70]

Conclusion

To architectural historian Paul Venable Turner, a unique feature of American universities is their inclusion of facilities and amenities geared towards the extracurricular experience.[71] In this chapter, we have seen how this emphasis on experience became embodied, or seen through the lens of bodily movement and physical health, in nineteenth-century America. At Vassar College, gymnasia and other spaces of physical instruction were designed to shape the student experience and, by extension, female student bodies. Yet the actual use of these buildings and the social and spatial significance created therein were more complex and ambivalent than their built forms suggest.

How, then, might we understand the collegiate gymnasium, as realized at Vassar and as a building type that emerged in the nineteenth century? First, physical education programmes and spaces, originating from concerns for student health and burgeoning scientific and public health theories and practices, both reflected and resisted popular anxieties. Physical education and health services, a twin endeavour in the nineteenth century, functioned as mechanisms of control, manifested through discourses and programmes employed to create 'ideal' student bodies, such as self-care regimens and the ordering and enclosure of new forms of bodily movement in college gymnasia and playing fields.[72] In particular, controlling female bodies on campus became, to many, a way to control the larger body politic by ensuring strong, healthy graduates capable of producing and raising healthy children.[73]

Yet, as demonstrated above, college gymnasia also offered an unprecedented forum for women to leverage their professional expertise to express different theories of women's health than their male counterparts promoted. In fact, gymnasia were spaces for professional freedom, innovation, and the assertion of specialized knowledge. These facts are not easily read in plans and sections, so a broader focus on the experience of gymnasia brings these layered and complex meanings to the fore to show how these spaces functioned as an *empowered* 'second sphere' where women exercised specialized expertise and pursued professional advancement.[74] This, then, is not simply a tale of the subjugation of women's bodies by popular scientific and medical understandings, but one of subjectivity and instrumentality. Further, as students engaged in daily exercise, gymnasia became a significant component of the collegiate experience, remarked upon in student diaries, letters, and scrapbooks highlighting the 'indelible memories' of campus.[75] Focusing on the experience of Vassar's gymnasia rightfully foregrounds these central spaces of campus life and, in so doing, informs a view of nineteenth-century education that tends to both mind and body.

Ultimately, this study proves the value of an experience-driven approach in historical scholarship, one that reads buildings as both cultural texts and active participants in social life. Indeed, historian Helen Lefkowitz Horowitz has noted that a focus on experience deepens questions of meaning, as buildings, not simply a single statement or hypothesis on the part of the designer, are re-framed, re-considered, and re-imagined through their continual use and active interpretation by a range of actors.[76] Thus, focusing on experience necessarily requires ones empathy for the voices that emerge in diaries, photos, articles, and other media to tell their tale of the places they inhabit and create through bodily and spatial practice. These sources are architectural, as much as social texts, and convey how a range of users continuously make and re-make spaces through their continual use, experience, and interpretation.

PART FIVE

Epilogue

CHAPTER TWELVE

Material, movement and memory: Some thoughts on architecture and experience in the age of mechanization

G. A. Bremner

I should like to draw all St Mark's, and all this Verona stone by stone, to eat it all up into my mind, touch by touch.[1]

—JOHN RUSKIN (1852)

The chapters comprising this volume have worked to reinforce the indelible connection between architecture and its experience. They have proven a useful reminder that the former can hardly be understood in all its complexity and variability without reference to the latter and vice versa. What is clear is that the idea of 'experience' in architecture comprises multiple and complex registers, ranging from the raw physical (visceral) to the sub-conscious psychological. How we *experience* architecture not only relates to being in or near a building or buildings (or representations thereof), but is also entirely subjective.

In concluding this volume, I want to offer some open-ended thoughts, or perhaps even speculate, on the role that certain fundamental characteristics of the Victorian age had on how we calibrate, and potentially extend, what we consider to be the relationship between 'architecture and experience'. I shall ask what are some of the underlying pre-conditions that led to the advent of what we now term Victorian architecture, such as mechanization and technical innovation, and how these might be factored into an interpretation that foregrounds the object nature of environments as a basic component of how we experience a building. The relationship between architecture and its materiality is a central theme in this speculation, but ideas of movement and memory emerge as equally important in articulating the narrower and wider parameters of what is understood by experience in this context.

In offering these thoughts I will deal specifically with architecture and building production during a time that corresponds roughly with the period spanning the early to mid-Victorian generation (c. 1830–85). This was a period when the advances in technology to which I shall refer were felt most starkly and forcefully. This period can be described quite properly as the first 'age' of full and efficient mechanization, propelled as it was by the effective harnessing of stream-powered locomotion.

Experiencing architecture: Subjective versus objective

The first thing that would perhaps strike anyone with more than a basic understanding of Victorian architecture is just how determined the Victorians were to 'manufacture' different types of prescribed behavioural experience through built form. This readiness to organize space in such a programmatic fashion relates to Victorian ideas concerning social reform and discipline, which were in turn associated with Victorian society's highly developed and religiously inflected sense of moral purpose. Architecturally speaking, Victorian views on the ordering of modern society were loosely translated through the propagation of bourgeois mantras such as 'improvement' and 'self-help', and made manifest in the planning of an array of institutional typologies, ranging from workhouses, prisons, and asylums, to schools, churches, factories, and museums.[2] The idea that one of architecture's primary functions was to act upon the body and the mind in a very deliberate manner was quite well understood during the Victorian age.[3] In this respect architecture was as much a quasi-social science as it was an art form; indeed, architecture was seen to have very real moral agency, not just passively but actively, too. This is something that sociologists have since come to describe as the built environment's capacity for behavioural 'structuration' and 'reproduction'.[4]

When speaking of such experience, however, we must also consider the full gamut of our senses. What is it, for example, to *hear*, *smell*, or even *touch* a Victorian building? What would it have been like to walk down a typical

Victorian street, where the incidence of large domesticated animals, such as horses, or the burning of fires, was much greater than it is today? Or, to enter a Victorian church, which was often poorly lit and dusty; or, in the case of Roman Catholic or High Anglican spaces, filled with the odour of incense? This recalls Eric Wilson's study of the sonic landscapes of seventeenth-century London, and how the sounds of the city were fundamental to its experience. Such experience is associated with what Wilson calls 'differentially inhabited space': spoken, touched, traversed, vacated, and so on, that constitutes the city more as an 'event' than as an object.[5]

The idea of architectural experience also forces us to consider the precise nature and extent of that experience, as the 'constituencies' or stakeholders involved enter and leave at various stages in the process, from design, through construction, to eventual use. These people, too, *experience* architecture in different ways, and at different times (not always coincident), whether in the abstract or more concretely.[6] Indeed, although it may be a commonplace to observe that the meaning of architecture shifts away from the architect and his intentions as it is ascribed and re-ascribed through use and experience, it is no less true. This pertains also to identity formation, and to what some have referred to as gender performance and self-fashioning, particularly in the Victorian age.[7]

And what about the emotional reception of architecture during the Victorian period, especially in relation to the pronouncements of critics such as John Ruskin, articulated as they often were in passionate and affected prose: to what extent is emotional response and attachment to buildings crucial to the way we understand our experience of architecture? Is not this emotional dimension fundamental?[8] This reminds one of the 'poetics of space', as Gaston Bachelard once described it, and how truly difficult it is to make sense of our experience of architecture, being at the 'fuzzy' intersection between time and space, memory and the present.[9] Bachelard hints at what might happen if we lose or are detached from our images and associations relating to architecture, especially the domestic scene or 'home': that some kind of psychosis will ensue. In other words, the images we absorb and store through our experience of home are in many ways essential to our core being.

Whether one wishes to understand architecture in this way is of course dependent upon whether one accepts its phenomenological potentiality. But where Bachelard was surely right, whatever perspective one wishes to take, is in stating that in order to get to the bottom of the problem of 'architectural experience' we must move beyond description and address what he terms the 'primal virtues' of architecture.[10]

This idea concerning the 'primal' may be understood as drawing us nearer a material engagement with the building as 'object'. Juhani Pallasmaa has observed, for instance, how recognition of the 'materiality' of buildings through our senses 'enables us to become convinced of the veracity of matter'. Natural materials such as stone, brick, and wood allow our senses to 'penetrate' their surfaces in various ways, with texture becoming important to how we interpret the objective nature of buildings. Such engagement evokes, among other things, the idea of time in the way these natural materials express their age and history through marks, erosion, wear, and staining. In this sense architecture has the capacity (indeed, responsibility, some would argue) to awaken our psychological need to experience the reality of our rootedness in the continuity of time.[11] It is precisely this desire to experience architecture in a multi-sensory way that highlights the quote by John Ruskin at the beginning of this chapter: seeing is only partially believing; full and verifiable experience requires sensory emersion, a kind of bodily intercourse with the object-nature of building.

But I would go one step further in ascribing a more radical objectivity to how we should understand the experience of architecture in the Victorian age. Such 'experience', I would argue, is fundamentally dictated by this material sensibility in its comprehension (witting or otherwise) of architecture as matter, leading us (the observer) to ponder the very nature of that matter. In other words, such an object-oriented approach helps us appreciate better the conditions that structure specific forms of experience and behaviour. Thus, if experiences associated with a Victorian building are perceived to be qualitatively different from that of any other, before or since, is it not the material specificity (object*ness*) of that building that plays a major role in both framing and characterizing those experiences?[12] This of course leads to a more basic question still: what *is* Victorian architecture? Or, to get rather more technical, what constitutes its ontology?

We have now set before us two distinct, if related, conditions of architectural 'experience': buildings as experienced in terms of time-space interaction (a kind of 'lived' or *sense*-experience), and the building as experiential artefact (material object/structure). Crudely put, this amounts to a fundamental dualism between subject and object. The one is concerned with social structuring and reproduction via subjective encounter and conditioning, the other with being and essence in the nature of object*ness*. As buildings are both made and capable of making, these forms of experience are not necessarily coincidental. While the former has more to do with the manipulation and negotiation of space by the subject *per se*, the latter is capable of impressing a certain quality on that space and its associated lived experience(s) merely in its being as the material object-entity which frames and gives shape to that experience. In its radical object*ness*, a building may be seen to become an essential, if oblivious, actor in the structuring of architectural experience.

In recognizing this dualism, I wish to explore briefly in this chapter two aspects of Victorian architecture as it pertains to experience: material and memory. My exploration of these aspects will be built loosely around the phenomenon of movement, which is a factor that not only became ever more prevalent, but also dominant during the Victorian period, encompassing everything from transportation to production. Indeed, this new age of mechanization, as it might be described, had by the mid-century come to characterize (if not capture) daily existence to a large extent, transforming both modes and means of living. Architecture, too, was subsumed by this phenomenon, leading, as will be discussed, to a whole new ecology of architectural procurement, fabrication, and assembly. If nothing else, this disrupted age-old ligatures between labour, materials, and location in the design and construction of buildings (particularly beyond vernacular tradition and practice), leading to a radically altered object status for architecture during this period – one from which it would never revert.

Moreover, the opening up and 'shrinking' of the wider world through the development of modern transport technology (rail and steamship) meant that growing numbers of Britons immigrated abroad, many to various parts of Britain's burgeoning colonial empire. As Lord Salisbury observed in 1871, the 'greater means of locomotion of the present day mark out the future to be one of great empires'.[13] But these increasingly easy, cheap, and speedy means of long-distance movement affected the sense-experience both of space and the built environment, connected as these means were with the amplification of perception and identity.[14] The potentiality of lived experience in the world suddenly became much greater for many more people. Here memory (of one's self and one's home) was engaged and exercised in ways, and at ever enhanced scales, that were peculiarly modern. On the one hand, this may have facilitated a certain continuity of experience, as one moved from, say, Manchester to Melbourne; but, on the other, it simultaneously created new challenges with respect to identity, belonging, and well-being. The hope of a new and more prosperous life beyond the British Isles may have beckoned, but the stress of severe dislocation also took its toll, for better or worse.

In what follows, both the material status of architecture and its memorial capacity are considered in the context of this underlying dynamic of movement, as a fundamental conditioning factor of modern experience.

Material matters: The new ontology of Victorian architecture

My first observation on this would simply be that much of what we call Victorian architecture today was a new kind of experience *in* and *of* itself, outside and beyond any interaction with it; that is, merely in its being. As mentioned earlier, by 'Victorian' here I mean Britain post c. 1830; by architecture, primarily architect- or engineer-designed structures, especially from the so-called High Victorian period (c. 1850–75) onwards. This sense of being was 'new' owing to the nature or essence of its objectness. In order to understand what is meant by this we need to approach Victorian architecture chiefly, and in the round, as the outcome of mechanized and energy-intense industrial processes. Although both steam power and mechanization were present to varying degrees prior to 1830, levels of consistency, reliability, and scale were comparatively insignificant. A typical building from the late Georgian period may have included some materials and processes reliant on mechanized technology, but speed and efficiency relating to these were low. Thus, working from the premise of the early twentieth-century historian and theorist Sigfried Giedion, the principal factor in making sense of this *new* condition is that of movement.[15] One of the seminal experiences of the Victorian age was the sensation and effects of the increased speed, frequency, and distance of movement. Indeed, as Giedion himself proclaimed in 1948, in explaining the history of industrial modernity we must 'begin with the concept of Movement'.[16]

In this schema 'movement' is directly associated with what may loosely be identified as 'mechanization'. This phenomenon of increased movement, according to Giedion, led to a kind of disorientation and dislocation; what he described as an increasing split between thought and feeling, which is what truly characterized 'modernity' and therefore modern experience. Although industrialization is often pointed to as a key driver of change in the Victorian landscape, both urban and rural, it was transportation technology in particular that was in so many ways, and at so many levels, the harbinger and agent of that change, not just practically and economically, but also visually and emotionally. One need only recall J. W. M. Turner's *Rain, Steam, and Speed* (1844) to get a sense of what is meant by this (Figure 12.1). There is not only something exhilarating about this picture, but also something quite foreboding and portentous. Like so many things Victorian, there are conflicting sentiments at play. On the one hand the painting captures the dynamism of a new age, as the locomotive punches through the mist and rain, suddenly emerging upon us; on the other, and at the same time, there would appear to be nothing we can do to halt its unrelenting progress – we feel trapped, if not paralysed, by its frenzied momentum. It evidently captures something of the 'disorientation and dislocation' that Giedion found so essential to the experience of modernity.

Steam power was of course responsible for this transport revolution. But, again, it is not its invention that matters here, as that had happened a long time before. Rather, as Lewis Mumford and others have observed, it was the effective and efficient harnessing of that power – on a massive, transformative scale – that mattered.[17] This is precisely what the Victorians mastered: inventing and refining processes that gave unprecedented access to huge quantities of energy and power, thus generating a *tipping point* with respect to the manner, speed, and quality of mechanized production. Needless to say, the effects of this transformation were felt widely and profoundly throughout the Victorian building world.

None of this is to suggest, however, that technology and its fetishization during the Victorian period was unproblematic (practically speaking), or taken wholly for granted, either by those who possessed it, or by the public who were its key beneficiary.[18] The rise of steam power and the

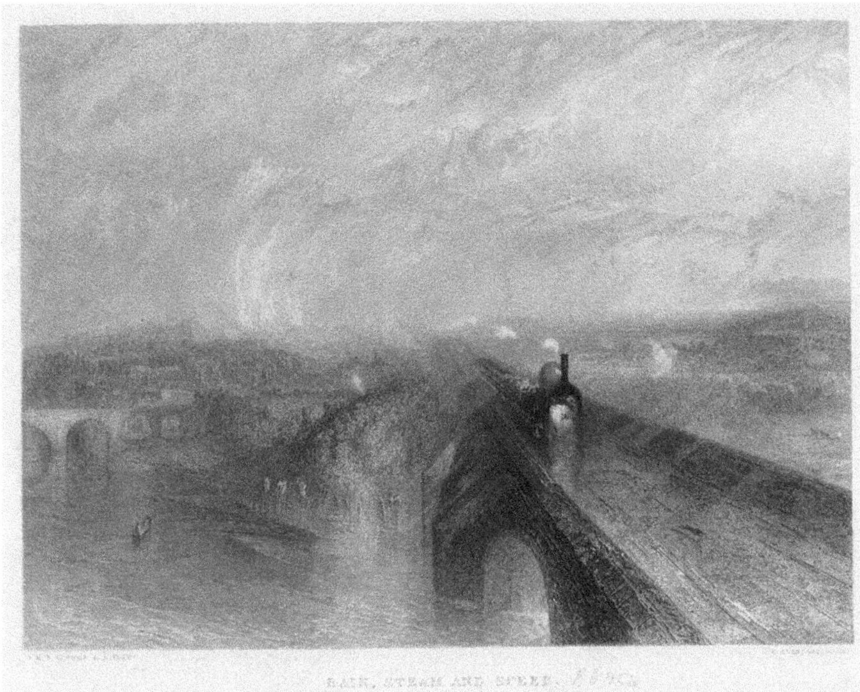

FIGURE 12.1 *J. M. W. Turner,* Rain, Steam and Speed, *engraving after Turner by R. Brandard, 1859–61. By permission of the Tate, London.*

technological transformations that accompanied it did not go unchallenged, nor was it appreciated in an unmediated manner. As Ben Marsden and Crosbie Smith have shown, although the sway of such technology was both demonstrative and acclaimed, trust was required to establish its claims to increased performance and productivity, and even then caution was often exercised.[19] Nevertheless, although the road to realizing the full capability of steam power was neither straight nor smooth, when we think of 'Victorian architecture' in this context, it is possible, if not desirable, to understand it as a peculiar outcome of this technological shift. The accumulated effects were the same, in a sense, as Giedion's explanation of something as mundane as the transformation in texture and appearance of bread following the introduction of industrial processes, and the symbolic implications that had as a fundamental marker of social and civilizational change; or, similarly, how Mumford pointed to pen technology in making the same point (Figure 12.2).[20]

In considering this technological shift in relation to Victorian architecture, I am not referring to the rather obvious formal transformations or material additions that literally changed the face of architecture at this time, such as the advent and availability of decorative cast iron in industrial quantities,

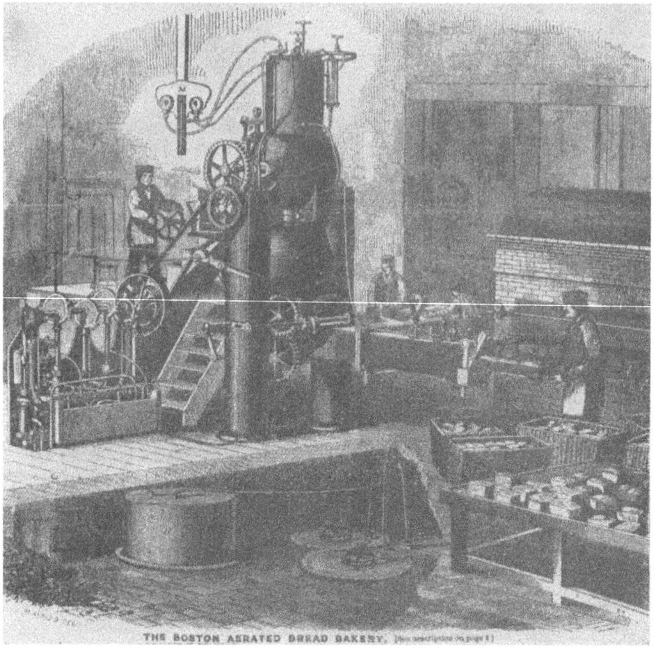

FIGURE 12.2 *'Dr. Dauglish's bread-making apparatus', early 1860s, from* American Artisan and Patent Record, *vol. 3 (May 1866). Although this device was not particularly successful, many like it changed the face of baking in the nineteenth century.*

although these changes can hardly be ignored. Rather, I am concerned with what might be described as a more fundamental, first-order transformation. In other words, not that decorative cast iron appeared, but why industrially produced materials like it appeared, and how this affects our understanding of Victorian architecture as a phenomenon.

A useful way of contextualizing this is via what professionals today call the embodied energy of building production and life-cycle analytics; or, in laymen's terms, what can be referred to as a building's 'carbon footprint'.[21] Consider stone, for instance: we tend to forget just how crucially the development of the Victorian stone industry (to take but one example) relied on new mechanized technologies developed in the Victorian era. The rather sudden appearance of a hitherto unobtainable array of decorative and common building stones, not just from within Britain, but from across Europe and the Mediterranean basin, in quantities and of a quality and at a cost that made them available for general use for the first time, was entirely dependent upon speed of movement resulting from a particular input of energy, whether in terms of new steam-driven cutting and polishing technology, or reliable steamship transportation, or indeed, the laying out of higher- and higher-speed rail networks. Having gone through these various processes, quarried and dressed stone, transported to site and ready for use, had accrued a considerable amount of embodied energy.

The same may be said for the humble brick. Cheap coal, in conjunction with fast and efficient transportation, led to the production and distribution of bricks on a previously unprecedented scale. Steam-powered manufacturing equipment, such as pressing machines, along with coal-fired kiln technology, meant a more consistent, reliable, and cheaper product that could be

TABLE 12.1 Coal production in England, Wales, and Scotland ('000 tons) and related statistics

	(1) 1560s	(2) 1700–9	(3) 1750–9	(4) 1800–9	(5) 1850–9
Coal production ('000 tons)					
England	177	2,200	4,295	11,195	51,650
Wales	20	140	220	1,850	13,400
Scotland	30	300	715	2,000	9,000
Total	**227**	**2,640**	**5,230**	**15,045**	**74,050**
Energy consumption, England and Wales (petajoules)					
Draught animals	21.1	32.8	33.6	34.3	50.1
Population	14.9	27.3	29.7	41.8	67.8
Firewood	21.5	22.5	22.6	18.5	2.2
Wind	0.2	1.4	2.8	12.7	24.4
Water	0.6	1.0	1.3	1.1	1.7
Coal	6.9	84.0	140.8	408.7	1,689.1
Total	**65.1**	**168.9**	**230.9**	**517.1**	**1,835.3**
Total less coal	**58.2**	**84.9**	**90.1**	**108.4**	**146.2**
Other related energy estimates, England and Wales					
Coal as a percentage of total energy consumption	10.6	49.7	61.0	79.0	92.0
Per caput energy consumption (gigajoules)	20.5	29.6	35.1	52.3	96.5

Source. E. A. Wrigley, *Energy and the English Industrial Revolution*, p. 37.

transported with relative ease wherever needed, leading to faster and more cost-effective construction.

Indeed, this is a scenario that could be applied to any number of common building materials and processes from the Victorian period, such as encaustic tiles, plate-glass, terracotta, or slate roofing, to name but a few. All required unprecedented inputs of energy and processing, either in their making or procurement, to attain the necessary tolerances in quality pertaining to their product-level status. Again, the key factor connecting all these various processes and procedures was movement; or more precisely, *mechanized* movement.

Thus, if we are to say that Victorian architecture is a truly different kind of architecture, offering a unique kind of experience, then it must relate to this basic question of ontology: that is to say, Victorian architecture's essential being as an object. This is firmly connected to the phenomenon of movement, and the systems created as a consequence of movement through new and evolving networks of production that acquired the power to facilitate novel forms of procurement and assemblage. In short, I am describing here what amounts to a fundamentally new dynamic in which disparate events and processes and even technologies, which in and of themselves may have seemed unimportant, or were perhaps not even connected previously, suddenly coalesce (as Giedion would have said) with explosive force. This was a dynamic forged quite literally in the heat of the permanent transformation of the British economy from an organic fungible one, to a mineral-based consumptive one, driven and dictated by coal-fired industry (see Table 12.1). This most crucial and decisive moment was that 'tipping point' which opened up a new world of possibilities in architecture, and with it a whole new array of experiences, not just of the buildings themselves, but through involvement in the process at every step along the chain of production (quarrymen, miners, train engineers, factory labourers, machine operators, builders, etc.).

Through an embracing of these changes, Victorian architecture took the embodied energy of architectural production to a whole new level, which is partly what makes it unique. It is so much the by-product of stream power and, in particular, of movement on a previously unimagined scale: materials coming from far away, procured under increasingly mechanized conditions, entailing the consumption of fossil-fuel energy in huge quantities. As a result, the *substance* of architecture was transformed. It was now a new kind of *product*, with novel material qualities. Scale, height, precision, speed, hardness, smoothness, colour, and consistency had all proliferated appreciably, just as architecture's network of supply lines had both stretched and converged. With this came new standards of measurement, accuracy, and thus predictability in construction practice, burdening architecture with the ever greater prospect of creating a better ordered and regulated society. This included the technological transformation of architecture itself, as buildings were subjected increasingly to scientific methods and scrutiny.[22]

The object-nature of architecture was utterly recast.[23] The energy inputs were considerable and exponential. In this sense Victorian architecture was a new and peculiarly modern kind of artefact: an 'architecture of energy'.

To get a sense of the rapidity and comprehensiveness of this transformation, one only need peruse the classified sections of the major architecture magazines and journals of the period, between about 1850 and 1860. The number and frequency of advertisements for mass-produced and/or machine-finished building componentry is precipitous. Indeed, the effects of specialized manufacturing and standardization – that which the likes of Ruskin and Morris riled so passionately against – on both the profession and industry of architecture were such that by the late 1850s one could find complete, generic specifications for middle-class suburban villas published in the leading architecture journals.[24] Such predictability and systematization was only possible owing to the assurances that came with the new ecologies of mechanization and movement that grew up around and thus constituted the Victorian building world, creating regimes of efficiency and economy that became increasingly difficult to deviate from in any meaningful way.[25]

It was precisely this problem that Ruskin and Morris came up against, leading ultimately to their call for a return to hand-craftsmanship to fall flat (at least for the majority). Smart architects like G. G. Scott, William Butterfield, G. F. Bodley, and G. E. Street understood the advantages of this new ecology for architecture, without forsaking design. Architecture became an 'art' that sought after a certain 'craftsmanship' through aim and assemblage rather than through procurement and production. As Michael Hall has recently observed in his study of G. F. Bodley, it was precisely the assemblage of new materials of this kind (both in terms of range and quantity, as well as technological precision) that made Victorian architecture 'modern'.[26] The precise combination of materials that comprised much Victorian architecture, both manufactured and mechanically procured, was simply not possible before this time. In short, the machine had triumphed: the architect had little choice but to respond.

Taking an outward glance to contemporary architectural discourse for a moment, we can see that such dramatic transformations in the possibilities for, and material conditions of, architecture played into ideas of 'development'. What seems important here is not so much that architects and theorists such as Benjamin Webb, A. J. B. Beresford Hope, and G. E. Street, among others, came up with this theory – that they spoke of architecture in their own age breaking the shackles of stylistic copyism by reaching out to varied and diverse traditions, the world over – but that they came up with it at all.[27] What, it might be asked, was their frame of reference? To begin with, the idea of development implied that of change. In this equation stasis was not only considered injurious, but fatal. Thus, the theory of 'development' was in many ways a consequence of outward pressures – material, intellectual, and economic – that had come to act upon architecture by the mid-century, resulting from this 'new world' that the Victorian's had constructed and come to inhabit, both literally and metaphorically. It was an expansive world, one that suddenly seemed smaller and within reach (and control) in ways that it had not before; a world that was at their disposal (or so they believed), providing new and enlarged horizons for architecture; a world that would bring wholly new experiences. Therefore, when Webb or Beresford Hope talked of adapting, manipulating, and/or camouflaging old (or 'pure') forms of architecture for novel and unprecedented purposes (and conditions), they were really responding to a world that had changed, recognizing that the discourses and practice of architecture had been left somewhat flatfooted by these changes. The impetus behind 'development' was at least in part about catching up and being modern.

Worlds beyond: Movement and memory in 'Greater Britain'

In knitting this world together, outward movement was also important, not just of people but of products, too. On one level this concerns the circulation of objects ('things') as part of a process of extending and thus reproducing the material presence (and experiences) of Victorian architecture abroad, whether into formal or informal imperial/colonial contexts. As Gary Magee and Andrew Thompson have recently observed, the export of decorative encaustic tiles to the wider British world, such as those produced by Mintons or Maw & Co., is evidence of imperially networked consumer habits at work, or the exercising of what they identify as a kind of 'transnational Anglo culture'.[28] This could apply to any number of British manufactured architectural products shipped abroad at this time, including the innumerable items of cast-iron that were exported to the colonies by manufacturers such as MacFarlane & Co. of Glasgow; or the distribution of stained-glass windows throughout the colonial world by the likes of Clayton & Bell.[29]

This extension, or outward movement, abroad also concerned sensory experience. Wherever one might have cared to go in the wider British world during the Victorian period, one would continually encounter strikingly familiar spatial experiences, whether in churches, domestic settings, shopping arcades, train stations, clubs, or government buildings. This pertained to certain behavioural patterns and expectations too, as well as the impressions affected by common decorative regimes or schemae. There was evidently a desire to create, or manufacture, certain kinds of experiential continuity across vast expanses of space, with such experiences becoming markers (symbols even) of that common 'Anglo culture' to which Magee and Thomson refer.

For instance, the noted English historian James Froude (1818-94), writing of Melbourne in the early 1880s, observed how 'it is English life over again: nothing strange, nothing exotic, nothing new or original ... All was the same

– dress, manners, talk, and appearance'.[30] Likewise, as noted in the *Home Friend* of the same city as early as 1853: 'To the immigrant from the United Kingdom this is not a *foreign* land'.[31] Again, although perhaps exaggerated, such witness suggests that, in many respects, there was both a desire and a practical need to create such experiential continuity.

However, despite this need for cultural continuity, acquiring it was not always so easy. The exponential movement of people and goods over vast distances that came to characterize the nineteenth century – the phenomenon James Belich has described as 'mass transfer' – also incurred a certain degree of what might be called loss of experience. [32] This was in effect a form of *dis*orientation produced via radical dislocation. The problems, indeed crises, that such acute dislocation was seen to cause in the refashioning of identity were, under certain circumstances, quite pronounced. Homesickness, and a yearning for the historically saturated environs of Europe, often caused a kind of neuroses with respect to residing in non-European lands. As we shall see, this anxiety had a distinct architectural dimension.

At the same time, relocation of this kind was also potentially re-constitutive, bearing the possibility of escape, reform, and renewal. Indeed, the very process of moving itself, whether across vast tracts of land or over great oceans, was an experience that led to a kind of transformation of personality and purpose that would ultimately affect attitudes towards architecture. This process of transfer often helped dissolve old, parochial, and local-communal concepts of identity while simultaneously, and by necessity, constructing new, larger, mass-composite ones. This was akin to people perhaps once identifying themselves as being from a particular town, say, in Yorkshire or Perthshire, and considering themselves English or Scottish, to suddenly seeing themselves as part of a much bigger 'British' world, what Charles Dilke conveniently termed 'Greater Britain'.[33]

The mechanisms of this transformative process have recently been explored by Tamson Pietsch through her reconstruction of the journeys of the Scotsman James Thomas Wilson in the 1880s from rural Dumfriesshire to the port cities of China and Australia.[34] What emerges from this example are two issues in particular, which are somewhat symbiotic. The first is that, again, the 'mass transfer' of people at this point in history, aided by mass-produced steam-powered shipping, brought people together from across the British Isles, into confined spaces, for long periods, in ways that they might not otherwise experience in their lives.[35] The second is the effect this had on their identities in these new worlds opening up before them. For some this movement was about new, life-changing and life-affirming opportunity; for others, like Dilke or Froude, a new kind of 'grand tour'. Either way, the result was an emergent and enlarged sense of identity.

For instance, as Pietsch observes, at the beginning Wilson was acutely aware of and sensitive to his Scottish heritage. In the journal from his first voyage to China in 1884 he records how 'I have realised the difference to me between a Scotsman & Englishman … Mr Moss the Chief Engineer is a

"Fifer" & we can generally find something to talk about. The difference is not only that of subject but of the very mode of thought'.[36] But as time went by, and from voyage to voyage, Wilson experienced very different peoples and places as he stopped off in Egypt, Sri Lanka, Singapore, and Hong Kong on his way to Australia. In the process Wilson's sense of parochial identity slowly gave way to recognition of a palpably common linguistic, political, cultural, and religious commonality between himself and his fellow passengers from the British Isles, one that he had not really considered before. They were no longer alien, but 'brothers' in a common cause. Pietsch articulates this transformation in the following terms:

> [H]is [Wilson's] journeys ... had directly shaped the way in which he understood himself and the world. In the shifting space of the ship he had encountered places and people against which he articulated his own identity, coming to see liberal Protestant Britain as the driving force of moral and material progress. Travelling the routes of global empire, he had translated his Scottish world into a British imperial one, and this gave him a way of thinking about himself that helped him negotiate its opportunities and expanses. ... Slipping between articulations of 'nation' and 'empire', for him the notion of a British 'organism' became a way to make sense of the spatial dislocations of his own life.[37]

Flicking through the pages of Froude's *Oceania* or Dilke's *Greater Britain*, one gets a very similar sense of the coming together of these different people and the effect this has: that these people are suddenly entering upon a world and an enterprise that is much bigger than themselves, beyond their local identities and concerns. Importantly, movement is the key medium through which they experience this realization and subsequent transformation.

As mentioned, such movement and its processes of self-reflection and identity transformation also had a negative dimension. For many of those making such a life-changing journey, what came with the huge excitement was an equally powerful sense of trepidation, if not downright fear. What was really on the other side, awaiting them, in what might as well have been another planet? They may well have had support in these new lands, a network of friends and relations, but could they really know what awaited them?

Here we arrive at the idea of absence, or what might be termed in this context the 'affliction of loss'. This takes us back to Bachelard, to the significance of 'home', and the power of memory that in so many ways constitutes our identity. What happens when home is suddenly absent? The effects of this were something that I came across quite frequently in the course of researching my book on the history of colonial church architecture.[38] This may be identified as a kind of sustained grief or trauma caused by what one historian has described as the 'tyranny of distance'.[39] There are many examples of this that one could point to, but an indicative one is the experience of the Rev. John Armstrong, who became bishop of Grahamstown in the Eastern Cape in 1853.

Armstrong had been plucked for the job from the bucolic bliss of Tidenham in rural Gloucestershire, where he was vicar of the local church. He was part of that new breed of colonial clergyman who had been raised on the bread and meat of Tractarianism. It was only natural that men like Armstrong carried with them ideas on architecture with which they had been inculcated while at Oxford or Cambridge. It was clear to such men that architecture had a certain mnemonic capacity in recalling to mind the time-honoured, if gentle, patterns of English civilization – patterns that, if increasingly traumatized by the assault of industrialization in Britain, might be recreated in new lands afresh.

Indeed, not long after arriving in southern Africa, the first Anglican bishop of the Cape Colony, Robert Gray, established a monthly publication entitled *The South African Church Magazine and Ecclesiastical Review*. Perusing this publication one is struck by what can only be described as the palpable anxiety over the colonial environment that characterizes its pages – a kind of hyper-urgent, even obsessive, desire to recreate the precepts of the old world in the new: to create history and culture where none were perceived to exist. Its editor, the indefatigable William Abiah Newman, was a keen ecclesiologist, regularly including articles on church architecture. His own writing on the subject was rather turgid, expressing a deeply romantic, near saccharine adoration for the image of English medieval architecture.[40] His prose is shot through with poetic yearnings:

> Though deprived of the pleasing delight we once had in our college long vacations, of a kind of pilgrimage to our old English Churches, tracing, or pleased to think that we traced, the pure specimens, and first gradations of the Saxon, Norman, early English, Perpendicular ... We have seen these venerable piles in all lights and shades, – in the stillness of the moonlight, – and beneath the glare of a noon day-sun; – and in every hour, and in every light, they are alike the same, – solemn, grand, sublime. They are still daguerreotyped on our minds. We see them yet, – years and distance and other scenes cannot erase them; they are *palimpsests*; – other impressions may for a time usurp their place, – but Memory's alchymy [*sic*] can in a moment restore them.[41]

Such evocative sentiments were no doubt exacerbated by the feelings of cultural and spiritual isolation Newman experienced upon his arrival in Africa. Not only were there few Anglican priests of his ilk, but even fewer Anglican churches worthy of the name (at least in his view). As with *The Ecclesiologist* magazine back in England, connections were regularly made in the *South African Church Magazine* between English medieval architecture and identity.[42] The suggestion here was that, although not perfect, English medieval forms were, to quote one of its authors, 'best adapted to the English national character in its noblest features, and so the best to be perpetuated in English colonies'.[43]

Perhaps forewarned of the emotional distress he would experience in a place like Africa, Armstrong came armed with a number of idyllic scenes containing churches that he had sketched before departing England. What is interesting about these sketches is that they do not seem to have been destined as models for new churches in the Cape, but instead something more akin to mementos, like some kind of emotional crutch or *aide-memoire*, to which he could turn during moments of homesickness. If not intended as the basis for future designs, these scenes would have provided psychological comfort by way of 'Memory's alchymy', to use Newman's term, amid the harsh, sun-scorched, and oftentimes barren environs of the Eastern Cape. Armstrong would later lament the trials of living in an environment destitute of 'antiquity', insisting that, 'no one knows what it is like to live in a country where there is nothing old 'til they have tried it'.[44] Armstrong's loss was a loss of architecture. What he experienced was, as Pallasmaa has argued elsewhere, recognition of how the formation of our identities is in continual dialogue with our physical and architectural settings.[45]

This experience obviously had quite an effect on Armstrong. His reaction is not uncommon. For instance, we might recall, among other such episodes, John Coleridge Patteson's initial encounter with the chapel at St John's College, Auckland, in 1855. Recognizing in it a certain familiarity, like a long-lost friend, he observed how the dim light of the interior likened it to a 'really good ecclesiastical building in England. ... Here my eye and mind rested contentedly and peacefully. ... [It] is already dear to me.'[46] This experience affected Patteson precisely because it stood in stark contrast to his other encounters in what was essentially a harsh and alien landscape.

To get a sense of what such experiences must have meant to sojourners like Armstrong, Newman, and Patteson, one need only consider the paintings of a colonial artist such as John Glover. The scenes of pioneering colonial endeavour in Van Diemen's Land captured by Glover accrue their power by a calculated staging of a nascent and fragile European civilization in its attempts to overcome and thus 'cultivate' the vast and bewildering landscapes of *terra australis*. There is something of the sublime here as, in many cases, the lineaments of European life – cottages, farmhouses, and insubstantial towns – are shown pitted against the awesome and potentially insuperable forces of the natural world (thick, impenetrable forests, and huge, apparently unending mountainous terrain). Although this unforgiving landscape might be wrested into submission, as Glover's images promise, the threat of reclamation by the wild and foreboding forces of nature seem ever present. The tension that comes with such colonial existence is palpable.[47]

Therefore, despite what Dilke, Froude, and others may have said about society in the colonies in terms of its resemblance to that of the 'mother country', there was always something disturbingly unfamiliar lurking in the shadows or just over the horizon. Thus, the uncanniness of colonial society was at once reassuring and unsettling. In this respect memory was key to establishing the perceptive registers by which meaningful experiential engagement with the colonial world could take place. This was both positive and negative, with the built environment being among the most significant and conspicuous determinants of that experience, as it harnessed the momentum of the modern world in its attempts to push back the frontiers of 'civilization'.

* * *

In conclusion, I would merely observe that these differing facets of architectural experience I have touched upon here, material and memory, may at first sight seem unrelated, if not opposed. But if looked at and understood through the prism of the fundamental, underlying phenomenon of increased mechanization and movement that so characterized the period in question, then they emerge as but different registers for experiencing the same general sensation of industrial modernity, and how this impacted on architecture: its production and use. This pertains not only to Victorian architecture as a new and basic form of experience *in* and *of* itself, but also how experience of such architecture (and architecture in that age) was truly global as opposed to merely local in both its aspirations and its reality.

NOTES

Introduction

1 As observed in Barry Bergdoll's lecture, 'Views across the Rhine: interchanges in French and German architectural thought, 1828-1879', delivered at the Museum of Architecture and Design, Ljubljana, Slovenia (26 February 2014).

2 The terms 'Enlightenment' and 'Industrial Revolution' are highly contested and it is not our intention to assess their validity here, but from an architectural perspective the increase of mechanized labour, industrial production techniques, and the construction of experimental, empirical frameworks of knowledge seem highly pertinent to our study.

3 See Carla Yanni, 'Development and display: Progressive evolution in British Victorian architecture and architectural theory', in Bernard Lightman and Bennett Zon (eds), *Evolution and Victorian Culture* (Cambridge: Cambridge University Press, 2014), 227–60; Carla Yanni, 'Nature and nomenclature: William Whewell and the production of architectural knowledge in early Victorian Britain', *Architectural History*, 40 (1997), 204–21.

4 On professionalism, see Frank Jenkins, 'The Victorian architectural profession', in Peter Ferriday (ed.), *Victorian Architecture* (London, 1963), 39–49; John Wilton-Ely, 'The Rise of the Professional Architect in England', in Spiro Kostof (ed.), *The Architect: Chapters in the History of the Profession* (New York: Oxford University Press, 1977), 180–208; Katherine Wheeler, *Victorian Perceptions of Renaissance Architecture* (Farnham: Routledge, 2014), 3–4; on scientific knowledge and architecture, see Edward J. Gillin, *The Victorian Palace of Science: Scientific Knowledge and the Building of the Houses of Parliament* (Cambridge: Cambridge University Press, 2017).

5 Barry Bergdoll, *European Architecture, 1750-1890* (Oxford: Oxford University Press, 2000), 2–3; on new building types, see 173–205; on technology and architecture, see 207–38; also see Thomas A. Markus, *Buildings and Power: Freedom and Control in the Origin of Modern Building Types* (London: Routledge, 1993), xix; on technology and knowledge, see Andrew Saint, *Architect and Engineer: A Study in Sibling Rivalry* (New Haven: Yale University Press, 2007), esp. 486–9; on history and architecture, see Frank Salmon, *Building on Ruins: The Rediscovery of Rome and English Architecture* (Aldershot: Lund Humphries Publishers, 2000).

6 Augustus Welby Pugin, *Contrasts: Or, a Parallel between the Noble Edifices of the Middle Ages, and Corresponding Buildings of the Present Day; Shewing the Present Decay of Taste* (London: Charles Dolman, 1841), 2–6.

7 Argued in John Ruskin, *The Nature of Gothic: A Chapter from the Stones of Venice* (London: G. Allen, 1900); on the implications of Ruskin's teachings, see Michael Hall, 'What Do Victorian Churches Mean? Symbolism and sacramentalism in Anglican Church architecture, 1850-1870', *Journal of the Society of Architectural Historians*, 59, no. 1 (March 2000), 78–95.

8 Michel Foucault, 'The Eye of Power', in Colin Gordon (ed.), *Power/Knowledge: Selected Interviews and Other Writings, 1972-1977*, trans. Colin Gordon, Leo Marshall, John Mepham, and Kate Soper (New York: Pantheon Books, 1980), 146–65, 148.

9 On the exertion of control through spatial apparatus, see Michel Foucault, *Discipline and Punish: The Birth of the Prison*, trans. Alan Sheridan (Harmondsworth: Penguin, 1977), 200–6; Paul Hirst, 'Foucault and Architecture', *AA Files*, no. 26 (Autumn 1993), 52–60, 56; on the architecture of eighteenth-century hospitals, see Michel Foucault, 'The incorporation of the hospital into modern technology', trans. Edgar Knowlton, Jr., William J. King, and Stuart Elden, in Jeremy W. Crampton and Stuart Elden (eds), *Foucault and Geography* (Aldershot: Ashgate, 2007), 141–51.

10 Foucault, 'The Eye of Power', 149.

11 Heghnar Zeitlian Watenpaugh, *The Image of an Ottoman City: Imperial Architecture and Urban Experience in Aleppo in the 16th and 17th Centuries* (Leiden: Brill, 2004), 26–7; also see Michel de Certeau, *The Practice of Everyday Life*, trans. Steven Rendall (Berkeley: University of California Press, 1984).

12 Thomas F. Gieryn, 'What buildings do', *Theory and Society*, 31, no. 1 (February 2002), 35–74, 41–4; for this constructivist approach to technology, see Thomas P. Hughes, *Human-Built World: How to Think About Technology and Culture* (Chicago: University of Chicago Press, 2004); also see William Whyte, 'How do buildings mean? Some issues of interpretation in the history of architecture', *History and Theory*, 45 (May 2006), 153–77.

13 Henri Lefebvre, *The Production of Space*, trans. Donald Nicholson-Smith (Oxford: Blackwell, 1991), 1–11, esp. 7; summarized well in, Chris Butler, *Henri Lefebvre: Spatial Politics, Everyday Life and the Right to the City* (Abingdon: Routledge, 2012), 37–54; usually 'space' and 'place' are differentiated by treating the former as an abstract and the latter as the specific. Casey challenges this assumption by arguing that rather than place devolving from space, place is itself primary, in Edward S. Casey, 'How to get from space to place in a fairly short stretch of time: Phenomenological prolegomena', in Steven Feld and Keith H. Basso (eds.), *Senses of Place* (Santa Fe: SAR Press, 1996), 13–52.

14 William Whyte, *Unlocking the Church: The Lost Secrets of Victorian Sacred Space* (Oxford: Oxford University Press, 2017), 23–4; compare to, Bonna D. Westcoat and Robert G. Ousterhout (eds.), *Architecture of the Sacred: Space, Ritual, and Experience from Classical Greece to Byzantium* (Cambridge: Cambridge University Press, 2012).

15 Laura H. Hollengreen, 'From medieval sacred place to modern secular space: Changing perspectives on the cathedral and town of Chartres', in Dana Arnold

and Andrew Ballantyne (eds), *Architecture as Experience: Radical Change in Spatial Practice* (London: Routledge, 2004), 81–108.

16 For example, we might refine the idea that, 'A city like any building or work of art is a text that can be read and is open to multiple and varied interpretations', in Dana Arnold, *Re-presenting the Metropolis: Architecture, Urban Experience and Social Life in London, 1800-1840* (Aldershot: Ashgate, 2000), xix.

17 Crosbie Smith and Jon Agar, 'Introduction: Making space for science', in Crosbie Smith and Jon Agar (eds), *Making Space for Science: Territorial Themes in the Shaping of Knowledge* (Basingstoke: Macmillan Press Ltd, 1998), 1–23; Charles W. J. Withers and David N. Livingstone, 'Thinking geographically about nineteenth-century science', in David N. Livingstone and Charles W. J. Withers (eds), *Geographies of Nineteenth-Century Science* (Chicago: University of Chicago Press, 2011), 1–19.

18 Carla Yanni, *Nature's Museums: Victorian Science and the Architecture of Display* (London: Athlone Press, 1999), 1–7; other excellent examples include, Simon Schaffer, 'Physics laboratories and the Victorian country house', in Smith and Agar (eds), *Making Space for Science*, 149–80; Sophie Forgan, '"But indifferently lodged ...": Perception and place in building for science in Victorian London', in Smith and Agar (eds.), *Making Space for Science*, 195–215; Peter Galison and Emily Thompson (eds.), *The Architecture of Science* (Cambridge, MA: MIT Press, 1999); Sophie Forgan, 'Context, image and function: A preliminary enquiry into the architecture of scientific societies', *British Journal for the History of Science*, 19, no. 1 (March 1986), 89–113, 91; Sophie Forgan, 'The architecture of display: Museums, universities and objects in nineteenth-century Britain', *History of Science*, 32, no. 2 (1994), 139–62; Graeme Gooday, 'Placing or replacing the laboratory in the history of science?', *Isis*, 99, no. 4 (December 2008), 783–95.

19 Whyte, *Unlocking the Church*, 29–30; Heinz Otto Sibum, 'Reworking the mechanical value of heat: Instruments of precision and gestures of accuracy in early-Victorian England', *Studies in History and Philosophy of Science*, 26, no. 1 (1995), 73–106.

20 Juhani Pallasmaa, *The Eyes of the Skin: Architecture and the Senses* (Chichester: Wiley, 2012), 13; experience can also be a form of knowledge, arguably opposite to the analysis of experts and consisting of wisdom accrued from failures and in response to changes. Experience, as a knowledge type, can be speculative, storytelling, narrative, or myth, as explored in James G. March, *The Ambiguities of Experience* (Ithaca: Cornell University Press, 2012), 1–4.

21 See also, Kate Goodwin, 'Curator's preface', in Kate Goodwin (ed.), *Sensing Spaces: Architecture Reimagined* (London: Royal Academy of Arts, 2014), 35–7; Philip Ursprung, 'Presence: The light touch of architecture', in Goodwin (ed.), *Sensing Spaces*, 39–53; Sarah Robinson and Juhani Pallasmaa (eds.) *Mind in Architecture: Neuroscience, Embodiment, and the Future of Design* (Cambridge, MA: MIT Press, 2015).

Chapter 1

1 James Fergusson, *The Illustrated Handbook of Architecture: Being a Concise and Popular Account of the Different Styles of Architecture Prevailing in All Ages and Countries* (London: John Murray, 1859), xxv.

2 Shadworth Hodgson, *Philosophy and Experience: An Address Delivered Before the Aristotelean Society October 26, 1885 (Being the Annual Presidential Address for the Seventh Session of the Society)* (London: Williams & Norgate, 1885), 6.

3 Shadworth Hodgson, *The Metaphysics of Experience* (London: Longmans, Green, 1898), 4 vols. On Hodgson, see W. J. Mander, 'The philosophy of Shadworth Hodgson', in W. J. Mander (ed.), *The Oxford Handbook of British Philosophy in the Nineteenth Century* (Oxford: Oxford University Press, 2014), 173–88.

4 Roger Dixon and Stefan Muthesius, *Victorian Architecture* (London: Thames and Hudson, 1985), 8.

5 See, for instance, Herbert Lindenberger, 'Experiencing history', *Scandinavian Studies*, 62, no. 1, 9 (Winter 1990), 7–23.

6 For a pioneering effort to integrate urban and sensory history to uncover the specificities of nineteenth-century experience, see Nicolas Kenny, *The Feel of the City: Experiences of Urban Transformation* (Toronto: University of Toronto Press, 2014).

7 David Anton Spurr, *Architecture and Modern Literature* (Ann Arbor: University of Michigan Press, 2012), 164.

8 Ellen Eve Frank, *Literary Architecture: Essays Towards a Tradition* (Berkeley: University of California Press, 1983), 117–33.

9 Marcel Proust, *The Way by Swann's,* trans. Lydia Davis (London: Penguin, 2003), 61–9. For the original version, see Marcel Proust, *À la recherches du temps perdu 1* (Paris: Gallimard, 1987), 58–66.

10 Jean Autret, William Burford, and Phillip J. Wolfe, ed. and trans. Marcel Proust, *On Reading Ruskin: Prefaces to La Bible d'Amiens and Sésame et les Lys with Selections from the Notes to the Translated Texts* (New Haven and London: Yale University Press, 1987).

11 Robert Fraser, *Proust and the Victorians: The Lamp of Memory* (London: St Martin's Press, 1994), 58.

12 John Ruskin, *Collected Works*, ed. E. T. Cook and Alexander Wedderburn, vol. 33 (London: George Allen, 1903–12), 130.

13 See, for instance, Emily Eells, *Proust's Cup of Tea: Homoeroticism and Victorian Culture* (London and New York: Routledge, 2002), 34–5.

14 On the link between these themes and associational psychology, see George L. Hersey, *High Victorian Gothic: A Study in Associationism* (Baltimore and London: Johns Hopkins University Press, 1972). There is, of course, a very rich literature on romanticism and the Gothic. Useful ways in, include Jan De Maeyer and Luc Verpoest (eds), *Gothic Revival: Religion, Architecture,*

and Style in Western Europe, 1815-1924 (Leuven: University of Leuven Press, 2000); Georg Germann, *Gothic Revival in Europe and Britain: Sources, Influences and Ideas*, trans. Gerald Onn (Boston: MIT Press, 1973); Rosemary Hill, *God's Architect: Pugin and the Building of Romantic England* (London: Allen Lane, 2007).

15 I explore some of this further in 'Architecture' in Joel Rasmussen, Judith Wolfe and Johannes Zachhuber (eds), *The Oxford Handbook of Nineteenth-Century Christian Thought* (Oxford: Oxford University Press, 2017), 171–84.

16 Arthur Schopenhauer, *The World as Will and Representation*, vol. i, trans. E. F. J. Payne (New York: Dover, 1969), 215.

17 In thinking about this topic, I have benefitted hugely from reading Zeynep Çelik Alexander's 'Kinaesthetic Impulses: Aesthetic experience, bodily knowledge, and pedagogical practices in Germany, 1871-1918' (PhD thesis, MIT, 2007), now published as *Kinaesthetic Knowing: Aesthetics, Epistemology, Modern Design* (Chicago and London: University of Chicago Press, 2017).

18 Harry Francis Mallgrave and Eleftheios Ikonomon (eds), *Empathy, Form, and Space: Problems in German Aesthetics, 1873-1893* (Santa Monica: Getty Center For The History Of Art, 1994).

19 Jonathan Crary, *Suspension of Perception: Attention, Spectacle, and Modern Vulture* (1999; Cambridge, MA and London: MIT Press, 2001), 29.

20 See also Christopher Curtis Mead, *Charles Garnier's Paris Opera: Architectural Empathy and the Renaissance of French Classicism* (Cambridge, MA: MIT Press, 1991), 253.

21 Sigfried Giedion, *Space, Time and Architecture: The Growth of a New Tradition* (5th ed.; Cambridge, MA: Harvard University Press, 1967), 2.

22 Ute Engel, 'The foundation of Pevsner's art history: Nikolaus Pevsner, 1902-1935', in Peter Draper (ed.), *Reassessing Nikolaus Pevsner* (Aldershot: Ashgate, 2004), 29–55. See also Marlete Halberstma, 'Nikolaus Pevsner and the end of a tradition: The legacy of Wilhelm Pinder', *Apollo*, 137 (1993), 107–9.

23 On this, see Michael Jackson, 'Introduction: Phenomenology, radical empiricism, and anthropological criqtue', in Michael Jackson (ed.), *Things As They Are: New Directions in Phenomenological Anthropology* (Bloomington and Indianapolis: Indiana University Press, 1996), 1–50.

24 Ruth Harris, *Lourdes: Body and Spirit in the Secular* Age (London: Allen Lane, 1999), xvii.

25 Ruth Harris, *The Man on Devil's Island: Alfred Dreyfus and the Affair that Divided France* (London: Allen Lane, 2010). On emotions more generally, see Jan Plumper, *The History of Emotions: An Introduction* (Oxford: Oxford University Press, 2012), trans. Keith Tribe.

26 Leif Jerrram, 'Space: A useless category for historical analysis?' *History and Theory*, 52 (2013), 400–19.

27 I explore this more fully in 'Buildings, landscapes, and regimes of materiality', in *Transactions of the Royal Historical Society* (forthcoming).

28 Dan Hicks and Mary C. Beaudry, 'Introduction: Material culture studies: A reactionary view', in Dan Hicks and Mary Beaudry (eds), *The Oxford*

Handbook of Material Culture Studies (Oxford: Oxford University Press, 2010), 1–24, 3.

29 Denis Hollier, *Against Architecture: The Writings of Georges Bataille*, trans. Betsy Wang (Cambridge, MA: MIT Press, 1989), ix.

30 Andrew Ballantyne, *Deleuze and Guattari for Architects* (Abingdon: Routledge, 2007).

31 W. J. T. Mitchell, *What Do Pictures Want? The Lives and Loves of Images* (Chicago: University of Chicago Press, 2005).

32 Gieryn, 'What Buildings Do', 37; Momin Rahman and Anne Witz, 'What really matters? The elusive quality of the material in feminist thought', *Feminist Theory*, 4 (2003), 243–61.

33 For a wonderfully rich range of readings, see Victor Buchli, *An Anthropology of Architecture* (London: Bloomsbury Academic, 2013).

34 Pierre Bourdieu, 'The Kabyle house or the world reversed', in *The Logic of Practice* (Oxford: Polity Press, 1980), 271–83.

35 Richard Jenkins, *Pierre Bourdieu* (London: Routledge 1992), 74.

36 Pierre Bourdieu, *Distinction: A Social Critique of the Judgement of Taste*, trans. Richard Nice (London: Routledge, 1986).

37 Stuart Elden, *Mapping the Present: Heidegger, Foucault and the Project of a Spatial History* (London: Bloomsbury, 2002), 3–4.

38 Tony Bennett and Patrick Joyce (eds), *Material Powers: Cultural Studies, History and the Material Turn* (London: Routledge, 2010).

39 Chris Philo, 'Michel Foucault', in Phil Hubbard and Rob Kitchin (eds), *Key Thinkers on Space and Place* (London: Sage, 2011), 162–70, 169.

40 This paragraph reuses material in my article, 'How do buildings mean', 153–77.

41 De Certeau, 'Spatial stories', 87.

42 Edward W. Soja, *Postmodern Geographies: The Reassertion of Space in Critical Social Theory* (London and New York: Verso, 1989), 247.

43 Lefebvre, *Production of space*, 7.

44 Amos Rappaport, *The Meaning of the Built Environment: A Nonverbal Communication Approach* (Tucson: University of Arizona Press, 1990).

45 Timothy Mitchell, *Rule of Experts: Egypt, Techno-Politics, Modernity* (Berkeley: University of California Press, 2002).

46 S. Gunn, *The Public Culture of the Victorian Middle Class* (New York: Manchester University Press, 2000), 53. See also Deborah Epstein Nord, *Walking the Victorian Streets: Women, Representation, and the City* (Ithaca and London: Cornell University Press, 1995), ch. 1 for an analysis which relies more on Baudrillard and Benjamin.

47 Patrick Joyce, 'What is the social in social history', *Past and Present*, 206 (2010), 213–48, 226–7. See also his *The State of Freedom: A Social History of the British State Since 1800* (Cambridge: Cambridge University Press, 2013), 19–20.

48 See my 'Re-enchanting the World: Buildings, Landscapes, and Regimes of Materiality'.

49 Bruno Latour, *Reassembling the Social: An Introduction to Actor-Network-Theory* (Oxford: Oxford University Press, 2005), 79.

50 Gieryn, 'What buildings do', 35–74.

51 Albena Yaneva, *The Making of a Building: A Pragmatist Approach to Architecture* (Oxford: Peter Lang, 2009), 199.

52 Helen Gittos, *Liturgy, Architecture, and Sacred Places in Anglo-Saxon England* (Oxford: Oxford University Press, 2013), 18.

53 Gieryn, 'What buildings do', 43.

54 Tim Ingold, *Making: Anthropology, Archaeology, Art and Architecture* (London: Routledge, 2013), 85.

55 Sewart Brand, *How Buildings Learn: What Happens After They're Built* (London: Penguin, 1995), 188.

56 Bruno Latour and Albena Yaneva, '"Give me a gun and I will make all buildings move": An ant's view of architecture', in Reto Geiser (ed.), *Explorations in Architecture: Teaching, Design, Research* (Basel: Birkhäuser GmbH, 2008), 80–9, 80.

57 Latour and Yaneva, '"Give me a gun and I will make all buildings move"', 84, 88.

58 Yaneva, *The Making of a Building*, 7.

59 Latour and Yaneva, '"Give me a gun and I will make all buildings move"', 88.

60 Tim Edensor, 'Entangled agencies, material networks, and repair in a building assemblage: The mutable stone of St Anne's Church, Manchester', *Transactions of the Institute of British Geographers*, 36 (2011), 238–52, 240.

61 Matthew Johnson, 'What Do Medieval Buildings Mean?' *History and Theory* 52 (2013), 380–99, 382.

62 Maurice Merleau-Ponty, *The Phenomenology of Perception*, trans. Donal A. Landes (London: Routledge, 2012), 209.

63 Martin Heidegger, 'Building, dwelling, thinking', in *Poetry, Language, Thought*, trans. Albert Hofstadter (New York: Harper Perennial, 1971), 141–59.

64 Merleau-Ponty, *The Phenomenology of Perception*, 103.

65 Edward S. Casey, *Getting Back into Place: Toward a Renewed Understanding of the Place-World* (Bloomington: Indiana University Press, 2009), 116.

66 William M. Taylor and Michael P. Levine, *Prospects for an Ethics of Architecture* (London: Routledge, 2011), 100.

67 Maurice Merleau-Ponty, *The Primacy of Perception*, ed. James M. Edie (Evanston: Northwestern University Press, 1964), 195.

68 Gaston Bachelard, *The Poetics of Space*, trans. Maria Jolas (Boston: Beacon Press, 1994), 173.

69 Joseph Rykwert, 'Foreword', in David Leatherbarrow (ed.), *The Roots of Architectural Invention: Site, Enclosure, Materials* (Cambridge, Cambridge University Press 1993), xviii.

70 Christian Norberg-Schulz, *Genius Loci, Towards a Phenomenology of Architecture* (London: Rizzoli International Publications, 1980).

71 David Leatherbarrow, *Uncommon Ground: Architecture, Technology, and Topography* (Cambridge, MA: MIT Press, 2000), 72.

72 Leatherbarrow, *Roots of Architectural Invention*, 218.

73 Edward S. Casey, *The Fate of Place: A Philosophical History* (Berkeley: University of California Press, 1997).

74 Andrew Sayer, 'The Difference that Space Makes', in Derek Gregory, and John Urry (eds), *Social Relations and Spatial Structures* (Basingstoke: Springer, 1985), 59.

75 Howard Davies, *The Culture of Building* (New York: Oxford University Press, 2006), 3.

76 See Whyte, 'Regimes of materiality'.

77 Robert Bork, *The Geometry of Creation: Architectural Drawing and the Dynamic of Gothic Design* (Farnham: Routledge, 2011), 2.

78 Marvin Trachtenberg, *Building-in-time: From Giotto to Alberti and Modern Oblivion* (New Haven and London: Yale University Press, 2010), 419. Though see Paul Binski, *Gothic Wonder: Art, Artifice, and the Decorated Style* (New Haven and London: Yale University Press, 2014), 55 for some scepticism about Trachtenberg's thesis.

79 Anthony Geraghty, 'After Colvin's *Canterbury Quadrangle*', in Malcolm Airs and William Whyte (eds), *Architectural History After Colvin* (Donington: Shaun Tyas, 2013), 42–57, 51.

80 Mary Carruthers, *The Craft of Thought: Meditation, Rhetoric and the Making of Images, 400–1200* (Cambridge: Cambridge University Press, 1998); *The Experience of Beauty in the Middle Ages* (Oxford: Oxford University Press, 2013).

81 See especially Binski, *Gothic Wonder*.

82 This is most charmingly illustrated in a neglected essay by Jane Harrison, 'The influence of Darwinism on the study of religions', in A. C. Seward (ed.), *Darwin and Modern Science; Essays in Commemoration of the Centenary of the Birth of Charles Darwin and of the Fiftieth Anniversary of the Publication of the Origin of Species* (Cambridge: Cambridge University Press, 1909).

83 See also Amanda Vickery, '"Neat and not too showy": Words and wallpaper in Regency England', in John Styles and Amanda Vickery (eds), *Gender, Taste and Material Culture in Britain and North America, 1700- 1830* (New Haven and London: Yale University Press, 2006), 201–24.

84 Rosemary Sweet, '"A neat structure with pillars": Changing perceptions of the Temple Church in the long eighteenth century', in Robin Griffiths-Jones and David Park (eds), *The Temple Church in London: History, Architecture, Art* (Woodbridge: Boydell and Brewer, 2010), 175–94.

85 I try to explore this further in Whyte, *Unlocking the Church*.

86 Crary, *Suspension of perception*, 284.

87 Hodgson, *Philosophy and Experience*, 9.

88 Gareth James, 'Discourse and experience: Interpretations of intellectual progress in nineteenth-century England' (Oxford: DPhil thesis, 2001), 163–5.

Chapter 2

1 Michael Hall, *George Frederick Bodley and the Later Gothic Revival in Britain and America* (London and New Haven: Yale University Press, 2014), 278–9.

2 For discussions on medievalism, art and labour, see Michael Alexander, *Medievalism: The Middle Ages in Modern England* (London and New Haven: Yale University Press, 2007) and Tim Barringer, *Men at Work: Art and Labour in Victorian Britain* (London and New Haven: Yale University Press, 2005).

3 On reading architecture and Victorian architectural history, see Hall, 'What do Victorian churches mean?', 78–95; Adrian Forty, *Words and Buildings* (London: Thames and Hudson, 2000), and William Whyte, *Unlocking the Victorian Church: The Lost Secrets of Victorian Sacred Space* (Oxford: Oxford University Press, 2017).

4 Elizabeth Wilson, 'Fashions and modernity', in Christopher Breward and Caroline Evans (eds), *Fashion and Modernity* (Oxford: Berg, 2005), 1.

5 John Maddison, *David Parr House Conservation Management Plan* (privately printed, 2016), 15.

6 Duncan Robinson and Stephen Wildman, *Morris and Company in Cambridge* (Cambridge: Fitzwilliam Museum, 1980), 31.

7 For more on Morris's designs and socialist politics, see Jeffrey Skoblow, 'The writings of William Morris' and Imogen Hart, 'The designs of William Morris', both in Elizabeth Prettejohn (ed.), *The Cambridge Companion to the Pre-Raphaelites* (Cambridge: Cambridge University Press, 2012), 197–227.

8 'From college cooks to artists and craftsmen: The story of a Cambridge dynasty', http://www.cam.ac.uk/news/from-college-cooks-to-artists-and-craftsmen-the-story-of-a-cambridge-dynasty (accessed 10 December 2017).

9 Glenn Adamson, *The Invention of Craft* (London: Bloomsbury, 2013), 18.

10 William Morris, 'The lesser arts of life', 1882, https://www.marxists.org/archive/morris/works/1882/life1.htm (accessed 19 December 2017).

11 Paul Thompson, *The Work of William Morris* (London: Oxford University Press, 1967), 36.

12 Linda Parry, *William Morris* (London: V&A, 1996), 151.

13 Elizabeth Woolley, '"Of only modest artistic quality": Reconsidering the significance of firm ecclesiastical wall painting in England, 1845-1920', in J. Bridgland (ed.), *ICOM-CC 18th Triennial Conference Preprints, Copenhagen, 4–8 September 2017,* 4

14 Adamson, *Invention*, 183.

15 Eileen Boris, *Art and Labour* (Philadelphia: Temple University Press, 1986), 3–12.

16 Robinson and Wildman, *Morris*, 37.

17 David Morgan, *The Embodied Eye: Religious Visual Culture and the Social Life of Feeling* (Berkeley: University of California Press, 2012), 198.

18 Caroline Dakers, *The Holland Park Circle* (London and New Haven: Yale University Press, 1999).

19 See Ayla Lepine, 'Living the gothic revival: William Burges and tower house', https://specialcollections-blog.lib.cam.ac.uk/?p=15167 (accessed 19 December 2017).

20 John Ruskin, *The Seven Lamps of Architecture*, (London: Smith, Elder, and Co., 1849), 213.

21 Ruskin, *The Seven Lamps of Architecture.*

22 The chronology can be found in full in Maddison, *DPH Conservation Plan*, Vol. 1, p. 44.

23 Historic England, 'Swan house', https://historicengland.org.uk/listing/the-list/list-entry/1294208 (accessed 19 December 2017).

24 Maddison, *DPH Conservation Report*, Vol. 2, p. 25.

25 Tamsin Wimhurst, 'Timely', http://davidparrhouse.org/timely/ (accessed 19 December 2017). For more on Sunderland plaques and examples of this inscription on domestic ceramics, see https://www.matesoundthepump.com/

26 George Herbert, *The Remains of that Sweet Singer of The Temple* (London: Pickering, 1836), 175.

27 F. W. Faber, 'There's a wideness in God's mercy', in *New English Hymnal* (London: Hymns Ancient and Modern, 1986), 461.

28 Faber, 'There's a wideness in God's mercy'.

29 James Trilling, *The Language of Ornament* (London: Thames and Hudson, 2001), 35, 137.

30 Maddison, *DPH Conservation Report*, Vol. 2, p. 42; Lewis F. Day, 'The Art of William Morris', *Easter Art Annual, Art Journal*, (1899), 22.

31 Ralph Adams Cram, Child's Bed, 1913, http://www.mfa.org/collections/object/childs-bed-45347 (accessed 19 December 2017).

32 Cheryl Buckley, *Designing Modern Britain* (London: Reaktion, 2007).

33 Quoted in Peter Davey, *Arts and Crafts Architecture: The Search for Earthly Paradise* (London: *Architectural* Press, 1980), 171.

34 Fiona MacCarthy, *Anarchy and Beauty: William Morris and His Legacy, 1860-1960* (London: National Portrait Gallery, 2014), 82, 153.

35 For a further discussion of Watts and Company, see Ayla Lepine, 'On the founding of Watts and Co, 1874', B*RANCH*, 2015, http://www.branchcollective.org/?ps_articles=ayla-lepine-on-the-founding-of-watts-co-1874 (accessed 10 October 2017).

36 Robinson and Wildman, *Morris*, 31.

37 James Elkins, *How to Use Your Eyes* (London: Routledge, 2000), 156.

Chapter 3

1 Numerous letters from Jane and Leland Stanford as well as letters from artists, architects, and administrators involved in the creation of the early campus are held in the Stanford University Archives (many of which are digitized and available online). Of the many scholarly histories of the university, by far the greatest for the interests of this chapter is Carol M. Osborne, *Museum Builders in the West* (Stanford: Stanford University Museum of Art, 1986). This chapter is much indebted to her extraordinary work and any new insights it provides are only the result of following the signposts she left for later scholars.

2 Richard Guy Wilson (ed.), *Jefferson's Academical Village* (Charlottesville: University of Virginia, 2009).

3 'Notes Explanatory of the Leading Motives of the Plan', typescript, 1888, Stanford University Archives, Architecture of Stanford University Collection.

4 The designs of the campus are discussed in detail in Richard Joncas, et al., *Stanford University: The Campus Guide* (New York: Princeton Architectural Press, 1999).

5 Willis L. Hall, *Stanford Memorial Church* (Palo Alto: [1917]1924), 24.

6 Joncas, *Stanford University,* 31.

7 Robert C. Gregg, et al., *Stanford Memorial Church: Glory of Angels* (Stanford: Stanford Alumni Assoc, 1995), 37.

8 Osborne, *Museum Builders in the West*, 57.

9 Gail Stockholm, 'The Stanfords' personal charity: Their vision for Stanford Memorial Church', typescript, Stanford University Archives, 4.

10 Bertha Berner, *Mrs Leland Stanford: An Intimate Account* (Stanford, CA: Stanford University Press, 1935), 58–9.

11 Laurie Ossman and Heather Ewing, *Carrère & Hastings: The Masterworks* (New York: Rizzoli, 2011), 30.

12 Osborne, *Museum Builders,* 31.

13 Reiko Hillyer, 'The New South in the ancient city: Flagler's St Augustine hotels and sectional reconciliation', *Journal of Decorative and Propaganda Arts*, 25 (2005), 104–35.

14 Berner, *Mrs Leland Stanford,* 51.

15 Joncas, *Stanford University,* 31.

16 Berner, *Mrs Leland Stanford*, 52.

17 California Academy of Sciences, 'Proceedings of the Agassiz memorial meeting', pamphlet, San Francisco (1874), 4.

18 Carla Yanni, *Nature's Museums: Victorian Science and the Architecture of Display* (London: Athlone, 1999), 31.

19 Ian F Bell, 'Divine patterns: Louis Aggasiz and American men of letters', *Journal of American Studies,*10, no. 3 (December 1976), 352.

20 Ezra Pound, *ABC of Reading* (New Haven: Yale University Press, 1934).

21 David Starr Jordan, *The Days of a Man,* vol. 1 (Yonkers, NY: World Book Company, 1922), 123.

22 Osborne, *Museum Builders,* 16.

23 Jordan, *Days of Man,* 123.

24 California Academy of Sciences, 'Proceedings', 5.

25 Ibid., 6.

26 Ibid., 8.

27 Ibid., 9 and 22.

28 Osborne, *Museum Builders,* 16–17.

29 Ibid.,15.

30 Osborne, *Museum Builders,* 50.

31 This was in 1901. Ibid., 80.

32 Ibid., 52.

33 George Edward Crothers, 'The Educational Ideals of Jane Lathrop Stanford', pamphlet (1933), 31.

34 Osborne, *Museum Builders,* 15.

35 Joncas, *Stanford University,* 34.

36 Ibid., 34.

37 Osborne, *Museum Builders,* 97.

38 Ibid., 101.

39 Joncas, *Stanford University,* 34.

40 Barksdale Maynard, *Princeton: America's Campus* (University Park: Penn State Press, 2012), 53.

41 For a history of the American art museum in this period, see Kathleen Curran, *The Invention of the American Art Museum: From Craft to Kulturgeschichte, 1870-1930* (Los Angeles: Getty, 2016). Mrs Stanford's secretary, Bertha Berner, recorded that the South Kensington Museum 'pleased Mrs Stanford the most of all the wonderful sites we had seen', when they were in London in 1897 for Queen Victoria's Diamond Jubilee. Berner, *Mrs Leland Stanford,* 112.

42 'The Leland Stanford Jr Museum: Origins and description', pamphlet (1886), Stanford University Archives, N781 A6 1886, 10.

43 'Origins and Description', 2.

44 Osborne, *Museum Builders,* 77.

45 Ibid., 17.

46 Ibid.

47 Ibid., 52–63.

48 Gregg, *Glory of Angels*, 11.

49 Hall, *Stanford Memorial Church,* 28.

50 Crothers, 'Educational Ideals', 31.

51 Berner, *Mrs Leland Stanford,* 53.

52 Osborne, *Museum Builders,* 74.

53 Gregg, *Glory of Angels*, 21–2

54 Osborne, *Museum Builders,* 40.

55 Letter, M Camerino to J Stanford, 14 April 1902, Stanford University Archives, Jane Stanford Papers.

56 Berner, *Mrs Leland Stanford,* 76.

57 Osborne, *Museum Builders,* 88.

58 Letter, Shepley Rutan & Coolidge to J Branner, 30 June 1910, Stanford University Archives. Architecture of Stanford University Collection.

59 Carol Osborne, 'The grandest museum in the world', *Sandstone & Tile,* 34, no. 2 (Spring/Summer 2010), 7–8.

60 Letter, Olmsted Brothers to Board of Trustees, 8 May 1914, Stanford University Archives, Architecture of Stanford University Collection.

61 Gunther W. Nagel, *Jane Stanford, Her Life and Letters* (Stanford, CA: Stanford Alumni Association, 1975), 186.

62 Benedetto Croce, *The Essence of Aesthetic* (London: William Heinemann, 1921), viii.

63 Croce, *The Essence of Aesthetic.*

64 Paul Goldberger, et al., *Berkeley: The Building of a College* (New Haven: Yale University, 1999), 6.

Chapter 4

1 The only recent study to which I am indebted is R. Lawrence, 'The evolution of the Victorian art school', *Journal of Architecture*, 19, no. 1 (2014), 81–107.

2 M. Tylecote, *The Mechanics' Institutes of Lancashire and Yorkshire before 1851* (Manchester: Manchester University Press, 1957), 72.

3 Q. Bell, *The Schools of Design* (London: Routledge & Kegan Paul, 1963), 68–73, 101–2. The committee published its report in 1836.

4 C. Ashwin, *Art Education: Documents and Policies, 1768-1975* (London: Society for Research Into Higher Education, 1975), 36–7, 42–9.

5 E. T. Cook and A. Wedderburn (eds), *Collected Works*, Library edition (London: George Allen and New York: Longmans Green) vol. 34, p. 511. Ruskin set up an art school in Oxford in 1871, following his own principles in opposition to the government-supported school there.

6 J. C. L Sparkes, *Schools of Art: Their Origin, History, Work and Influence* (London, 1884), 92.

7 S. Macdonald, *The History and Philosophy of Art Education* (London: University of London Press, 1970), 182.

8 D. Jeremiah, *A Hundred Years and More* (Manchester: Manchester Polytechnic, 1980), 3.

9 B. Clapp, *The University of Exeter: A History* (Exeter: University of Exeter, 1982), 4–5.

10 Macdonald, *Art Education*, 173.

11 C. Jones, *A History of Nottingham School of Design* (Nottingham: Nottingham Trent University, 1993), 20.

12 Spokes, *Schools of Art*, 94(n).

13 Jones, *Nottingham School of Design.*, 13–14.

14 *Building News* (hereafter *BN*,) 21 October 1876. The architect was J. G. Gibbons.

15 D. Boswell, 'Arts with crafts', in C. Miller (ed.), *Behind the Mosaic* (Leeds: Leeds Museums and Galleries, 2013), 17–18; *Builder*, 1867, 696–7.

16 G. Waterfield, *The People's Galleries* (New Haven and London: Yale University Press, 2015), 230–1; *Builder*, 4 June 1864, 415.

17 See S. Gunn, *The Public Culture of the Victorian Middle Class* (Manchester: Manchester University Press, 2000), 26–30 and *passim*.

18 N. Pevsner, *Academies of Art Past and Present* (Cambridge: Cambridge University Press, 1940), 185–6.

19 J. Physick, *The Victoria and Albert Museum* (Oxford: Phaidon Christies, 1982), 102–4, 124–8.

20 C. Ashwin, *Art Education: Documents and Policies, 1768-1975* (London: Society for Research into Higher Education, 1975), 42–4.

21 Laura Knight, *Oil Paint and Grease Paint* (Macmillan Company, 1936), 47.

22 Macdonald, *Art Education*, 298–30.

23 H. Muthesius, *The English House*, ed. D. Sharp (Oxford: BSP Professional Books, 1979), 14–15.

24 Macdonald, *Art Education*, 185; Lawrence, 'Victorian art school', 84.

25 *BN*, 4 February 1881.

26 E. D. Mackerness, 'The early history of the Sheffield (*sic*) school of art', in S. Pollard and C. Holmes (eds), *Essays in the Economic and Social History of South Yorkshire* (Sheffield: South Yorkshire County Council, 1976), 258. It was demolished after bombing in 1940.

27 Jones, *Nottingham School of Design*, 39–40, 44.

28 D. Verey and A. Brooks, *The Buildings of England: Gloucestershire* 2 (New Haven and London: Yale University Press, 2002), 463; *Builder*, 17 January 1871, 466–7; *BN*, 9 June 1877.

29 *BN*, 9 June 1877.

30 Birmingham City University (BCU) Art & Design Archives, SA/AD/8/1-2 (bound volumes of printed programmes, 1878–1909); J. Swift, *Changing Fortunes: The Birmingham School of Art Building, 1880-1995* (Birmingham: ARTicle Press, 1996), 14.

31 Macdonald, *Art Education*, 184. Redmayne's first design is illustrated in *BN*, 1 November 1878.

32 Jeremiah, *A Hundred Years and More*, 20, 28–30.

33 For Chamberlain and Martin, see P. Ballard (ed.), *Birmingham's Victorian and Edwardian Architects* (Birmingham: Oblong Creative, Ltd, 2009), 153–81, 339–63.

34 Diary, 5 November 1904, King's College, Cambridge, quoted in A. Crawford (ed.), *By Hammer and Hand: the Arts and Crafts Movement in Birmingham* (Birmingham: Birmingham Museums and Art Gallery, 1984), 27.

35 J. Swift, *Changing Fortunes*, 19–20; Lawrence, 'Victorian art school', 90–4.

36 BCU, SA/AD/8/1-2 Swift, *Changing Fortunes*, 13–14; Lawrence, 'Victorian art school', 94–7.

37 BCU, SA/AD/8/2.

38 W. Buchanan (ed.), *Mackintosh's Masterwork: The Glasgow School of Art* (London: A & C Black, Glasgow School of Art Press, 2004), 5; A. Crawford, *Charles Rennie Mackintosh* (London: Thames and Hudson, 1995), 31. See also R. Macleod, *Charles Rennie Mackintosh: Architect and Artist* (London: Collins, 1983), 48–61, 120–40.

39 Lawrence, 'Victorian art school', 103.

40 Glasgow School of Art archives, reproduced in Buchanan, *Mackintosh's Masterwork*, 50–5, 112. Mackintosh's plans, elevations and sections of 1907 and 1910 (Glasgow School of Art Collection) are reproduced on pp. 58–69.

41 Buchanan, *Mackintosh's Masterwork*, 38.

42 R. Banham, *The Architecture of the Well-Tempered Environment* (London: Architectural Press, 1969), 84.

43 D. Hawkes, *The Environmental Imagination* (London: Routledge, 2008), 19–29.

44 Boswell, in C. Miller, *Behind the Mosaic*, 22. For Bedford and Kitson, see D. Boswell in C. Webster (ed.), *Building a Great Victorian Vity* (Leeds: Northern Heritage Publications, 2011), 293–312.

45 Architect of, *inter alia*, the City Hall at Cardiff and the Methodist Central Hall close to Westminster Abbey.

46 *BN*, 13 October 1905; *Architectural Review*, 18 (1905), 65; R. Fellows, *Edwardian Architecture: Style and Technology* (London: Lund Humphries, 1995), 134–7.

47 *BN*, 4 February 1881; www.liobans.org/documents/collegeofart.pdf. (conservation statement, 2012). They went on to design the Cunard Building at the Pier Head, one of the main monuments to the city's maritime prestige.

48 *Prospect*, 51 (1994), 10, quoted in D. C. MacDowell, 'Drawing (*sic*) on the past: The Edinburgh college of art', *Architectural Heritage*, 13 (2002), 136.

49 BCU, School of Art Management sub-committee minute book 3 (1890–3), 15–16 (Report of Museum and School of Art committee, 6 May 1890).

50 Jeremiah, *A Hundred Years and More*, 19, 25.

51 www.picturesheffield; North East Midlands Photographic Archive.

52 A. Conan Doyle, *The Memoirs of Sherlock Holmes* (London, 1911), 7 (https://sherlock-holm.es/stories/pdf/a4/1-sided/nava.pdf).

Chapter 5

1 Henry James, 'A small boy and others', in Frederick Dupee (ed.), *Autobiography* (1913; New York: Criterion Books, 1956), 198–9.

2 Andrew McClellan argues that the Louvre is understood to be an exemplary museum, 'arguably the world's most famous' and 'in the context of museum history, it is important as a model for the public art museums that have become a necessary ornament of nation-states and self-respecting cities the world over'. 'Musée du Louvre, Paris: Palace of the people, art for all,' in Carol Paul (ed.), *The First Modern Museums of Art* (Los Angeles: J Paul Getty Museum, 2012), 213.

3 Andrew McClellan traces the changing hang of the Louvre in his foundational and important book, *Inventing the Louvre: Art, Politics and the Origins of the Modern Museum in 18th Century Paris* (Cambridge: Cambridge University Press, 1988). See also Dominique Poulot, *Une Histoire des Musées en France* (Paris: Editions de la Découverte, 2005). For collectors see Krzystof Pomian, *Collectors and Curiosities: Paris and Venice, 1500-1800,* trans. Elizabeth Wiles-Porier (Cambridge: Polity Press, 1990) and Dominque Pety, *Poétique de la collection au XIXe siècle* (Paris: Presses Universitaires de Paris Ouest, 2010).

4 Timothy M. O'Sullivan, 'The mind in motion: Walking and metaphorical travel in the roman villa', *Classical Philology*, 101, no. 2 (April 2006), 133–52.

5 O'Sullivan, 'The mind in motion', 140.

6 Frances Gage, 'Exercise for mind and body: Giulio Mancini, collecting, and landscape painting in the seventeenth century', *Renaissance Quarterly*, 61, no. 4 (Winter 2008),1170.

7 Gage, 'Exercise for mind and body', 1177–83.

8 Helen Leahy, *Museum Bodies* (Farnham: Ashgate, 2012), 15. For further studies of touch in museums, see also Fiona Candlin, *Art Museums and Touch* (Manchester: Manchester University Press, 2010), Sandra Dudley, ed., *Museum Objects/Museum Materialities* (London and New York: Routledge, 2012), and Constance Classen, *Museum of Senses: Experiencing Art and Collections* (London: Bloomsbury Academic, 2017).

9 Constance Classen, 'Museum manners: The sensory life of the early museum', *Journal of Social History*, 40, no. 4 (Summer 2007), 895–914.

10 Constance Classen, *The Deepest Sense: A Cultural History of Touch* (Chicago: University of Illinois Press, 2012), 136.

11 Leahy, *Museum Bodies,* 134.

12 Andrew McClellan highlights the tensions between private collections and public museums in his article 'Vive l'amateur! The Goncourt House revisited', in Melissa Lee Hyde and Katie Scott (eds), *Rococo Echo* (Oxford: Oxford

University Press, 2014), 87–107. See also Anne Higonnet, *A Museum of one's own* (New York: Prestel Publishing, 2009).

13 James L. Connelly, 'The grand gallery of the Louvre and the Museum project: Architectural problems', *Journal of the Society of Architectural Historians,* 31, no. 2 (May 1972), 120–32. Connelly presents the early projects of the transformation of the grande galerie from an architectural point of view.

14 Marquis de Vasselot, *Répertoire des vues des salles du Musée du Louvre*, Archives de l'art Français (Paris: Amand Colin, 1946).

15 Charles Baudelaire, 'Le peintre de la vie moderne,' in *Curiosités Esthétique* (Paris: Editions du Milieu du Monde [1863]), 529.

16 See Rosalys Coope, 'The "long gallery": Its origins, development, use and decoration', *Architectural History*, 29 (1986), 45–72, as well as her 'The gallery in England: Names and meanings', *Architectural History*, 27 (1984), 446–55. The gallery could be a space for decorative programmes: See Antoine Schnapper, 'The king as collector in the seventeenth century', *Journal of Interdisciplinary History*, XVII, no. I (Summer 1986), 186–202. Isabelle Tillerot argues that the gallery as a space of collection was less common in the eighteenth century than in the seventeenth. *Jean de Jullienne et les collectionneurs de son temps* (Paris: Éditions de la Maison des sciences de l'homme, 2005), 206–7.

17 Anthony Blunt, 'Poussin studies VI: Poussin's decoration of the long gallery in the Louvre', *The Burlington Magazine*, 93, no. 585 (December 1951), 369–77.

18 Blunt, 'Poussin studies VI', 372.

19 T. Jessup, *Journal d'un voyage à Paris en Septembre-Octobre 1820* (Paris, 1828), 57 as quoted in McClellan, *Inventing the Louvre*, 198.

20 Henry James, *The American*, in *Novels*, 1871-1880 (1877; New York: Library of America, 1983), 515. See discussion by Jonah Siegel, *The Haunted Museum: Longing, Travel & The Art-Romance Tradition* (Princeton and Oxford: Princeton University Press, 2005), 113–47.

21 As I have argued elsewhere, such guidebooks as Théophile Gautier's *Guide to the Louvre* led the visitor on a directed, logical, and historically oriented itinerary. Valerie Mendelson, 'Metaphors of collecting in nineteenth century Paris', *Open Library of Humanities*, 2, no. 1 (2016), e15, 1–33. DOI http://dx.doi.org/10.16995/olh.71.

22 As quoted in Leahy, *Museum Bodies,* 128.

23 Quatremère de Quincy argued against the museum stating that 'to make of such a gathering [of monuments] a practical course in modern chronology: This is to constitute ourselves as a dead nation'. *Considérations Morales* (Paris, 1815), 47. The image of death is taken up by Goethe and Théophile Thoré. David Carrier places these writers in the sceptical tradition. *Museum Skepticism: A History of the Display of Art in Public Galleries* (Durham and London: Duke University Press, 2006), 51–73. Also important is the comparison of Hegel and Quatremère de Quincy in Didier Maleuvre's *Museum Memories* (Stanford: Stanford University Press, 1999), 21–30.

24 For the relationship between collecting and interior design, see Anca Lasc, 'Interior decorating in the age of historicism: Popular advice manuals and the pattern books of Édouard Bajot,' *Journal of Design History,* 26, no. 1 (2013), 1–24.

25 For the relationship between social change and collecting in the nineteenth century, see Charles Blanc, *Le Trésor de la curiosité, tire des catalogues de vente de tableaux, dessins, estampes, livres, marbres, bronzes, ivories, terres cuites, vitraux, médailles, armes, porcelains, meubles, émaux; laques et autres objets d'art, avec diverses notes et notices historiques et biographiques*, with a preface by Adolphe Thibaudeau, 2 vols (Paris: Vve J. Renouard, 1857–8) and *Collections et Marché de L'Art en France 1789-1848* (Rennes: Presses Universitaires de Rennes, 2005).

26 'Secrétan Sale Closed,' *The New York Times*, 3 July 1889.

27 For discussion of the Pourtalès Collection, particularly its antiquities, see Olivier Boisset, 'Les antiques du comte James-Alexandre de Pourtalès-Gorgier (1776-1855): Une introduction', in *Collections et Marché de L'art en France 1789-1848* (Rennes: Presses Universitaires de Rennes, 2003), 187–206. See also Robin Middleton, 'Hotel Pourtalès-Gorgier, 7 rue Tronchet, Paris,' *AA Files*, 33 (Summer 1997), 52–71.

28 Pamela Warner describes the artistry of their home in terms of framing, symmetry and contrast. 'Framing, symmetry and contrast in Edmond de Goncourt's aesthetic interior', *Studies in the Decorative Arts*, 15 (2008), 36–64. See also Elizabeth Emery, *Photojournalism and the Origins of the French Writer House Museum (1881-1914)*, (Surrey, UK and Burlington, VT: Ashgate, 2012) and McClellan, 'Vive l'amateur!'

29 'Ma volonté est que mes dessins, mes estampes, mes bibelots, mes livres, enfin les choses d'art qui ont fait le bonheur de ma vie, n'aient pas la froide tombe d'un musée, et le regard bête du passant indiffèrent, et je demande qu'elles soient toutes éparpillées sous les coups de marteau du commissaire-priseur et que la jouissance que m'a procuré l'acquisition de chacune d'elles, soit redonnée, pour chacune d'elles, à un heritier de mes gouts.' *Collections des Goncourts, Estampes Modernes, Aquarelles et Dessins* (Paris: Drouot, 1897), i.

30 As Jonathan Crary underlines, Henri Bergson linked the movement of the body to perception and the degree attention to one's perceptions 'decides ... the degree of freedom of one's own existence.' Crary, *Suspensions of Perception*, 317.

31 Paul Mantz, 'Préface', *Collection Rothan* (Paris: Georges Petit, 1890), xii–xiii. 'A ceux qui vivent dans les travaux de l'esprit, les oeuvres d'art donnent des consolations et, quelquefois, les conseils. Gustave Rothan avait su faire à son sérieux labeur d'historien un cadre superbe.' For more on Gustave Rothan, see his *Souvenirs diplomatiques; l'affaire du Luxembourg; la prélude de la guerre de 1870* (Paris: Calmann Lévy, 1882).

32 Mantz, 'Préface', xiii. 'les excellent tableaux qui, pendant tant d'années, ont fait la joie de notre ami et qui ont presque été ses collaborateurs.'

33 *Collection Merlin*, (Paris: Drouot, 1900), n.p. 'Peu soucieux des caprices de la mode en matière de beaux-arts, il aimait et admirait les tableaux exclusivement

pour eux-mêmes, allant surtout à ceux vers qui il se sentait personnellement attiré. Aussi, une fois admis dans sa collection, les considérait-il et les traitait-il comme des amis.'

34 A large literature on the psychology of collecting treats collecting as a symptom of various psycho-sexual drives. See Susan Pearce for an overview. *On Collecting: An Investigation into Collecting in the European Tradition* (London and New York: Routledge, 1995).

35 *Collection M le Cte Daupias* (Paris: Georges Petit, 1892), 5. 'le comte Daupias n'obéissait pas à un devoir d'historien méthodique; il voulait surtout satisfaire son besoin de plaisir élevé; il voulait faire éclater autour de lui comme la joie des yeux.'

36 *Collection Alfred Feydeau* (Paris: Drouot, 1902), 5. [il] 'les avait réunies avec un soin éclairé; il les avait gardées par devers lui avec une tendresse jalouse; elles représentaient ce que son goût de l'art lui disait d'aimer, et il ne les regardait pas sans une émotion où se mêlait à une jouissance esthétique jamais blasée le souvenir de la grande bataille de l'école de 1830 à laquelle il avait pris part.'

37 L. Roger-Milès, 'Preface', *Collection Auguste Rousseau* (Paris: Georges Petit, 1900), 6. 'Il connait l'adorable joie de reposer ses yeux sur des oeuvres qu'il aime, et que seul il a le droit d'aimer. ..il s'est créé une volupté à lui, jalouse, silencieuse; chaque jour il est revenu à ces petites merveilles, dont il est le gardien plein de sollicitude et chaque jour, depuis quarante ans, il a découvert en elles des qualités insoupçonnées la veille, des aperçus qui lui avaient échappé, des clartés subtiles dont son oeil n'avait pas encore décliné la caresse.'

38 *Catalogue des livres précieux de M. Ambroise Firmin-Didot*. Introduction by M. Paulin (Paris: Drouot, 1878), vii. 'Quand ... il était devenu l'heureux possesseur d'un de rares volumes qu'il avait longtemps couvé les yeux, il ne s'en séparait ni le jour ni la nuit. Une place lui était ménagée sous son oreiller et, il n'était réuni aux autres joyaux du même genre qu'à l'arrivée d'un nouveau rival, à son tour accueilli avec la même effusion de tendresse.'

39 Classen, *The Deepest Sense*, 130.

40 Caroline Juler, *Les orientalistes de l'école italienne* (acr-edition.com, 1994), 156.

41 From the start, collectors have been linked to voyage, travelling far and wide to amass their collection. See Dominique Poulot, *Une Histoire des Musées*, 21. The Grand Tour was well known for encouraging wealthy Europeans and Americans to collect art along the way. See Bruce Redford, *Dilettanti: The Antic and the Antique in Eighteenth-Century England* (Los Angeles: Getty Publications, 2008).

42 André Michel, 'Preface to the sales catalogue of Jean Dollfus', *Collection Jean Dollfus* (Paris: Georges Petit, 1912), 5. For more on André Michel see his entry in the *Dictionary of Art Historians, https://dictionaryofarthistorians.org/michela.htm*. For more on Jean Dollfus see Samuel Rocheblave, *Un Grand Collectionneur Alsacien, Jean Dollfus* (1823-1911) (Strasbourg: Revue Alsacienne Illustré, 1912).

43 *Collection de Bériot*, preface by Pascal Forthuny (Paris: Drouot, 1901), n.p. 'Je viens de vivres quelques heures au milieu de la collection de Bériot.' 'I have just come from living for several hours in the middle of the Bériot collection.'

44 Ibid., 'tout au long de cette promenade, aucune fatigue, aucune contrainte ne me sont venues et que, de toile en panneau, rarement voyage ne me fut plus agréable et plus reposant.'

45 Ibid., 'Et pourtant, quelle route sinueuse, compliquée, quel vagabond chemin de poètes ne me fallut-il pas suivre? Quels aspects de nature infiniment variés, quels sites changeants, me fut-il donné de traverser; enfin quel réconfortant bain de plein air, depuis les prairies fécondes, les limpides rivières d'une plantureuse Normandie, jusqu'aux décors gris des paysages, accroupis sous les basses nuées de Hollande, en passant par les vallées si grassement pittoresques du pays Bourbonnais où m'égara l'harmonieux talent du plus poète peut-être de nos peintres de France!'

46 Nancy Forgione discusses the relationship between walking and looking in her 'The art of walking in late-nineteenth-century Paris', *The Art Bulletin*, 87, no. 4 (December 2005), 664–87.

47 Martha Ward, 'Impressionist installations and private exhibitions', *Art Bulletin*, 73, no. 4 (1991), 599–622.

48 For more on Valtesse, see Yolaine de la Bigne, *Valtesse de la Bigne ou Le pouvoir de la volupté* (Paris: Perrin, 1999) and more recently Catherine Hewitt, *The Mistress of Paris* (New York: St. Martin's Press, 2015).

49 *Collection de Valtesse de la Bigne* (Paris, 1902), ii. 'Les amateurs qui viendront aux jours d'exposition à l'hôtel du boulevard Malesherbes, auront de quoi satisfaire leur curiosité :tableaux, bijoux et argenterie, objets d'art, meubles, tapisserie, sièges en bois sculptés recouverts de tapisserie, coussins, tentures, étoffes, tapis, voitures, que sais-je? C'est une infinité d'œuvres et de choses de haut goût qui s'offriront à eux dans le cadre luxueux, où la main, la plus experte aux élégances, s'était plu à les réunir, à les grouper, à les harmoniser, si je puis m'exprimer ainsi, pour le plaisir de l'œil.'

50 Prince Demidoff had inherited a fabulous collection from his father which he sold in 1880. For more information on Demidoff see Helen Cooper, 'Prince Demidoff's Greek slave', *Nineteenth-Century Art Worldwide,* 15, no. 2 (Summer 2016).

51 *Catalogue de Vente de Palais de San Donato*, Florence, 1880.

52 'Prince Demidoff and the San Donato Sale', *The Art Amateur*, 2, no. 5 (1880), 98–9. Many museums bought from this sale, including the Louvre, which dispatched Both de Tauzia to acquire art. Silvia Davoli, 'Renaissance art from the Both de Tauzia collection, now at the Wallace Collection', *Journal of the History of Collections*, 25, no. 3 (November 2013), 391–405.

53 *Catalogue des estampes et des dessins de J.-L. Forain, Constantin Guys et H. de Toulouse-Lautrec composant la collection de M. A. Ragault ...* / [expert] Loys Delteil, 1910.

54 *Catalogue d'un important mobilier* (Paris, 1890).

55 His collection is discussed in Davoli, 'Renaissance art from the Both de Tauzia collection', 391. According to her, D'Armaillé's collection was renowned and particularly strong in 'arts and crafts'. She points to the description of his home as palatial and a 'museum'.

56 *Catalogue des objets d'art provenant de la collection de M. le comte d'Armaillé* (Paris, 1890).

57 *Catalogue de Vente de la collection M. le comte d'Armaillé* (Paris: Sedelmeyer, 1890).

58 *Catalogue de Vente de la collection Mme la baronne Hauzeur de Ciply* (Paris, 1891). Some other examples include *Catalogue de Vente de la collection Mme Oppenheim* (Paris, 1890), Catalogue de vente après décès de M. et Mme Benou (Paris, 1890); *Catalogue de Vente de la Collection de M. de Leemans* (Paris, 1891).

59 See *Collection Roslin* (Écouen, 1890) and *Collection Mme de Grandville* (Orne, 1906).

60 *Catalogue de vente de la collection de Mme Roslin. n.p.*

Chapter 6

I am grateful to Mary Saunders for her help with archival material and images for this chapter.

1 Robert Dunn, 'Saving college graduates: The clubs of the various universities in New York, and how they ease the tasks of young men in the city', *Outing Magazine* (April 1908), 21–31.

2 The work of Peter Dopkin Hall has been particularly important to my thinking on this subject. See 'Rediscovering the Bourgeoisie: Higher education and governing-class formation in the United States, 1870-1914', in Sven Beckert and Julia B. Rosenbaum (eds), *The American Bourgeoisie: Distinction and Identity in the Nineteenth Century* (New York: Palgrave, 2010), 167–87; and *The Organisation of American Culture, 1700-1900: Private Institutions, Elites, and the Origins of American Nationality* (New York: New York University Press, 1984). Historical sociologists have also produced notable work in this area. For example, Jerome Karabel, *The Chosen: The Hidden History of Admission and Exclusion at Harvard, Yale, and Princeton* (Boston: Houghton Mifflin, 2006); and E. D. Baltzell, *The Protestant Establishment: Aristocracy & Caste in America* (1964; New Haven: Yale University Press, 1987), 135–42.

3 For the growth of alumni associations see James Axtell, *Wisdom's Workshop: The Rise of the Modern University* (Princeton: Princeton University Press, 2016), 292–3; and Eric Hobsbawm, 'Mass-Producing Traditions: Europe, 1870-1914', in Eric Hobsbawm and Terence Ranger (eds), *The Invention of Tradition* 20th printing (Cambridge: Cambridge University Press, 2012), 294–6.

4 I am indebted here and elsewhere to Ormonde de Kay's club history, *From the Age that Is Past: Harvard Club of New York City, A History* (New York:

The Club, 1994), 1–42. For membership numbers see 'membership', loose file, Harvard Club of New York Archives [hereafter HCNY].

5 Of the seventeen members who signed the club's bill of incorporation in 1887, which granted the organization the right to hold property in common, three quarters were born in New England. For the record they were Edward King, Charles C. Beaman, Edmund Wetmore, Edward L. Parris, Thomas F. Brownell, Nathaniel A. Prentiss, George S. Greene, Jr., James W. Hawes, Amos K. Fiske, Clement Cleveland, William Montgomery, Jr., Nathaniel S. Smith, Camillus G. Kidder, William S. Seamans, Eugene D. Hawkins, William A. Purrington, and Samuel H. Ordway. *Harvard Class of 1861, Sixth Report* (1892); *Report of the Class of 1860* (1895); *Class of 1865, Seventh Secretaries Report* (1890); *Class of 1865, Ten Report of the Secretary* (1907); *Class of 1862, Fiftieth Anniversary Report* (1912); *Report of the class of 1860* (1915); *Class of 1866, The tenth secretary's report* (1901); *The twentieth secretary's report of the class of 1866* (1922); *Class of 1867, Secretary's Report* (1907); *Class of 1867, Secretary's Report* (1918); *Tenth Report of the Class of 1869* (1908); *Class of 1872, Secretary's Tenth Report* (1917);*Class of 1887, Seventh Report* (1917); *Class of 1881, Fortieth Anniversary Report* (1921); *The Ninth Report of the Secretary of the Class of 1873* (1913); Obituary of Samuel H. Ordway, *New York Times,* 20 April 1934.

6 Quoted in Hall, 'Rediscovering the Bourgeoisie', 168–9.

7 On the development of Harvard under Eliot, see Hugh Hawkins, *Between Harvard and America: The Educational Leadership of Charles W. Eliot* (New York: Oxford University Press, 1972); Samuel Eliot Morison, *The Development of Harvard University since the Inauguration of President Eliot, 1869-1929* (Cambridge, MA: Harvard University Press, 1930); and Andrew Schlesinger, *Veritas: Harvard College and the American Experience* (Chicago: Ivan R. Dee, 2005).

8 'Report of the Committee on the Elective System' (1886), 5, HCNY.

9 On Harvard University governance and the club's campaign for representation, see de Kay, *From the Age that is Past,* 32–42; 'Report of a Committee of the Harvard Club of New York City on the Eligibility of Graduates Residing Without the Commonwealth of Massachusetts to Membership in the Board of Overseers of Harvard College', 8 October 1878, HUD (3605.624 A), Harvard University Archives [hereafter HUA]; and Morison, *The Development of Harvard University since the Inauguration of President Eliot*, xxv–xxxviii.

10 Quoted in *The Harvard Register: An Illustrated Monthly*, 3, no. 2 (February 1881), 156–7.

11 My account of New York's social and economic history is based on Sven Beckert, *The Monied Metropolis: New York City and the Consolidation of the American Bourgeoisie, 1850-1896* (Cambridge and New York: Cambridge University Press, 2001), especially 237–72; and Mike Wallace, *Greater Gotham: A History of New York City from 1898 to 1919* (Oxford: Oxford University Press, 2018), 15–76; see also Thomas Kessner, *Capital City: New York City and the Men Behind America's Rise to Economic Dominance, 1860-1900* (New York: Simon & Schuster, 2003); and Clifton Hood, *In Pursuit*

of Privilege: A History of New York City's Upper Class and the Making of a Metropolis (New York: Columbia University Press, 2017), 171–250.

12 'Report of the Committee on the Elective System'.

13 Quoted in de Kay, *From the Age that is Past*, 46.

14 Ibid., 34.

15 Ibid., 46–7.

16 Ibid., 52.

17 Lloyd McKim Garrison, 'New York's Harvard House', *Harvard Graduates' Magazine,* September 1894, 24.

18 de Kay, *From the Age that is Past,* 43. A good overview of the building type can be found in Charles Lockwood's *Bricks and Brownstone: The New York Row House, 1783-1929* (New York: Abbeville Press, 1972).

19 Garrison, 'New York's Harvard House', 24.

20 King's grandfather, Rufus King, was the Massachusetts signer of the United States Constitution and the first in the family to attend Harvard (class of 1777). Rufus's descendants moved to New York and New Jersey, where they established reputations as both politicians and bankers, while continuing to send their sons to Harvard. *Report of the Harvard Class of 1853* (Cambridge, MA: Harvard University Press, 1913), 167–72.

21 'Note made by Bamortin of President's remarks about Edward King at a meeting of the Harvard Club held 27 Jun 1909,' Folder K17-B, Erving-King Family Papers [hereafter EKFP] (MS 204), Box 18, New-York Historical Society [hereafter NYHS].

22 For a comparison of Harvard and Yale's approaches, see Hall, 'Rediscovering the Bourgeoisie', 167–89.

23 Other Writings, Speeches at Harvard, Columbia, Yale, and Princeton, fo. K15-B, Box 17, EKFP, NYHS.

24 'Princeton men at dinner', *New York Times,* 16 January 1891.

25 The speeches are untitled and undated, but the intended audiences are indicated in the opening paragraphs. Other Writings, Speeches at Harvard, Columbia, Yale, and Princeton. fo. K15-B, Box 17, EKFP, NYHS.

26 Leland M. Roth, *McKim, Mead and White: Architects* (New York: Thames & Hudson, 1983), 147.

27 The 1905 remodelling and addition substantially changed the plan and character of the original building. My description of the building draw on several contemporary reviews, including 'The Harvard Club House in New York' *The Outlook,* 30 June 1894; James Pooton, 'The Harvard Club', *New York Times,* 23 May 1897; and 'Harvard House', *The Critic: A Weekly Review of Literature and the Arts,* 14 July 1894.

28 Quoted in Garrison, 'New York's Harvard House', 26.

29 Ibid.

30 Ibid., 30.

31 Charles F. McKim – Edward King, n.d., file KB, Box 16, EKFP, NYHS.

32 Quoted in Garrison, 'New York's Harvard House', 25.

33 Ex-secretary A. Chevalier Haseltine, republished letter in the *Harvard Graduates' Magazine*, September 1893, 113.

34 Letter from descendent of King to Francis R. Appleton, 10 February 1917, fo. K17-B, Box 18, EKFP, NYHS.

35 Text of speech for first dinner in Harvard Hall, 1908, fo. K15-A, Box 17, EKFP (MS 204), NYHS.

36 Garrison, 'New York's Harvard House', 28.

37 Addressed to T. Frank Brownell, 28 April 1889, Folder 1887–88 and 1892, Standing File, HCNY.

38 Addressed to T. Frank Brownell, 21 February 1889, Ibid.

39 Harvard Club Secretary – Eliot, 1 October 1893, Charles W. Eliot Papers [hereafter CWEP], Harvard Club Correspondence, HUA.

40 Greene – Slocum, 23 January 1906, CWEP, Harvard Club Correspondence, HUA.

41 Slocum – Greene, 24 January 1906, CWEP, Harvard Club Correspondence, HUA.

42 Untitled text, fo. K15-B, Box 17, EKFP, NYHS.

Chapter 7

1 Thomas Roger Smith, *A Rudimentary Treatise on the Acoustics of Public Buildings; or, The Principles of the Science of Sound Applied to the Purposes of the Architect and Builder* (London: John Weale, 1861), 1–2. This was republished with an addition index as *Acoustics in Relation to Architecture and Building: The Laws of Sound as Applied to the Arrangement of Buildings* (London: Crosby Lockwood and Son, 1878). A third edition with minor additions was published as *Acoustics in Relation to Architecture and Building: The Laws of Sound as Applied to the Arrangement of Buildings* (London: Crosby Lockwood and Son, 1895). Both later editions contain the same epigraph quotation at the pages marked. All page references to Smith, *Acoustics*, below are identical for all three editions, unless otherwise specified.

2 Thomas Roger Smith, *Architecture, Gothic and Renaissance* (London: Sampson Low, Marston, Searle & Rivington, 1884), 8. See also Thomas Roger Smith and John Slater, *Architecture, Classic and Early Christian* (London: Sampson Low, Marston, Searle & Rivington, 1888).

3 For a discussion of the symbiosis between the writing of architectural history and the professionalization of architecture in the nineteenth century, see Wheeler, *Victorian Perceptions of Renaissance Architecture*. While Wheeler discusses Smith's historical writings, her study does not include acoustics. By

contrast, for a discussion of acoustic issues in design of state-funded public building in the 1840s, see Gillin, *The Victorian Palace of Science,* 30–1 and 140. For the deliberations of the select committee on the Houses of Commons' buildings, see *Parliamentary Papers*, 269 (1833), 11–13.

4 Emily Thompson, *The Soundscape of Modernity: Architectural Acoustics and the Culture of Listening in America,* 1900–1933 (Princeton, NJ: Princeton University Press, 2002), 33–42.

5 Emily Thompson, 'Listening to/for modernity architectural acoustics and the development of modern spaces in America', in Emily Thompson and Peter Galison (eds), *The Architecture of Science* (Cambridge, MA: MIT Press, 1999), 253–80 on 258.

6 George Saunders, *A Treatise on Theatres* (London: I & J Taylor, 1790), esp. 4–29 on acoustics. Discussed in Smith, *Acoustics*, 33–6 and in Thompson, *The Soundscape of Modernity,* 21–4.

7 Smith, *Acoustics*, 136.

8 T. B 'The acoustic properties of rooms', *The Builder*, 19(1861), 469–70. One possible identification of T. B is Thomas Talbot Bury (c. 1809–77). W. Tregellas (2004-09-23). Thomas Talbot Bury (bap. 1809, d. 1877), architect and engraver. *Oxford Dictionary of National Biography*. Retrieved 4 January 2018, from http://0-www.oxforddnb.com.wam.leeds.ac.uk/view/10.1093/ref:odnb/9780198614128.001.0001/odnb-9780198614128-e-4156

9 Smith, *Acoustics*, 134.

10 Rachel Milestone, 'The monstrosity of bricks and mortar: The town hall as a music venue in nineteenth-century Stalybridge', in Rachel Cowgill and Peter Holman (eds), *Music in the British provinces, 1690-1914* (Aldershot, England; Burlington, VT: Ashgate Pub. Limited, 2007), 295–323, 309 and 311.

11 The Belfast city hall completed in 1906 had problematic acoustics attributed to its high roof; see [Anon] 'Acoustic properties', *Architects Magazine,* 6, no. 71 (September 1906), 203. For later discussion on problems at London County Hall, see 'Defective acoustics', *Times* (24 July 1922), 13.

12 The Pump-room's dimensions were given by: inside length, 86 feet 6 inches; width, 33 feet 0 inches; height to ceiling line, 22 feet 7 inches; and height to centre, 24 feet 2 inches. The architect in question was John Clark of Leeds (1798/9–1857), see Derek Linstrum, 'Clark, John (1798/9–1857)', *Oxford Dictionary of National Biography* (Oxford: Oxford University Press, 2004). http://0-www.oxforddnb.com.wam.leeds.ac.uk/view/article/63001, accessed 6 September 2017, http://www.harrogatepeopleandplaces.info/publications/hollins1866/006-The%20Cheltenham%20Pump%20Room.htm Known latterly as the Royal Pump-room, this was repurposed in 1953 as a museum, http://www.yorkshirepost.co.uk/news/through-the-years-taking-the-waters-in-harrogate-1-6728565

13 Smith *Acoustics* 139–41, T. B 'The acoustic properties of rooms', 470. The *Builder* had published a review of Smith's book the previous week (see below) 433–44, and a friendly adviser had clearly drawn T. B's attention to this volume at a late stage in the writing of this letter to the *Builder.*

14 'To-day the QUEEN opens a magnificent edifice', [Editorial] *The Times*, Wednesday, 29 March 1871, 9; see discussion in 'St Pauls Cathedral and the science of acoustics' *Building News,* 20 (31 March 1871), 249–50.

15 The velarium was a type of awning used in Roman times, stretched over amphitheatres to protect spectators from the elements – not for acoustic purposes.

16 Henry Y. D. Scott and John Tyndall, 'The acoustics of the royal Albert Hall', *Times* (1 April 1871), 11. Henry Y. D. Scott, 'The acoustic qualities of the Albert-Hall', *The Times* (Monday, 01 May 1871), 12. 'The echo in the Albert Hall', *Building News*, 20 (9 June 1871), 461. See additional critical discussion in the same source 352–3, 477, 500. Leslie Chew, et al., *The Daily Book of Classical Music: 365 Readings that Teach, Inspire & Entertain* (Irvine, CA: Walter Foster Publishing, 2010), 35.

17 Smith, *Acoustics* (1895), 157–8.

18 Paul Waterhouse, 'Smith, Thomas Roger (1830–1903)', Rev. John Elliott, *Oxford Dictionary of National Biography* (Oxford: Oxford University Press, 2004); online edn, May 2006. http://0-www.oxforddnb.com.wam.leeds.ac.uk/view/article/36163 (accessed 28 February 2016). J. Mordaunt Crook, 'Architecture and history', *Architectural History,* 27 (1984), 555–78, especially 560–1; Thomas R. Metcalf, 'Architecture and the representation of empire: India, 1860-1910', *Representations,* 6 (Spring 1984), 37–65.

19 Sophie Forgan, 'Bricks and bones: Architecture and science in Victorian Britain', in Emily Thompson and Peter Galison (eds), *The Architecture of Science* (Cambridge, MA: MIT Press, 1999), 181–208.

20 Thomas Roger Smith, 'On acoustics', *Transactions of the Royal Institute of British Architects*, (1860–1), 73–96 (including discussion) republished as Thomas Roger Smith, 'On acoustics', *The Building News*, 6 (1860), 992–7. Page references to 'On Acoustics' below are to the *Building News* publication. For discussion of his early lectures on acoustics in 1858–60, see Smith, *Acoustics* (1878), 160 and *Acoustics* (1895), 162.

21 Theodore Lachéz, *Acoustique et Optique des Salles de Réunions Publiques* (Paris, 1848) Saunders, *A Treatise on Theatres*. J. G. Rhode, *Théorie der Verbreitung des Schalles für Baukünstler* (Berlin, 1800) and E. Chldani, *Traité d/Acoustique* (Paris, 1909).

22 John F. W. Herschel, *Treatises on Physical Astronomy, Light and Sound Contributed to the Encyclopaedia Metropolitana* (London and Glasgow: Richard Griffin & Co., 30 vols. 1817–45); Mary Somerville's *On the Connexion of the Physical Sciences* (London: John Murray, 1834).

23 Smith, 'On acoustics', 993.

24 Ibid., 994.

25 John Blackburn, 'Description of a sounding board in Attercliffe invented by the Rev. John Blackburn Minister of Attercliffe-Cum-Darnall, Sheffield', *Philosophical Transactions of the Royal Society of London*, 118 (1828), 361–3. At his RIBA lecture Smith showed a model of this sounding board which had previously been donated to UCL.

26 Smith, 'On acoustics', 996.

27 Smith, *Acoustics* (1878), 152.

28 Smith, *Acoustics*, 43 and 104. John Scott Russell, 'Elementary considerations of some principles in the construction of buildings designed to accommodate spectators and auditors', *Edinburgh New Philosophical Journal*, 27 (April–October 1839), 131–6 and *Transactions of the Royal Scottish Society of Arts*, 1 (1841), 314–19. See discussion in Jeanne Halgren Kilde, *When Church Became Theatre: The Transformation of Evangelical Architecture and Worship in Nineteenth-century America* (Oxford: Oxford University Press, 2002), 48–57 and 234. For the broader history of the Royal Institution's architecture, see Frank James and Anthony Peers, 'Constructing space for science at the Royal Institution of Great Britain', *Physics in Perspective*, 9 (2007), 130–85.

29 'Books Received: *A rudimentary treatise on the acoustics of public buildings*', *The Builder*, 19 (1861), 433–4.

30 H. W. Burrows, 'Sound in its relation to buildings'. *Journal of the Royal Society of British Architects*, (3rd series) 2 (1895), 353–75.

31 As Emily Thompson notes, the definitive version of 'Reverberation' was reproduced as single article in Wallace Clement Sabine, *Collected Papers on Acoustics* (Cambridge, MA and London: Harvard University Press, 1922), 3–68.

32 By comparison Sabine claimed the ideal resonance time for a concert hall was around two seconds. The Sander theatre had been designed to mark the centenary of US independence by Harvard graduates William Robert Ware and Henry Van Brunt for the University's Memorial Building. Their model had been Oxford University's Sheldonian Building.

33 Thompson, *The Soundscape of Modernity,* 69–74. I thank Horatio Joyce for pointing out that it was Sabine's work with the Boston Symphony Orchestra and architect Charles F. McKim launched Sabine's consulting career before he left Harvard. See Thompson, *The Soundscape of Modernity*, 69.

34 For early praise of Sabine in the UK, see [Anon] 'Acoustics and architecture: Reverberation and absorption', *Architects Magazine,* 1, no. 5 (March 1901), 85.

35 See discussions of this in the Builder's Journal; see also [Anon] 'Architectural acoustics', *Architects Magazine*, 7, no. 73 (November 1906), 15.

36 [Anon] 'Acoustics of buildings a difficult problem', *Journal of the Society of Architects*, 4, no. 46 (August 1911), 372–3.

37 Clement Sabine, *Collected Papers on Acoustics.*

38 Hope Bagenal, 'Acoustics applied to buildings', *Journal of the Society of Architects,* 1922, 15, no. 2 (December 1921), 34–46. David Trevor-Jones, 'Bagenal, (Philip) Hope Edward (1888–1979)', *Oxford Dictionary of National Biography* (Oxford: Oxford University Press, 2004), http://www.oxforddnb.com/view/article/63126 (accessed 10 September 2017).

39 Alexander Wood, 'Architecture and acoustics', *Architecture*, 16, no. 1 (November 1922), 40–2. On the collaboration of these two leading interwar

UK acousticians, see Hope Bagenal and Alexander Wood, *Planning for Good Acoustics* (London: Methuen, 1931).

40 Ian Stewart, *Seventeen Equations that Changed the World* (London: Profile Books, 2012).

41 Smith, *Acoustics*, 2.

42 Ibid.

43 Emily Thompson, 'Listening to/for modernity', 258 and 273. The 1895 debate was reported in the *Royal Institute of British Architects Journal* (3rd series), 4 (6 May 1897), 323.

44 The publisher's prefatory note to this revised edition of 1895 specified that 'the text has been revised by him in a few places, and additions made [on electrical transmission of sound and on the Albert Hall's defects]. Otherwise the text remains as in previous editions, the engagements of Professor Roger Smith having prevented his undertaking any comprehensive revision of the work'. Smith, *Acoustics*, 3rd edition, iv.

45 Thompson, *The Soundscape of Modernity*.

46 Smith, *Acoustics*, 40. Kamptulicon had been patented by Elijah Galloway in 1843/4: see entry on 'Floorcloth' in Encyclopaedia Britannica, 11th edition, Volume 10, http://gutenberg.readingroo.ms/3/5/7/4/35747/35747-h/35747-h.htm#ar24

47 Obituary' [Thomas Roger Smith & others], *The Times* (Saturday, 14 March 1903), 12.

Chapter 8

1 Report of Select Committee on Houses of Parliament (HC 1844, 448); Note: Select Committees are committees composed of Members of Parliament and are appointed to conduct inquiries into a particular issue or areas.

2 Fergus Nicol and Susan Roaf, 'Rethinking thermal comfort', *Building Research Information*, (March 2017), 1–5; Adrian Leaman and Bill Bordass, 'Assessing building performance in use: The Probe occupant surveys and their implications', *Building Research and Information*, 29 (2001), 129–43; Wolfgang F. E. Preiser and Andrea Hardy, 'Historical review of building performance evaluation', in Wolfgang F. E. Preiser Aaron Davis, Andrea Hardy and Ashraf Salama (eds), *Architecture Beyond Criticism Expert Judgment and Performance Evaluation* (Abington: Routledge, 2015), 147–59.

3 David Boswell Reid, *Illustrations of the Theory and Practice of Ventilation* (London, 1844); David Boswell Reid, *Ventilation in American Dwellings* (New York, 1858).

4 Hugo Reid, *Memoir of the Late David Boswell Reid* (Edinburgh: R. Grant and Son, 1863).

5 Reid's inquiries into air quality, including his use of Co_2 concentration as an index for air quality, can has been explored in Colin Porteous, 'Sensing

a Historic Low-CO2 Future', in Nicolas Mazzeo (ed.), *Chemistry, Emission Control, Radioactive Pollution and Indoor Air Quality* (Rijeka: InTech, 2011), 213–46; Letter from Reid to the Council of the University College, London, 1837 in *Testimonials regarding Dr. Reid's qualification as a lecturer in chemistry and teacher of practical chemistry*, April 1837 (UCL Library, Hume Tracts).

6 David Boswell Reid, 'The revision of architecture in connection with the useful arts', *Builder* (5 May 1855), 208f; David Boswell Reid, 'Eight lectures by David Boswell Reid on 'Progress of architecture in relation to ventilation, warming, lighting, fire-proofing, acoustics, and the general preservation of health', *Smithsonian Annual Reports* (1856), 147–86.

7 David Boswell Reid, *Rudiments of Chemistry* (Edinburgh: William and Robert Chambers, 1836); David Boswell Reid, *Elements of Practical Chemistry* (Edinburgh: Maclachlan and Stewart, 1830).

8 Report of the Select Committee on the Ventilation of the Houses of Parliament, (HC 1835, 583).

9 David Boswell Reid, *Brief Outlines Illustrative of the Alterations in the House of Commons, in Reference to the Acoustic and Ventilating Arrangements* (Edinburgh, 1837).

10 Ventilation of the House. Letter from Dr. Reid to the Viscount Duncannon, 28 March 1838 (HC 1837–38, 277); 'Philosophical society', *Caledonian Mercury* (28 July 1836).

11 Christine Ridings and Jacqueline Riding, *The Houses of Parliament: History, Art, Architecture* (London: Merrel, 2000).

12 As I have explored in Henrik Schoenefeldt, 'The temporary houses of parliament and David Boswell Reid's Architecture of Experimentation', *Architectural History*, 57 (2014), 175–215.

13 Report of Select Committee on Houses of Parliament (HC SC 1844, 448). A modern definition of thermal comfort is 'that condition of mind that expresses satisfaction with the environment'. *Environmental Design CIBSE Guide A* (London: CIBSE, 2007), Sections 1.1 to 1.7.

14 Gustav Theodor Fechner, *Elemente der Psychophysik* (Leipzig: Breitkopf & Härtel, 1860).

15 Reid, *Illustrations of the Theory and Practice of Ventilation*, 185.

16 Second report from the Select Committee on Ventilation and Lighting of the House (HC 1852, 402), Q361.

17 Report from the Select Committee on Lighting the House (HC 1839, 501).

18 Reid, *Illustrations of the Theory and Practice of Ventilation*, 184–7.

19 Second Report of the Select Committee on Ventilation and Lighting of the House, (HC 1852, 402), Q642.

20 David Boswell Reid, *Extract from Official Documents, Reports and Papers Referring to the Progress of Dr. Reid's Plans for Ventilation, Undated* (National Archives: Work 11-16, nr. 88); David Boswell Reid, *Narrative of Facts as to the New Houses of Parliament* (London: Longmans, 1839).

21 Report of Select Committee appointed to consider a plan for a more convenient temporary accommodation for the House of Lords, 3 July 1835 (Parliamentary Archives: Arc/Pro/Work 11/10/2 nr. 450).

22 Letter from Lord Campbell, 11 September 1843, in Extracts from official documents, reports (UCL Library, Hume Tracts); 'Progress of the new houses of parliament', HL Deb, 24 April 1846, vol. 85, cc970-6.

23 'The new houses of parliament', HL Deb, 21 February 1843, vol. 66, cc1033-6.

24 'Progress of the new houses of parliament', HL Deb, 24 April 1846, vol. 85, cc970-6; Letter from Lord Campbell, 11 September 1843, in Extracts from official documents, reports (UCL Library, Hume Tracts).

25 'Maynooth College Bill – Ajourned debate', HL Deb, 3 June 1845, vol. 80, cc1298; 'Maynooth College Bill', HL Deb, 2 June 1845, vol. 80, cc11160-231; 'Maynooth College Bill – Ajourned debate', HL Deb, 4 June 1845, vol. 81, cc6-120.

26 'The new houses of parliament', HL Deb, 05 June 1845, vol. 81, cc120-2.

27 Report of the Select Committee on the Houses of Parliament (HC 448, 1844), Q317-28, 387.

28 Oral Statement given by Reid, 26 July 1842, Report from the Select Committee on Ventilation of the New Houses of Parliament, (HC 1842, 536), Q14.

29 Oral Statement given by Reid, 17 June 1844, (HC 448, 1844) Q320–387.

30 For example, ceiling above equalizing chamber with supply tubes, valves, and flaps, 28 June 1851 (Work 29/3100); Section through centre Gangway, raised platforms and seats, 10 January 1851 (Work 29/3093); Set of drawings, dated 10 January 1851, showing perforated floor at the back of the benches. (Work 29/3093).

31 A description of Reid's original ventilation system in the Permanent House of Commons is provided in: Henrik Schoenefeldt, 'Reid's Short-lived ventilation system for the Permanent House of Commons', *Studies in the History of Construction* (Cambridge: CHS, 2015), 167–82. A detailed anatomical reconstruction of the lost chamber is provided in the forthcoming article: Henrik Schoenefeldt, 'The historic ventilation system of the house of commons', 1840–52: revisiting David Boswell Reid's environmental legacy, *Journal of the Society of Antiquaries*, 98–2018.

32 Registers of temperature control and ventilation for the House of Commons 1853–4 (Parliamentary Archives: OOW/5).

33 Statement explanatory of the arrangements for warming and ventilating the New House of Commons, 5 April 1852, in Second report from the Select Committee on Ventilation and Lighting of the House (HC 1852, 402), pp. 545–8; Oral statement given by Reid 20 April 1852 (HC 1852, 402), Q597-8.

34 Oral Statement given by Charles Barry, 30 March 1852, Second report from the Select Committee on Ventilation and Lighting of the House (HC 1852, 402), Q788-91.

35 Alfred Meeson, First Report on the State of the warming, and ventilation and lighting of the Houses of Parliament, 8 January 1853 (National Archives: Work 11/14, nr. 768-81).

36 Plan of Principal Floor, 1852 (Strategic Estates Archives, Westminster); Plan and Section of Ventilation Office in South-West angle of House Lobby, November 1852, (National Archives: Work 29/3110).

37 Plan and Section of offices for ventilation, 22 September 1851; (National Archives: Work 29/3106); Plan of ground floor, 1852 (Strategic Estates Archives, Westminster) 22 September 1851 (National Archives: Work 29/3106).

38 Second report from the Select Committee on Ventilation and Lighting of the House (HC 1852, 402), Q255.

39 Registers of temperature control and ventilation for the House of Commons 1853-4 (Parliamentary Archives, OOW/5).

40 These included Select Committee of House of Commons on Ventilation and Lighting of the House, 1852; Select Committee on Ventilation of the House of Commons, 1854; Select Committee of the House of Lords, appointed to inquire into the possibility of improving the ventilation and the lighting of the House, 1854. A detailed examination of the technical and managerial issues underlying Reid's system can be found in Henrik Schoenefeldt, 'The lost (first) chamber of the house of commons', *AA Files*, 72 (June 2016), 44–56.

41 For example, Ventilation of the House, HC Deb 06 February 1852 vol. 119 cc231-4 231; The Queen's Speech – Report of Address, HC Deb, 4 February 1852, vol. 119, cc162-72; Imperial Parliament, *Daily News* (5 February 1852), 3; 'The science of ventilation has at length been', *The Times* (9 February 1852), 4; Ventilation of the House, HC Deb, 11 February 1852, vol. 119, cc400-16; Editorial, Builder, 10-471, 14 February 1852, 97; Ventilation of the House, HC Deb, 16 March 1852, vol. 119, cc1147-50 1147.

42 'Imperial parliament', *Daily News* (5 February 1852), 3.

43 Second report of Mr Goldsworthy Gurney on the ventilation of the new House of Commons, (HC 1852, 252 (371).

44 Second report from the Select Committee on Ventilation and Lighting of the House (HC 1852, 402), Q153-57.

45 Ventilation of the House, HC Deb, 11 February 1852, vol. 119, cc400-16.

46 Temperature at the House of Commons, taken by the messenger of the Serjeant-at-Arms, 22 March–4 May 1852 (HC 1852 (402).

47 Historic paintings show that MPs wore heavy clothing during debates. Modern standards recommend temperatures of 20 °C–23 °C in winter and 22 °C to 26 °C in summer (ASHRAE, 2004), but if the historic clothing levels are taken into consideration these temperatures come close to current standards. According to ASHREA Standard 55 an air temperature of 65 °F is optimal for thermal comfort at clothing levels of 1.5 clo.

48 Second report from the Select Committee on Ventilation and Lighting of the House (HC 1852, 402), Q124-38.

49 Oral statement given by the Speaker of the House of Commons, 26 March 1852, (HC 1852, 402), Q316.

50 Oral statement given by John Leslie, 27 April 1852 (HC 1852, 402), Q3137-73.

51 Second report of Mr Goldsworthy Gurney on the ventilation of the new House of Commons, (HC 1852, 252 (371)).

52 For a more detailed study of technical problems, see Schoenefeldt, 'Reid's Short-lived ventilation system for the Permanent House of Commons', 167–82.

53 David Boswell Reid, *Report of Measures Required for the Health and Comfort of the Honourable House of Commons, in Obedience to Resolution of the* House, 10 March 1852 (National Archives: Work 11/14 nr. 711-14).

54 Temperature at the House of Commons, taken by the messenger of the Serjeant-at-Arms, 22 March–4 May 1852 (HC 1852 (402).

55 Alfred Meeson, *First Report on the State of the Warming, Ventilating, and Lighting Arrangements Throughout the Building*, December 1852 (National Archives: Work 11/14, nr. 768-81).

56 Report of the Standing Committee on the Ventilating and Lighting the House of Commons; (HC 1852-53, 911); Report of Mr Goldsworthy Gurney to the Commissioners of Works, respecting the lighting of the House of Commons.

57 Report of Mr Goldsworthy Gurney to the Commissioners of Works, respecting the lighting of the House of Commons (HC 1852-53, 911).

58 Ventilation of the House, HC Deb, 17 February 1853, vol. 124 cc180-1; 'Supply', HC Deb 19 May 1853 vol 127 cc388-422; Ventilation of the House, *The Times* (11 March 1854), 7; Ventilation of the House, Morning Chronicle, 6 May 1853; Imperial Parliament, *Daily News* (20 May 1853), 3; Ventilation of the House, *Daily News* (1 March 1854), 2; Ventilation of the House, *Morning Chronicle* (6 May 1853); Imperial Parliament, *Daily News* (20 May 1853), 3.

59 Second Report from the Select Committee on Ventilation of the House of Commons (HC 1854, 270); Third report from the Select Committee on Ventilation of the House (HC 1854, 403).

60 Oral statement given by Goldsworthy Gurney, 23 May 1854 (HC 2704), Q206-9; Oral statement given by Gurney, 8 May 1854 (HL 1854, 384) Q618-81; 'The New House of Commons', *Morning Chronicle* (29 April 1854), 5.

61 Report from the Select Committee of the House of Lords, appointed to inquire into the possibility of improving the ventilation and the lighting of the House (HL 1854, 384)

62 First Report from the Select Committee on Ventilation, (HC 1854, 149); Letter from Works to Gurney, 7 April 1854 (National Archives: Work 11/14 nr. 850); Letter from Gurney to Works, 7 April 1854 (National Archives: Work 11/14 nr. 842); Letter from Gurney to Office of Works, 10 April 1854 (National Archives: Work 11/14 nr. 847)

63 Report from the Select Committee of the House of Lords, appointed to inquire into the possibility of improving the ventilation and the lighting of the House (HL 1854, 384) Q839-81.

64 Second Report *of* Select Committee on Ventilation of House of Commons (HC 1854 270), iii–ix.

65 William Heberden, An account of the heat of July, 1825, together with some remarks upon sensible cold, *Philosophical Transactions of the Royal Society*,

2-1826, pp. 69–74; Thomas Tredgold, *Principles of Warming and Ventilating Public Buildings* (London: J. Taylor, 1824), 3–17.

66 Thomas Bedford, *The Warmth Factor in Comfort at Work. A Physiological Study of Heating and Ventilation* (London: HMSO: 1936), 10–11.

Chapter 9

1 A. H. Beavan, *Imperial London* (London: J.M. Dent & Co.; New York: E.P. Dutton & Co., 1901).

2 *The Hotel World* (November 1898), 501.

3 Although Pevsner argues that since 1840, 'America led the world in hotel building' (Nikolaus Pevsner, *A History of Building Types* (Princeton: Princeton University Press, 1976), 176), there were crucial differences between US and London grand hotels. London establishments claimed to be more cosmopolitan, drawing on the best of American, European, and British hotel-keeping cultures, and were not used as centres of commerce, with the consequence that the ground floors of US hotels were often raucous, male-dominated spaces. See Molly W. Berger, *Hotel Dreams: Luxury, Technology and Urban Ambition in American, 1829-1929* (Baltimore: Johns Hopkins University Press, 2011).

4 Thorstein Veblen, *The Theory of the Leisure Class: An Economic Study of Institutions* (London: Allen & Unwin, 1899).

5 As Bourdieu notes, 'taste classifies and it classifies the classifier', and the form of visible 'cultural consumption' found in luxury hotels fulfilled the function of legitimating social differences which aimed to keep out undesirables. Pierre Bourdieu, *Distinction: A Social Critique of the Judgement of Taste* (London: Routledge & Kegan Paul, 1984), 6–7; Markus identifies the importance of restricting access in semi-public, shared spaces for leisure, such as clubs and hotels. These spaces also required freedom and visibility once within, so that occupants might meet and socialize freely. Markus, *Buildings & Power*, 157.

6 David Bowie, 'Pure diffusion? The great English hotel charges debate', *The Times*, 1853', *Business History*, 58, no. 2 (2015), 159–78; Albert Smith, *The English Hotel Nuisance* (London: David Bryce, 1855), 6.

7 Charles Dickens, *Household Words* (16 February 1856), 97–103; 23 February 1856, 141–4 and 1 March 1856, 148–54; Anthony Trollope, *North America* (Philadelphia: J.B. Lippincott & Co., 1862), 55.

8 For the history of railway hotels, see Jack Simmons, 'Railways, hotels and tourism in Great Britain, 1839-1914', *Journal of Contemporary History*, 19 (1984), 201–22; 'The new hotel system', *The London Review* (27 June 1863), 687.

9 Christine Amsler, Robin Bartlett, and Craig Bolton, 'Thoughts of some British economists on early limited liability and corporate legislation', *History of Political Economy*, 13 (1981), 774–93.

10 *Modern London; or London as it Is* (London: John Murray, 1879), 48.

11 *The Langham Hotel Guide* (London, 1872), 17.

12 As well as *Murray's Guide*, these also included *The 'Tariff-Frame' Hotel Guide* (London: Hotel and General Advertising Company Ltd, 1894) and Karl Baedeker, *London and its Environs* (Leipzig: 1889) and other editions.

13 *The Langham Hotel Guide* (London, 1881), 7–10.

14 For the place of women in the retail world, see Erika Rappaport, *Shopping for Pleasure: Women in the Making of the West End* (Princeton, NJ; Chichester: Princeton University Press, 2001); for the growth of respectability in restaurants and cafes, see Rachel Rich, *Bourgeois Consumption: Food, Space and Identity in London and Paris, 1850-1914* (Manchester: Manchester University Press, 2011); for the use of domestic design references in Victorian theatre interiors, see Hugh Maguire, 'The Victorian theatre as a home from home', *Journal of Design History*, 13 (2000), 107–21.

15 'The Langham Hotel', *The Builder* (25 June 1865), 532; 'The Grand Hotel, Charing Cross', *The Builder* (29 March 1879), 342.

16 Charles Rice, *The Emergence of the Interior: Architecture, Modernity, Domesticity* (London: Routledge, 2007), 57.

17 Baedeker, *London*, 7. The 1898 edition records 109 hotels; 1900 edition – 114 hotels; 1905 edition – 116 hotels.

18 'The prospects of hotels in London', *The Hotel World* (February 1898), 12.

19 For the development of changing ideas of luxury, see Linda Levy Peck, *Consuming Splendor: Society and Culture in Seventeenth-Century* England (Cambridge: Cambridge University Press, 2005) and Jan de Vries, 'Luxury in the Dutch golden age in theory and practice', in M. Berg and E. Eger (eds.) *Luxury in the Eighteenth Century: Debates, Desires and Delectable Goods* (Basingstoke: Palgrave Macmillan, 2003).

20 Seven hundred bedrooms at 100 per cent capacity would equate to 255,000 room-nights. An 80 per cent occupancy rate (expected for twenty-first-century luxury hotels) would equate to 204,000.

21 Veblen, *The Theory of the Leisure Class*.

22 Jean-Noel Kapferer, 'Abundant rarity: The key to luxury growth', *Business Horizons*, 55 (2012), 453–62, citing John Groth and Stephen McDaniel, 'The exclusive value principle: The basis for prestige racing', *Journal of Consumer Marketing*, 10, no. 1 (1993), 10–16.

23 *Manchester Guardian* (21 May 1885), 4.

24 *The Art Journal* (July 1889), 50; *Daily Telegraph* (31 July 1889), 3.

25 *The Savoy Souvenir* (London, 1889), 24–6; 'The Hotel Coburg', *The Caterer* (December 1896), 598; 'The Coburg Hotel', *Illustrated London News* (23 January 1897), 130.

26 'The old inn and the modern hotel', *The Queen* (4 April 1891), 518.

27 'Hotel Coburg', *The Caterer* (December 1896), 598.

28 The three great Edwardian London grand hotels – the Ritz (1906), The Piccadilly (1908), and the Waldorf (1908) – were all neoclassical in design, with the Waldorf in particular bearing a striking resemblance to the Great Western.

29 Andrew Wynter, *Subtle Brains and Lissom Fingers* (originally published London: 1863; revised and enlarged by Andrew Steinmetz, 1877), 69.

30 'Monster hotels', *London Reader* (27 October 1866), 689; *The Langham Hotel Guide* (London, 1872), 9; *British Architect* (20 October 1882), 501; 'Big London hotels', *The Caterer* (March 1889), 107.

31 Nathaniel Newnham-Davis, *Dinners and Diners: Where and How to Dine in London* (London: Grant Richards, 1899), 37.

32 'The uniform oft proclaims the hotel', *The Hotel World* (February 1897), 7.

33 Douglas Tallack, '"Waiting, waiting": The hotel lobby in the modern city', in Neil Leach (ed.) *The Hieroglyphics of Space: Reading and Experiencing the Modern Metropolis,* (London: Routledge, 2002), 142.

34 'Some of the first-class hotels in the West End only receive travellers when the room has been ordered beforehand or when the visitors are provided with an introduction'. Karl Baedeker, *London and its Environs* (Leipzig, 1888), 7; 'Hotel Mems – the American hotel clerk', *The Caterer* (15 January 1897), 2; 'English hotels', *The Caterer* (15 September 1893), 375.

35 For the role of the hotel lobby or lounge, and its function as a site of anonymity in the modern metropolis, see Siegfried Kracauer, *The Mass Ornament: Weimar Essays* (Cambridge, MA: Harvard University Press, 1995) and Franziska Bollerey, 'Beyond the lobby: Setting the stage for modernity – the cosmos of the hotel', in Tom Avermaete and Anne Massey (eds), *Hotel Lobbies and Lounges* (London: Routledge, 2013).

36 For the innovative construction in hotels and clubs, see Jonathan Clarke, *Early Structural Steel in London Buildings: A Discreet Revolution* (Swindon: English Heritage, 2014) particularly Chapters 4 and 10.

37 *The Langham Hotel Guide* (1872), 9; *The Langham Hotel Guide* (1881), 4.

38 See Augusta McMahon, 'Space, sound and light: Toward a sensory experience of ancient monumental architecture', *American Journal of Archaeology*, 117 (2013), 163–79, 169.

39 Mrs Humphry, 'A historical hotel', in *Homes of the Passing Show* (London: Savoy Press, 1900), 57.

40 *Hotel Cecil, London* (London: 1906), 7. A guidebook for the use of guests.

41 A similar technique was adopted in other spaces for leisure, where the suggestion of status was an essential part of the luxury proposal, and consequent cost, of the venue; see Andrew P. Haley, *Turning the Tables: Restaurants and the Rise of the American Middle Class, 1880-1920* (Chapel Hill: University of North Carolina Press, 2011), 40.

42 'The Grand Hotel, Charing-Cross', *Illustrated London News* (19 June 1880), 598.

43 'The Hotel Metropole', *The Times* (London, England), 1 June 1885, 6.

44 *Hotel Cecil* (1906), 7; *The Architect and Contract Reporter* (8 May 1896), 298; The Ballroom at 17 Grosvenor Place, London (1890) decorated by the firm of Duveen for Sir Arthur Wilson (Nicholas Cooper, *The Opulent Eye: Late Victorian and Edwardian Taste in Interior* Design (London: Architectural Press, 1976), 57) has a similar frieze and ceiling.

45 Marie Ritz, *César Ritz, Host to the World* (London: G. G. Harrap, 1938), 152.

46 'Hotel Mems', *The Caterer* (June 1895), 239.

47 *London Metropolitan Archives*: Presented Papers: LCC/min/10906. Letter from Charles Francis Munro, secretary of the Savoy Hotel Limited, to H de La Hooke Esq, clerk of the London County Council, 27 October 1893; *London Metropolitan Archives*: GLC/AR/BR/19/0164. LCC Architects Department. Entertainment licence application for the Hotel Cecil, 15 March 1899.

48 'The Langham Hotel', *Illustrated London News* (8 May 1886), 481.

49 'A kind of inn in Eastern countries where caravans put up ... a large quadrangular building with a spacious court in the middle'. *Murray's New English Dictionary* (Oxford: Clarendon Press, 1888), 106; for discussions of the range of meanings associated with cosmopolitanism from 'the pejorative to the progressive', see Tanya Agathocleous and Jason R. Ruby, 'Victorian cosmopolitanisms: Introduction', *Victorian Literature and Culture*, 38 (2010), 389–97.

50 *The Times* (London, England, 3 November 1855), 7; Evening Telegraph and Star and Sheffield, *Daily Times* (13 June 1889), 3; 'The furnishing of the new Claridge's', *Furniture and Decoration* (December 1898), 194.

51 The *New York Times* often reported the activities of Americans staying at the London hotels. See 'How American society will be represented', *New York Times* (22 June 1902), 4 and 'What Americans are doing in London', *New York Times* (15 June 1902), 17; these exotic guests are listed in *Hotel Cecil* (1906), 10.

52 See Judith R. Walkowitz, 'Cosmopolitanism, feminism, and the moving body', *Victorian Literature and Culture*, 38 (2010), 427–49; for a more detailed argument of the role of women in restaurants, see Mary-Louise Roberts, 'Gender, consumption and commodity culture', *American Historical Review*, 103 (1993), 817–44.

53 Ritz, *César Ritz,* 98 and 184.

54 'The Carlton Hotel', *Daily Telegraph* (12 July 1899), 10.

55 Well-known French chefs included Escoffier and Echenard at the Savoy, Antoine Coste at the Cecil, and M. Malley at the Ritz; 'Englishmen ... are little employed at hotels simply because they won't learn foreign languages. In a large hotel, 85% of the cooks are French, and French is the *lingua franca* of the kitchen'. Carl Ritz, 'The mechanism of a modern hotel', *The Review of Reviews* (26 November 1902), 509; Brenda Assael, 'Gastro-cosmopolitanism and the restaurant in late Victorian and Edwardian London', *Historical Journal*, 56 (2013), 681–706, 683;

56 According to the Census records, at the Savoy in 1891, the thirteen waiters registered were mostly German or French, (one Italian, one Belgian, and one Swiss). In 1901 all waiters were German. See also Stefan Manz and Panikos Panayi, 'The rise and fall of Germans in the British hospitality industry c1880-1920', *Food & History*, 11, no. 2 (2013), 243–66.

57 An Indian curry chef , for example, was employed at the Cecil. Newnham-Davis, *Dinners and Diners*, 39; 'Menu for the Diamond Jubilee dinner at

the Savoy on 4 March 1897', in *University of Las Vegas Digital Collection: Menus: The Art of Dining*, http://digital.library.unlv.edu/collections/menus (accessed 14 December 2017); *The Savoy Souvenir* (1889), 24.

58 'The decadence of the political club', *Pall Mall Gazette* (16 June 1887), 1.

59 See the reference to 'lounging' in the earlier quotation from *The Hotel World* (November 1898), 501.

60 *Homes of the Passing Show* (London: The Savoy Press, 1900) was a collection of articles and sketches by well-known authors and artists, promoting the Savoy Group of hotels, which included the Savoy, Claridge's, and the Berkeley, as well as a number of European venues.

61 *The Langham Hotel Guide* (1872), 5.

62 *Building News* (18 November 1898), 714.

63 *Builders Journal* (6 June 1900), 328.

64 Beavan, *Imperial London*, 456; 'A fashionable resort of today: The Palm Court at the Carlton Hotel', *Illustrated London News* (5 August 1899), 190; Ritz, *César Ritz*, 274.

65 Mrs Hardy, 'The hotel drawing room', *The Queen* (21 September 1895), 525.

66 Robert Machray, *The Night Side of London* (Philadelphia: J.B. Lippincott & Co., 1902), 79.

Chapter 10

1 Anthony Trollope, *Can You Forgive Her?*, 1864–5, ed. Stephen Wall, (London: Penguin, 2004), 480.

2 Whyte, *Unlocking the Church*, 23–4.

3 For examples, see M. H. Port (ed.), *The Houses of Parliament* (New Haven: Yale University Press, 1976); Roland Quinault, 'Westminster and the Victorian constitution', *Transactions of the Royal Historical Society*, 2 (1992), 79–104.

4 There are risks to using literature for historical analysis, but such material can prove productive; for example, see Julian Wolfreys, *Writing London Volume 3: Inventions of the City* (Basingstoke: Palgrave Macmillan, 2007), 1–7; Julian Wolfreys, 'Dickensian architextures or, the city and the ineffable', in Ruth Robbins and Julian Wolfreys (eds), *Victorian Identities: Social and Cultural Formations in Nineteenth-Century Literature*, (Basingstoke: Palgrave Macmillan, 1996), 199–214, 201 and 209–11; Elizabeth A. Bridgham, *Spaces of the Sacred and Profane: Dickens, Trollope, and the Victorian Cathedral Town* (New York: Routledge, 2008), 1–7 and 43–44; David Spur, *Architecture and Modern Literature*, 4; comparing the symmetrical organization of buildings and text, see Susan Bernstein, *Housing Problems: Writing and Architecture in Goethe, Walpole, Freud, and Heidegger* (Stanford: Stanford University Press, 2008).

5 Elaine Hadley, *Living Liberalism: Practical Citizenship in Mid-Victorian Britain* (Chicago: University of Chicago Press, 2010), 33–6.

6 Anthony Trollope, *Autobiography of Anthony Trollope* (London: Oxford University Press, 1883), 240.

7 Ibid., 102–3.

8 Anthony Trollope, *Phineas Finn*, 1869, ed. John Sutherland (London: Penguin, 1972), 296.

9 (Anon.), 'Trollope's Irish Novels', *Dublin Review*, 65 (October 1869), 361; George Levine, 'Can you forgive him? Trollope's "Can you forgive her?" And the myth of realism', *Victorian Studies*, 18, no. 1 (September 1974), 5–30, 14; George Levine, *The Realistic Imagination: English Fiction from Frankenstein to Lady Chatterley* (Chicago: Chicago University Press, 1981), 4.

10 (Anon.), 'Mr Anthony Trollope', *Edinburgh Review*, 166 (October 1877), 455.

11 James Kincaid, *The Novels of Anthony Trollope*, (Oxford: Oxford University Press, 1977), 49; Ayelet Ben-Yishai, 'The fact of a rumor: Anthony Trollope's *The Eustace Diamonds*', *Nineteenth-Century Literature*, 62, no. 1, (June 2007), 88–120, 118 and 90–4; also see J. Hillis Miller, *The Ethics of Reading: Kant, de Man, Eliot, Trollope, James, and Benjamin* (New York: Columbia University Press, 1987).

12 Simon Eliot, 'The business of Victorian publishing', in Deirdre David (ed.), *The Cambridge Companion to the Victorian Novel* (Cambridge: Cambridge University Press, 2012), 36–61, 48–9.

13 Alvar Ellegard, 'The readership of the periodical press in mid-Victorian Britain: II. Directory', *Victorian Periodicals Newsletter*, 13, (Vol. 4, No.3), (September 1971), 3–22, 13, 19 and 20–1.

14 Jonathan Parry, *The Rise and Fall of Liberal Government in Victorian Britain* (New Haven: Yale University Press, 1993), 221; also see Robert Saunders, *Democracy and the Vote in British Politics, 1848-1867: The Making of the Second Reform Act* (Farnham: Routledge, 2011).

15 John N. Hall, 'Trollope, Anthony (1815–1882)', *Oxford Dictionary of National Biography* (Oxford: Oxford University Press, 2004); online edn, September 2012, http://www.oxforddnb.com/view/article/27748 (accessed 12 March 2017); John N. Hall, *Trollope: A Biography* (Oxford: Clarendon Press, 1991).

16 Trollope, *Autobiography*, 222.

17 Jill Felicity Durey, *Trollope and the Church of England* (Basingstoke: Palgrave Macmillan, 2002), 179 and 166.

18 Trollope, *The New Zealander* (Oxford: Oxford University Press, 1972), 192–3.

19 Trollope, *Can You Forgive Her?*, 479.

20 Trollope, *Phineas Finn*, 104 and 473.

21 Ibid., 214–5 and 218.

22 Anthony Trollope, *Phineas Redux*, 1874, ed. Gregg A. Hecimovich (London: Penguin, 2003), 13.

23 Trollope, *Can You Forgive Her?*, 482–3.

24 Trollope, *Phineas Redux*, 259; also see John N. Hall (ed.), *The Letters of Anthony Trollope*, vol. I (Stanford: Stanford University Press, 1983), 49.

25 Anthony Trollope, *The Way We Live Now*, vol. I of II (London: Chapman and Hall, 1875), 219 and 277–8; also see Shirley Robin Letwin, *The Gentleman in Trollope: Individuality and Moral Conduct* (Basingstoke: Palgrave Macmillan, 1982), 175–7.

26 Anthony Trollope, *The Way We Live Now*, vol. II of II (London: Chapman and Hall, 1875), 119.

27 Anthony Trollope, *The Prime Minister*, 1875–6, ed. David Skilton (London: Penguin, 1994), 584.

28 Parliamentary Papers (1833) 269; 'Report from the select committee on the House of Commons' Buildings; with the minutes of evidence taken before them', 28–9.

29 Ibid., 33 and 12; also see Charles T. Goodsell, 'The architecture of parliaments: Legislative houses and political culture', *British Journal of Political Science*, 18, no. 3 (July 1988), 287–302.

30 See W. J. Rorabaugh, 'Politics and the architectural competition for the Houses of Parliament, 1834–1837', *Victorian Studies*, 17, no. 2 (1973), 155–75, 159; George H. Weitzman, 'The utilitarians and the houses of parliament', *Journal of the Society of Architectural Historians*, 20, no. 3 (October 1961), 99–107; Andrea Fredericksen, 'Parliament's genius loci: The politics of place after the 1834 fire', in Christine Riding and Jacqueline Riding (eds), *The Houses of Parliament: History, Art, Architecture* (London: Merrell Publishers, 2000), 99–111.

31 Trollope in *St Paul's: A Monthly Magazine*, vol. 3 (October 1868–March 1869, London, 1869), 538–9.

32 Trollope, *Phineas Finn*, 99; Anthony Trollope, *The Duke's Children*, 1880, ed. Dinah Birch (London: Penguin, 1995), 478.

33 Trollope, *Can You Forgive Her?*, 289.

34 Trollope, *Phineas Finn*, 58.

35 John Halperin, *Trollope and Politics: A Study of the Pallisers and Others* (Basingstoke: Palgrave Macmillan, 1977), 88.

36 Trollope, *Phineas Redux*, 289.

37 Trollope, *Autobiography*, 225; on his earlier ideas, see David M. Craig, 'Advanced conservative liberalism: Party and principle in Trollope's parliamentary novels', *Victorian Literature and Culture*, 38 (2010), 355–71, 366.

38 Courtney C. Berger, 'Partying with the opposition: Social politics in *The Prime Minister*', *Texas Studies in Literature and Language*, 45, no. 3 (Fall 2003), 315–36, 320.

39 Ibid., 323 and 329.

40 Trollope, *The Prime Minister*, 71 and 66.

41 Ibid., 163.

42 Ibid., 351, 102, and 613.

43 Anthony Trollope, *North America*, 1862, ed. Donald Smalley and Bradford Allen Booth (New York: Knopf, 1951), 328.

44 Trollope, *North America*, 1862, 329–30.

45 Ibid., 337 and 330.

46 Trollope, *Can You Forgive Her?*, 447–8.

47 Anthony Trollope, *The Eustace Diamonds*, 4th edn (London: Chapman and Hall, 1876), 424.

48 Trollope, *The Prime Minister*, 492.

49 Trollope, *Phineas Redux*, 264.

50 Trollope, *The Duke's Children*, 132 and 162.

51 On gender, see Margaret Hewitt, 'Anthony Trollope: Historian and sociologist', *The British Journal of Sociology*, 14, no. 3 (September 1963), 226–39, 227; Ramona L. Denton, '"That cage" of femininity: Trollope's Lady Laura', *South Atlantic Bulletin*, 45, no. 1 (January 1980), 1–10; Suzanne Keen, 'Quaker dress, sexuality, and the domestication of reform in the Victorian novel', *Victorian Literature and Culture*, 30, no. 1 (2002), 211–36.

52 Trollope, *Phineas Redux*, 266; also see Mark W. Turner, *Trollope and the Magazines: Gendered Issues in Mid-Victorian Britain* (Basingstoke: Palgrave Macmillan, 2000), 141–82.

53 Trollope, *Can You Forgive Her?*, 258.

54 Trollope, *Phineas Finn*, 127 and 98.

55 Trollope, *Phineas Redux*, 319.

56 Trollope, *The Prime Minister*, 52, 55, 90, and 171.

57 Ibid., 98–9.

58 Gillin, *The Victorian Palace of Science*.

Chapter 11

1 For a more extensive study on this topic, see Caitlin DeClercq, 'Sound bodies for sound minds: Architectural interventions to ameliorate the sedentary life of scholars on college campuses, 1865-2016' (PhD diss., University of California, Berkeley, 2017).

2 John Raymond, 'Vassar college, a sketch of its foundation', 1873, in David J. Rothman and Sheila M. Rothman (eds), *The Dangers of Education: Sexism and the Origin of Women's Colleges* (New York: Garland Press, 1987), 5.

3 Vassar warned in 1861 that 'it is related of one of the most noted female seminaries … that incalculable injury is being done to the health of pupils, under the plea of thorough discipline, and by ill-ventilated apartments, and over-taxation of their brains.' Matthew Vassar, communication to Trustees, 26 February 1861, in Harriet Ballintine, compiled materials regarding the physical education history of Vassar College, Physical Education Collection, Box 4, Vassar College Archives and Special Collections, Poughkeepsie, New York.

4 Rebecca Edwards, '"To unfold such powers": Nineteenth-century America women's rights, women's education, and the founding of Vassar College',

2011, https://specialcollections.vassar.edu/exhibit-highlights/2011-2015/sesquicentennial/1900s_american_womens_rights.html (accessed 6 January 2017).

5 Daphne Spain, *Gendered Spaces* (Chapel Hill: The University of North Carolina Press, 1992), 143–60. By 1900, only about 3 per cent of college-aged women were enrolled in college. See also Edwards, 'To unfold such powers'.

6 Terry S. Kogan, 'Sex separation: The cure-all for Victorian social anxiety', in Harvey Molotch and Laura Norén (eds), *Toilet: Public Restrooms and the Politics of Sharing* (New York: New York University Press, 2010), 145.

7 According to Mabel Newcomer, 'It was contended that women were mentally inferior to men and would be quite unable to meet the standards set for men's higher education.' Mabel Newcomer, *A Century of Higher Education for American Women* (New York: Harper and Brothers, 1959), 26–8.

8 Scientific work of the era included 'discoveries' that women were weaker than men both intellectually and physically. These findings justified the 'separate-spheres' ideology and were used to bolster social and spatial practices aimed at protecting women's bodies. See Roberta Park, 'Sport, gender, and society in a transatlantic Victorian perspective', *History of Sport*, 24 (2007), 1571–5; Kogan, 'Sex separation'.

9 Susan K. Cahn, *Coming on Strong: Gender and Sexuality in Twentieth-Century Women's Sport* (Cambridge: Harvard University Press, 1994), 13.

10 Edward Hammond Clarke, *Sex in Education; or A Fair Chance for the Girls* (New York: Arno Press, 1873), 127.

11 Carroll Smith-Rosenberg and Charles E. Rosenberg, 'The female animal: Medical and biological views of woman and her role in nineteenth-century America', in Judith Walzer Leavitt (ed.), *Women and Health in America: Historical Readings*, 2nd edn (Madison: University of Wisconsin Press, 1999), 116.

12 Mary Taylor Bissell, *Physical Exercise and Development for Women* (New York: Dodd, Mead and Co., 1891).

13 Roberta Park, 'The contributions of women to exercise science and sports medicine, 1870-1994', *Women in Sport and Physical Activity Journal,* 4, no. 1 (1995), 4. Male physicians and physical educators also advocated physical education for women. See Dudley Allen Sargent, *Physical Education* (Boston: Ginn and Co., 1906); Dioclesian Lewis, *New Gymnastics for Men, Women, and Children* (Boston: Ticknor & Fields, 1862).

14 Physical education was leveraged towards different ends for men and women. To educate men to be the future leaders of the nation required edified minds, strong bodies, and, in the words of Edward Hitchcock, the first professor of physical education at an American college, control of baser 'animal spirits'. Larry Owens, 'Pure and sound government: Laboratories, playing fields, and gymnasia in the nineteenth-century search for order', *The History of Science Society*, 76 (1985), 189. Historian Janice Ross argues that Catharine Beecher's calisthenic system aimed to 'correct the female form' and prepare women physically for … motherhood and domestic matters'. Janice Ross, *Moving Lessons: Margaret H'Doubler and the Beginning of Dance in American Education* (Madison: The University of Wisconsin Press, 2000), 63.

15 Spain, *Gendered Spaces,* 153.

16 Mary Taylor Bissell and others stressed that women should develop strong, not large, muscles to conform to an ideal feminine form while obtaining physical strength. Bissell, *Physical Exercise and Development for Women,* 16, 60.

17 Patricia Vertinsky, 'Introduction', in Patricia Vertinsky and Sherry McKay (eds), *Disciplining Bodies in the Gymnasium: Memory, Monument, Modernism* (London: Routledge, 2004), 3.

18 Matthew Vassar called sound minds in sound bodies 'a first truth among educators' of the era. Proceedings of the Trustees, 30 June 1863, in Ballintine, compiled materials, Vassar College Archives and Special Collections, Poughkeepsie, New York.

19 By the late nineteenth century, women's presence in workplaces gave rise to concerns about the dangers of over-work to their health and that of their progeny. Thus, historian Terry Kogan has observed, policymakers in the late 1880s enacted laws to mandate sex-segregated bathrooms in workplaces. Such laws 'can best be understood as an attempt by legislatures to re-create the separate-spheres ideology within the public realm. If women could not be forced back into the home, substitute protective havens would instead be created in the workplace by requiring the separation of water closets, dressing rooms, [and] resting rooms'. Kogan, 'Sex Separation', 163; Cahn, *Coming on Strong,* 26.

20 'Emic' is an anthropological term, connoting a definition that is internally derived from a cultural or historical context, rather than imposed by an outside researcher or from an external perspective.

21 Heather Munro Prescott, *Student Bodies: The Influence of Student Health Services in American Society and Medicine* (Ann Arbor: The University of Michigan Press, 2007), 14.

22 Vassar Female College, 'Prospectus of Vassar female college', May 1865, in Rothman and Rothman, *The Dangers of Education,* 4. See also Elizabeth Daniels, *Main to Mudd: An Informal History of College Buildings* (Poughkeepsie: Vassar College, 1987).

23 Vassar Female College, 'Prospectus', 5.

24 'The prospectus exhibited the titles of studies to be taught in the college, grouped together loosely in ten departments of instruction. But it was added: "This scheme must be regarded as merely tentative. The board reserves its final decision on the distribution of studies until experience has developed the wants" of campus members.' Raymond, 'Vassar college', 23.

25 For more on the intention and experience of architecture, see Annmarie Adams, 'The Eichler home: Intention and experience in postwar suburbia', *Perspectives in Vernacular Architecture,* 5 (1995), 164–78; Helen Lefkowitz Horowitz, *Alma Mater: Design and Experience in the Women's Colleges from their Nineteenth-Century Beginnings to 1933,* 2nd edn (Amherst: University of Massachusetts Press, 1984).

26 Vassar Female College, 'Prospectus', 4.

27 Matthew Vassar looked to the seminary 'system of female protection'. Horowitz, *Alma Mater,* 28–36. Indeed, Vassar had several direct ties to

women's seminaries, particularly his relationship with Milo P. Jewett, Vassar's first president, who founded a women's seminary in 1839. Daniels, *Main to Mudd*, 12. Additionally, Vassar's own niece, Lydia Booth, ran a seminary for girls in Poughkeepsie, New York. Edwards, 'To unfold such powers'.

28 All of these activities would be overseen by a 'Lady-Principal'. Vassar Female College, 'Prospectus', 4–5.

29 First catalogue of Vassar College, 1865–6, in Ballintine, compiled materials, Vassar College Archives and Special Collections, Poughkeepsie, New York.

30 Frederick Law Olmsted and Calvert Vaux saw Central Park (1858), the quintessential Pleasure Ground, as a site for moral recreational pursuits and a means to combat the sickening miasmatic forces of city life. Galen Cranz, *The Politics of Park Design: A History of Urban Parks in America* (Cambridge: The MIT Press, 1984). In the 1860s, outdoor exercise – the 'air cure' – was seen as an antidote to the perils of sedentary life and the use of corsets. Harvey Green, *Fit for America: Health, Fitness, Sport, and American Society* (New York: Pantheon Books, 1986). See also Anna C. Brackett, 'Vassar College', *Harper's*, 1875, 360.

31 Architectural historian Paul Venable Turner argues that the rural setting, single-building plans and family-like domestic arrangement of women's colleges 'reflected ideas about women and their education'. Paul Venable Turner, *Campus: An American Planning Tradition* (Cambridge: The MIT Press, 1984), 140.

32 H. H. McFarland, 'What are they doing at Vassar?', *Scribner's Monthly*, 2 (1870–1), 337.

33 Turner, *Campus*, 137–8.

34 Matthew Vassar employed the use of vibrant, complementary colours in Main's slate mansard roof as a way to convey both the innovation and optimism his namesake college represented. Karen Van Lengen and Lisa Reilly, *Vassar College: An Architectural Tour* (New York: Princeton Architectural Press, 2004), 48.

35 Ibid, 47. Historian Elizabeth Daniels suggests that Main Hall was an architectural experiment, given Vassar's novelty as the first college for women. Daniels, *Main to Mudd*, 15.

36 Brackett, 'Vassar College', 350.

37 Daily exercise was an important part of hygienic, healthy living and a centrepiece of collegiate physical education programmes in the late 1800s.

38 Brackett, 'Vassar College', 360.

39 Green, *Fit for America*.

40 Brackett, 'Vassar College', 360.

41 First catalogue of Vassar College, 1865–6, in Ballintine, compiled materials, Vassar College Archives and Special Collections, Poughkeepsie, New York.

42 Vassar, communications to Trustees, 25 June 1867, in Ballintine, compiled materials, Vassar College Archives and Special Collections, Poughkeepsie, New York.

43 Daniels, *Main to Mudd,* 21.

44 McFarland, 'What are they doing at Vassar?'

45 Anna Brackett quotes Vassar as saying: 'I wish to give one sex all of the advantages too long monopolized by the other … [and] this I conceive, may be fully accomplished within the rational limits of true womanliness, and without the slightest hazard to the attractiveness of her character.' Vassar added: 'We are already defeated before we commence if such development be in the least dangerous to the dearest attributes of her sex.' Brackett, *Vassar College*, 356. See also Vassar Female College, 'Prospectus', 5.

46 Kogan, 'Sex separation'.

47 First catalogue of Vassar College, 1865–6, in Ballintine, compiled materials, Vassar College Archives and Special Collections, Poughkeepsie, New York.

48 Ross, *Moving Lessons,* p. 56.

49 For more on Elizabeth Cady Stanton, see Park, 'Sport, gender, and society'.

50 First catalogue of Vassar College 1865–6 and second catalogue 1866–7, in Ballintine, compiled materials, Vassar College Archives and Special Collections, Poughkeepsie, New York.

51 Annie Houts, letter to John Houts, November 1866, and Harriette A. Warner, letter to mother, October 1866. Digital Collections Library, Student Letters, Vassar College Archives and Special Collections, Poughkeepsie, New York.

52 Addie Thompson, letter to parents, April 1876. Ibid.

53 By the late 1880s, Vassar's physical educators also used Dudley Allen Sargent's anthropometric charts to measure students' physical proportions and development. These examinations and measurements were indicative of a belief that women's experiences could be quantified and read on the body.

54 Annie G. Howes, 'Health statistics of women college graduates: A special committee of the association of collegiate alumnae', 1885, in Rothman and Rothman, *The Dangers of Education*, 9.

55 Harriet Ballintine, gymnasium report to President Taylor, 1899, Physical Education Collection, Box 4.98, Vassar College Archives and Special Collections, Poughkeepsie, New York.

56 Howes, 'Health statistics', 18.

57 In 1889, the Vassar Alumnae Association's Committee on Physical Culture wrote that 'Statistics amply demonstrate the large possibilities of improving the average physical development at a period in their lives when properly directed exercise is a potent factor in their future health and well-being.' Yet the Calisthenium was, to the Committee, 'entirely inadequate for the purpose'. Achsah M. Ely, 'Report of the gymnasium building committee of the association of alumnae of Vassar college', 11 June 1889, *The Vassar Miscellany*, 18, no. 1 (1889/9), 346.

58 The Committee included Dr Mary Taylor Bissell, Alumna of Vassar (1875). Ely, 'Report', 348; see also 'The old gymnasium has its story', *Listening In: Extra Gym Edition*, November 1930, Buildings and Grounds Collection, Box 11, Vassar College Archives and Special Collections, Poughkeepsie, New York.

59 Ely, 'Report', 348.

60 Students, alumnae, and the campus dramatic society (which desired space for dramatic productions in the new building) contributed funds to pay for the new gymnasium. Daniels, *Main to Mudd*, 28.

61 Bissell saw air, ventilation, heating, and lack of overcrowding as important considerations in 'school hygiene'. Mary Taylor Bissell, *A Manual of Hygiene* (New York: The Baker & Taylor Company, 1894), 277–8.

62 Ely, 'Report', 348.

63 This was necessitated in part by the practice of posture photos, which required specialized equipment and space.

64 For example, in 1899, physical education department head Alice Bridgeman wrote to President Taylor about students' observed gains in physical strength: 'The progress made in all cases has been satisfactory, and in some cases quite remarkable.' Anna J. Bridgeman, letter to President Taylor, 1899, Physical Education Collection, Box 4.98, Vassar College Archives and Special Collections, Poughkeepsie, New York. Student Adelaide Mansfield wrote to her mother about the experience of such exams: 'Did I tell you that I had my second physical examination in the gymnasium? My back and legs are quite a little stronger, and everything else has improved, except my right hand which has decreased.' Adelaide Mansfield, letter to mother, 25 March 1894. Digital Collections Library, Student Letters, Vassar College Archives and Special Collections, Poughkeepsie, New York.

65 The only exception was a 'field day', meant to celebrate the year's athletic work and with a public spectacle. Park, 'Sport, gender, and society', 1594–5.

66 Kogan, 'Sex separation'.

67 A student referenced a curfew in her 1871 diary: 'The prohibition on walking after five o'clock has been removed'. Bertha Keffer, April 1851, Digital Collections Library, Student Diaries, Vassar College Archives and Special Collections, Poughkeepsie, New York.

68 In an 1871 diary entry, student Mary Pidgeon-Kiersted wrote: 'Abbie and I took an hours exercise on the Observatory walk.' Ibid.

69 Ross, *Moving Lessons*, 24.

70 Smith-Rosenberg and Rosenberg, 'The female animal', 114.

71 Turner, *Campus*, 3. These extracurricular amenities include housing, activities, and gymnasia.

72 Owens, 'Pure and sound government'.

73 Heather Prescott has argued that college health services, originating in response to concern about vulnerable female bodies, have long been a mechanism to cope with a diversifying student body. Prescott, *Student Bodies*, 14.

74 Roberta Park suggests that 'in co-educational institutions, the women's physical education department was [an enclave] that males were not encouraged to enter … much as the Victorian home had been a sheltered refuge in a competitive and male-dominated society.' Park, 'Sport, gender,

and society', 1590. Female faculty developed new pedagogical practices for bodily instruction and took on leadership roles on campus and in professional organizations (such as Vassar's Helen C. Putnam, who became one of the Vice Presidents of the American Association for the Advancement of Physical Education). Park, 'The contribution of women to exercise science and sports medicine'.

75 'Indelible Photographs' photo album, c. 1890, Photographs, Folder 17.31, Vassar College Archives and Special Collections, Poughkeepsie, New York.

76 Horowitz, *Alma Mater*, xx.

Chapter 12

1 This quote can be found in the 'Minor Ruskiniana' section to the 1904 edition of *The Stones of Venice*, and comes from a letter by Ruskin to his father from Verona of June 1852. See John Ruskin, *The Stones of Venice*, vol. II (London: George Allen, 1904), xxv.

2 For the idea of 'improvement' and the Victorians, see A. Briggs, *The Age of Improvement, 1783-1867*, 2nd edn (London: Routledge, 1999). For 'self-help', see Samuel Smiles, *Self-Help, with Illustrations of Conduct and Perseverance* (London: John Murray, 1859).

3 Take, for instance, architecture associated with education, as outlined in E. R. Robson's classic primer on the subject, *School Architecture, being Practical Remarks on the Planning, Designing, Building, and Furnishing of School-Houses* (1874). For more on this, see Deborah E. B. Weiner, *Architecture and Social Reform in Late-Victorian London* (Manchester: Manchester University Press, 1994).

4 For an overview of these concepts in reference to Anthony Giddens and Pierre Bourdieu, see Gieryn, 'What buildings do', 35–45.

5 Eric Wilson, 'Plagues, friars, and street cries: Sounding out society and space in early modern London', *Modern Language Studies*, 25, no. 3 (1995), 1–42. For a more general critique of the 'ocularcentric' paradigm in modern architecture and the value of alternate sensory experience, see J. Pallasmaa, *The Eyes of the Skin: Architecture and the Senses* (London: Academy Editions, 1996). A book that charts in part the general decline in scopic regimes in Western thought, and one that affords consideration for architectural historians in this context, is Martin Jay's *Downcast Eyes: The Denigration of Vision in Twentieth-Century French Thought* (Berkeley: University of California Press, 1993).

6 Gieryn, 'What buildings do', 42. This idea of experience is also somewhat coincident with William Whyte's notion of the understanding of meaning in architecture, where there is no single meaning, but rather a series of 'meanings' that are revealed through a process of 'translation' and 'transposition' of recognizable architectural genres instead of a direct 'reading' of them. See Whyte, 'How do buildings mean?, 153–77.

7 For example John Tosh, *A Man's Place: Masculinity and the Middle-Class Home in Victorian England* (New Haven and London: Yale University Press, 1999). See also James Eli Adams, *Dandies and Desert Saints: Styles of Victorian Masculinity* (Ithaca: Cornell University Press, 1995). I wish to thank Erin Hammond for reminding me of these ideas.

8 For a recent exploration on the relationship between architecture and feeling in the Victorian age, see Karen L. Burns, 'The awakening conscience: Christian sentiment, salvation, and spectatorship in mid-Victorian Britain', *19: Interdisciplinary Studies in the Long Nineteenth Century*, 23 (2016). DOI: http://doi.org/10.16995/ntn.769

9 Gaston Bachelard, *The Poetics of Space*, trans. Maria Jolas (New York: Orion Press, 1964).

10 Bachelard, *The Poetics of Space*, 3–4.

11 Pallasmaa, *Eyes of the Skin*, 23–4.

12 This notion may be related to Structuration theory in so far as the material conditions for the containment of space (and thus its 'structure') are responsible in part at least for the possibilities of action within that space, and therefore may be seen to 'characterize' the experience thereof. For a working example of Structuration theory vis-à-vis space, see 'Time, Space, Context' in A. Giddens, *The Constitution of Society: Outline of the Theory of Structuration* (Cambridge: Polity Press, 1984), 132–9.

13 C. B. Davis, K. E. Wilburn, and R. E. Robinson, *Railway Imperialism* (New York: Greenwood, 1991), 2–3. I wish to thank Lucia Juarez for bringing this quote to my attention. For the cultural understanding and impact of technologies such as steam power and telegraphy, see Ben Marsden and Crosbie Smith, *Engineering Empires: A Cultural History of Technology in Nineteenth-Century Britain* (London: Palgrave Macmillan, 2005).

14 For example Duncan Bell, *The Idea of Greater Britain: Empire and the Future of World Order, 1860-1900* (Princeton: Princeton University Press, 2007), 74–91.

15 Siegfried Giedion, *Mechanisation Takes Command: A Contribution to Anonymous History* (New York: Oxford University Press, 1948).

16 Giedion, *Mechanisation Takes Command*, 5.

17 L. Mumford, *Technics and Civilization* (London: Harcourt, 1934). For a more recent elucidation of this critical moment and its consequences, see E. A. Wrigley, *Energy and the English Industrial Revolution* (Cambridge: Cambridge University Press, 2010). See also J. Mokyr, 'Editor's introduction', in J. Mokyr (ed.), *The British Industrial Revolution: An Economic Perspective* (Boulder: Westview Press, 1993), 20.

18 For the fetish aspect of this, see Andreas Malm, *Fossil Capital: The Rise of Steam Power and the Roots of Global Warming* (London: Verso Books, 2016), 194–222.

19 In this respect Marsden and Smith approach technological endeavour as 'fluid practice' rather than 'solid product'. See Marsden and Smith, *Engineering*

Empires, 4. See also, Crosbie Smith and Anne Scott, '"Trust in providence": Building confidence into the cunard line of steamers', *Technology and Culture*, 48, no. 3 (2007), 471–96.

20 Giedion, *Mechanisation*, 172-208; Mumford, *Technics*, 110.

21 Embodied energy is described specifically as 'the sum of the energy requirements associated, directly or indirectly, with the delivery of a good or service'. See J. Cleveland and C. G. Morris (eds), *Dictionary of Energy* (Amsterdam: Elsevier, 2009), 191.

22 For instance, consider the Houses of Parliament. See Gillin, *The Victorian Palace of Science*.

23 As Simon Schaffer has pointed out in relation to the rise and ideological power of metrology in Victorian Britain, new standards of measurement and accuracy brought with them new values relating to order, regulation, and commerce. See S. Schaffer, 'Metrology, metrication, and Victorian values', in B. Lightman (ed.), *Victorian Science in Context* (Chicago: University of Chicago Press, 1997), 438–74.

24 For example *The Building News* (7 October 1859), 899–910.

25 For these regimes, see Malm, *Fossil Capital*.

26 Hall, *George Frederick Bodley and the Later Gothic Revival in Britain and America*, 72–4.

27 The theories that I am talking about here can be found in, among other sources, B. Webb, 'On the adaptation of pointed architecture to tropical climates', *Transactions of the Cambridge Camden Society, 1843–45* (1845), 199–218; 'Past and future developments in architecture', *The Ecclesiologist* (February 1846), 48–53; G. E. Street, 'The true principles of architecture and the possibility of development', *The Ecclesiologist* (August 1852), 247–62; and *The English Cathedral of the Nineteenth Century* (London: John Murray, 1861). For scholarship on these theories, see J. M. Crook, 'Progressive eclecticism: The case of Beresford Hope', *Architectural Design*, 53, no. 7–8 (1983), 56–62; M. Hall, '"Our own": Thomas Hope, A. J. B. Beresford Hope and the creation of the high Victorian style', in R. Hill and M. Hall (eds), *The 1840s, Studies in Victorian Architecture and Design*, vol. 1 (London: Victorian Society, 2008), 61–75; Yanni, 'Development and display', 227–60.

28 G. B. Magee and A. S. Thompson, *Empire and Globalisation: Networks of People, Goods and Capital in the British World, c.1850–1914* (Cambridge: Cambridge University Press, 2010), 118.

29 For cast-iron, see Gavin Stamp's introduction to John Gay, *Cast Iron: Architecture and Ornament, Function and Fantasy* (London: John Murray, 1985); L. Juarez, 'Scottish cast iron in Argentina: Its role in the British informal imperial system', in P. Dobraszczyk and P. Sealy (eds), *Function and Fantasy: Iron Architecture in the Long Nineteenth Century* (Abingdon: Ashgate, 2016), 141–62. For stained glass, see J. Holliday, *Stories in Glass: The Stained Glass Heritage of Bombay* (Mumbai: India Eminence Designs, 2012); J. Zimmer, *Stained Glass in Australia* (Melbourne: Oxford University Press, 1984); J. Allen, *Windows for the World: Nineteenth-Century Stained Glass and the*

International Exhibitions, 1851-1900 (Manchester: Manchester University Press, 2018).

30 J. A. Froude, *Oceana, or England and Her Colonies* (London: Longmans, Green, & Co., 1886), 89. Froude went on to say how he found Australians '*ipsis Anglicis Angliciores*' (131).

31 Quoted in A. Briggs, *Victorian Cities* (Harmondsworth: Penguin Books, 1968), 295.

32 James Belich, *Replenishing the Earth: The Settler Revolution and the Rise of the Anglo-World, 1783-1939* (Oxford: Oxford University Press, 2009), 106–44.

33 This is a phenomenon that J. G. A. Pocock earlier described as the phenomenon of 'global Britishness'. See J. G. A. Pocock, *The Discovery of Islands: Essays in British History* (Cambridge: Cambridge University Press, 2005), 20. Something of a balancing act occurred in this process, as Scots, for instance, could come to identify themselves as 'British' without forgetting their Scottishness. See Andrew Mackillop, 'European, Britons, and Scots: Scottish sojourning networks and identities in Asia, 1700-1815', in Angela McCarthy (ed.), *A Global Clan: Scottish Migrant Networks and Identities since the Eighteenth Century* (London: I. B. Tauris, 2006), 19–47.

34 See Tamson Pietsch, 'A British sea: Making sense of global space in the late nineteenth century', *Journal of Global History*, 5, no. 3 (2010), 423–46. 'Greater Britain' is a phenomenon that J. G. A. Pocock earlier described as the phenomenon of 'global Britishness'. See Pocock, *The Discovery of Islands*, 20.

35 For steam shipping and empire in general, see Douglas Burgess, *Engines of Empire: Steamships and the Victorian Imagination* (Stanford: Stanford University Press, 2016).

36 Pietsch, 'A British sea', 433.

37 Ibid., 442, 445.

38 G. A. Bremner, *Imperial Gothic: Religious Architecture and High Anglican Culture in the British Empire, c.1840-1870* (New Haven and London: Yale University Press, 2013).

39 Geoffrey Blainey, *The Tyranny of Distance: How Distance Shaped Australia's History* (Melbourne: Macmillan, 1968).

40 For instance, see *South African Church Magazine and Ecclesiastical Review*, 1, no. 2 (1850), 33–40, 167–75.

41 Ibid., 34–5.

42 For instance, *The Ecclesiologist* had itself praised Walter Scott for his 'truthful and attractive pictures' of medieval life in Britain. See White, *The Cambridge Movement*, 8.

43 H. M. White in the *South African Church Magazine and Ecclesiastical Review*, new ser., 1 (1853), 131.

44 See John Armstrong, 'Notes from South Africa', *Bodleian Library* (Oxford: USPG Archive, D7b), 94.

45 Recalling Maurice Merleau-Ponty, Pallasmaa observes: 'spaces and places are not mere stages for our lives, as they are "chiasmatically" intertwined'. See Juhani Pallasmaa, 'Newness, tradition and identity: Essential context and meaning in architecture', *Architectural Design*, 82, no. 6 (2012), 18.

46 Patteson quoted in Ian Lochhead, 'Remembering the middle ages: Responses to the gothic revival in Colonial New Zealand', in J. Anderson (ed.), *Crossing Cultures: Conflict, Migration and Convergence. The Proceedings of the 32nd International Congress in the History of Art* (Carlton, VIC: Miegunyah Press, 2009), 537. Patteson would become the first Bishop of Melanesia. It is also worth referring here to a like passage by William Newman: 'It is with much satisfaction that we are enabled to inform our readers, that the English Churches now building at Rondebosch, George, Graff-Reinet, Colesberg, and elsewhere in this colony [South Africa], will be in a style calculated to recall the "goodly fabrics" in which we have been accustomed to worship in other lands …'. *The South African Church Magazine*, 1 (February 1850), 33.

47 For Glover, see David Hansen (ed.), *John Glover and the Colonial Picturesque* (Hobart: Tasmanian Museum and Art Gallery, 2003).

INDEX

Note: Page locators in italics refer to illustrations.

Lightning Source UK Ltd.
Milton Keynes UK
UKHW020147040720
365968UK00004B/146

9 781350 159709